THE NEW FREEDOM

THE NEW FREEDOM

Individualism and Collectivism in the Social Lives of Americans

William A. Donohue

Transaction Publishers
New Brunswick (U.S.A.) and London (U.K.)

Library of Congress Catalog Number: 89-34597
ISBN: 0-88738-298-3
Printed in the United States of America

Library of Congress Cataloging-in-Publication Data

Donohue, William A., 1947-
   The new freedom : individualism and collectivism in the social
lives of Americans / William A. Donohue.
      p.   cm.
   Bibliography: p.
   Includes index.
   ISBN 0-88738-298-3
   1. United States—Social conditions—1980-   2. Individualism.
I. Title.
HN65.D66   1989
302.5'4—dc20
                                                      89-34597
                                                         CIP

This book is dedicated to my wife, Valerie

Contents

Acknowledgments

Parts of this book were previously published or appeared in slightly different form:

Chapter 1 was published as "The Limits of Liberty: Individual Freedom and Social Disorders," *The Heritage Lectures* 147, December 1987.

Chapter 3 appeared in a slightly different form as "The Social Consequences of the Rights Revolution," *Intercollegiate Studies Review*, Spring 1987.

Chapter 7 first appeared as "Children's Rights: The Ideological Road to Sweden," *The Family in America*, November 1988.

Chapter 9 was adapted from "Failed Formulas: Teen Pregnancy and the New Freedom," *The Family in America*, September 1989.

Chapter 12 was published as "Why Schools Fail: Reclaiming the Moral Dimension in Education," *The Heritage Lectures* 172, June 1988.

Chapter 13 is adapted from "Religion in the Age of the New Freedom," *Social Justice Review*, July/August 1989.

I would like to thank The Heritage Foundation for giving me the opportunity to spend a year in residence, 1987–1988, so that I could complete this book expeditiously. In particular, I would like to thank Charles Heatherly, Vice-President for Academic Affairs. Chuck made available to me all the resources a writer would want. Thanks, too, to John Charba, who did an outstanding job as my research assistant. And a special thanks to The Lynde and Harry Bradley Foundation for funding my stay at Heritage.

I am indebted to Esther Luckett for her dedicated editorial work. And without the support of Irving Louis Horowitz, President of Transaction and Hannah Arendt Professor of Sociology and Political Science at Rutgers University, this book would not have been published. Never afraid of controversy, Professor Horowitz is a model of what a publisher should be, but unfortunately seldom is.

My wife, Valerie, was unflinching in her total support of this effort, and to a considerable extent is responsible for the energy that went into the book.

PART I

INTRODUCTION

1

The Ultimate Revolution

In 1986 Dr. David A. Hamburg, president of the Carnegie Corporation, announced the launching of a new national council on adolescent development. "An alarming proportion of America's teen-agers drop out of school, commit crimes, become pregnant, abuse drugs or alcohol, commit suicide or die from injuries and become disabled mentally and physically," Dr. Hamburg said.[1] As an index of problems facing young people, Dr. Hamburg's assessment is excellent. But to get a handle on the magnitude of the overall level of social problems facing American society, mention must also be made of the high rates of child abuse, runaways, homelessness, separation, divorce, herpes, and AIDS. The final tally is not encouraging.

Not coincidentally, there has been an explosion in the number of men, women, and children seeking professional help. Indeed, there are more people paying more money for advice, analysis, counseling, and treatment than ever before. In response to the demand, an entire industry has taken root: the Helping Professions. Something has gone wrong.

The enormousness of the psychological and social disorders affecting the United States threatens to undermine the political and economic progress that has been made toward the production of a free and democratic society. If people do not have the psychological means to enjoy their rights, or their bounty, freedom becomes an empty gesture, worthy of little respect or vigilance. Liberty was meant to be enjoyed, not endured.

Politically, it can be said that the American experiment in democracy has been a success. Individual rights have been extended to virtually every segment of the population. Those who govern continue to do so with the consent of the governed. Our system of checks and balances has been repeatedly tested and found solvent. Economically, Americans enjoy a standard of living that is the world's envy. Despite the recurrent problems of inflation, recession, and budget deficits, the state of the economy has proven to be more resilient and capable of reform than that of any of the Western

3

nations. Our technology continues to advance, solving what only yesterday was thought unsolvable. But all this isn't enough if social relationships come undone, personal problems mount, and social discord flourishes.

There are social and cultural requisites of a free and democratic society, as well as political and economic ones. Our mistake has been to neglect sorely the social and cultural context in which individual liberty can be meaningfully exercised. We have assumed, falsely, that a republican form of government and a market economy are all that is needed to make freedom a reality. The price we pay for this misjudgment is evident in the unraveling of the social fabric.

Self-government cannot be ordered into being. A written constitution that provides for a separation of powers is the beginning, not the end, of free society. Self-government is predicated on civic responsibility, on a willingness of the citizenry to participate in the chores of community. Citizens are not likely to do so if saddled with their own personal problems.

The reason that American society suffers from a surfeit of psychological and social disorders has little, if anything, to do with such popular explanations as income inequality, competitiveness, or the trials and tribulations of youth. Yet the appeal that these arguments have seems almost irresistible. The point cannot be made too strongly that neither economic analysis nor psychological inquiry better explains why we suffer from such a high degree of social disorder. And neither offers a compelling case for understanding why the rates of disorder have jumped precipitously since the 1960s.

Thirty, fifty, or a hundred years ago, when the level of social pathologies was quite low, income distribution was more unequal than it is today. And if noncash transfer benefits are counted, there is even less inequality today than there was then. Moreover, we have always been a competitive people, and are arguably less so today than we were a hundred years ago; the 1880s were the heyday of unbridled capitalism and laissez-faire economics. Yet families remained intact and social problems were manageable. In short, trying to pin the blame on capitalism just doesn't work. Japan is also a capitalist country, yet it has only a fraction of the social problems we have. It is culture, not the economy, that best explains the characterological outcomes of individuals in any society.

As common sense ought to inform, the travails of youth are not unique to our age. "Raging hormones" is surely an expression of the eighties, but it no more accurately describes a phenomenon of youth today than in the past; hormones raged with just as much intensity among young people in the fifties, the difference being, however, that social pressure kept them from being recklessly ventilated. Similarly, short time horizons, impulsiveness, and risk taking were not invented in the 1980s. They have historically been properties of youth in any age. What's changed is the degree to which these tendencies have gone unchecked.

My thesis is that the wide range of psychological and social disorders that currently plague American society are traceable to a flawed conception of freedom. Since the late 1960s, American culture has defined freedom as the abandonment of constraint. Although this concept of freedom as something inherently adverse to the social order is quite old in philosophical terms, it wasn't until the 1960s that it took hold as the dominant viewpoint of our cultural elites: the universities, media, entertainment industry, and publishing world. Therein lies the genesis of our psychological ailments, moral failings, and social problems.

Americans have always prized liberty; it is the most defining characteristic of what it is to be an American. But only in recent years has freedom come to mean freedom from constraint. Beginning in the 1960s, an increasing number of Americans began to interpret burdens of any kind as an unjust infringement on their liberty. The new freedom sees the idea of limits as an unfair abridgment of human liberty. Inescapably, such logic views the normative order, loaded as it is with dos and don'ts, as repressive. Moral codes, which are by their very nature restrictive, are cast as the enemy of freedom. In this environment, appeals to responsibility and restraint are greeted with cynicism and derision.

It would be a mistake to suggest that all Americans share this idea of freedom. They do not. But it is the ascendant idea, the one that screams the loudest and grabs the most attention. Those who choose not to embrace this "value system" (or lack thereof) are required to reject it. No one escapes its influence.

The contemporary idea of freedom is evident in art, music, television, movies, plays, books, and magazines. It finds expression in the home, at school, and on the job. It colors relationships between men and women and among children and adolescents. It affects our values as well as our behavior. It defines our society. It is not a viewpoint struggling to influence the establishment; it *is* the establishment.

Freedom in the West was never defined as promiscuously as it is today. Beginning with the Greeks, to be free meant to be free from arbitrary and capricious rule. It did not mean freedom from social sanctions. It meant that individuals could freely pursue their own interests, consistent always with respect for the rights of others and in deference to the general interests of society. The principle of constitutional government and rule by law, it was decided, would be the model upon which the Western idea of freedom would be based.

The new freedom bears little resemblance to this time-honored interpretation. The contemporary definition can best be described as neo-Millian. It was John Stuart Mill, in his classic 1859 essay "On Liberty," who elevated individual autonomy to extreme heights, and thereby paved the way intellectually for the current assault on community and the normative order. "From the Greenwich Village of the early twentieth century," writes sociologist Robert Nisbet, "to the contemporary chaos of cultural anarchy, hedonism, narcissism, and generalized flouting of idols there is a straight line best defined as Mill's one very simple principle."[2]

Mill's "one very simple principle"—that short of directly harming another person every individual should be accorded total freedom to do as he wishes—has proven to be the most seductive and irresistible doctrine of our time. Even those who never heard of Mill understand exactly what this doctrine means: it means (a) the individual should triumph over society, (b) moral neutrality should triumph over a moral hierarchy, and (c) self-actualization should triumph over self-discipline. Mill may have intended to promote individual independence, but his real progeny remains license.

It is true, as Harry V. Jaffa has written, that "Mill is very clear that he presupposes moral characters already formed, and not only able to distinguish right from wrong but disposed toward the right by a decent upbringing."[3] But by casting liberty and discipline as opposites, and by relentlessly criticizing social constraints, Mill undermined the moral basis of a free society. And by doing so, he made untenable the social and cultural context in which self-restraint and responsibility to others are learned. It will not do to say that he never counseled against self-control, or against a sense of civic responsibility. We need to know how he expected these requisites of liberty to be realized in an environment hostile to social constraints.

The present chaos in culture has a Freudian element in it as well. Though Freud is well known for his admonition that civilization requires the subordination of individual appetites to the common good, it is less well recognized that he thought this condition is as unfortunate as it is necessary. His real preference was for a freedom that abandons all cultural strictures and man-made codes of conduct. "Primitive man," he maintained, "was better off in knowing no restrictions of instinct." But Freud's longing for primordial freedom was dashed by the reality that "integration in, or adaptation to, a human community appears as a scarcely avoidable condition which must be fulfilled. . . ." Tellingly, he couldn't resist adding, "If it could be done without that condition, it would perhaps be preferable."[4]

So if it is true that Freud knew that freedom in a civilized society cannot be attained without paying the price of moral restraints, it is also true that he was discontent with paying the bill. Exponents of the new freedom take this logic to the next step by defining the existence of cultural prohibitions as obstacles to freedom. They regard such inexplicably human characteristics as defense mechanisms, taboos, guilt, shame, stigma, anxiety, and stress as standing in the way of true emancipation. This perspective sees tradition, custom, and social convention as unwarranted social pressure. It is fundamentally hostile to the psychological and social trappings of what it is to be human.

This amounts to a revolution—a revolution against society itself. Previous revolutions have been waged against persons held to be oppressors: slave against master; peasant against lord; working class against upper class; new elite against old elite. This revolution is different: it is man against society. Previous revolutions have been motivated out of despair against poverty, misery, and injustice. This revolution is different: it is motivated out of despair against the limitations of the human condition. It is the ultimate revolution.

It won't work. Man is not suited to endure such a reckless idea of freedom. It is one thing to imagine a state of freedom, quite another to live it. The mind is capable of painting freedom as infinity but no one has the emotional staying power to realize it. By throwing off tradition, custom, and social convention as the yoke of repression, man is essentially going to war against himself. It is a war he cannot hope to win.

It is not as though we haven't been warned. Most students of freedom have emphasized that "true freedom" consists in doing what is right and good, that is, it is dependent on virtuous action. Aristotle said it best: "Every man should be responsible to others, nor should any be allowed to do just as he pleases; for where absolute freedom is allowed there is nothing to restrain the evil which is inherent in man."[5]

The idea of absolute freedom is a canard, a cruel hoax sold to men and women in search of self-fulfillment. "The *extreme* of liberty (which is its abstract perfection, but its real fault)" wrote Edmund Burke, "obtains nowhere, nor ought to obtain anywhere; because extremes . . . are destructive both to virtue and enjoyment."[6] Exactly. But for many people, such admonitions are tantamount to heresy. They sincerely believe that the road to freedom is marked by the number of "experiences" one can endure; the more extreme the experience, the greater the sense of exhilaration and emancipation. Nothing is off-limits to today's free spirits. This is what the new freedom is all about.

The new freedom is made manifest in two principal ways: (a) in our monistic fixation on individual rights, and (b) in our embrace of the doctrine of moral neutrality. Individual rights have always been central to any Western definition of freedom, but only in the late twentieth century have they been seen as a sufficient cause of freedom. Similarly, freedom from excessive social scrutiny has always been indispensable to any concept of individual liberty, but never has it been defined more radically than today. What makes the new freedom so unique is its insistence that every individual has a right to be totally liberated from everything that constrains him.

The new freedom creates so many problems because it cuts against the grain of society. No society, free or unfree, can exist without a modicum of civility and community. As sociological analysis confirms, both of these properties are dependent upon the subordination of the individual to the social, that is, on the willingness of the individual to submit to the interests of society. But the new freedom is predicated on precisely the opposite principle: it elevates the individual above all else, paying lip service, at best, to the needs of society. In short, the pursuit of individual freedom is on a collision course with the public weal. Hence, the unprecedented level of social pathologies.

The number of social problems a society has is a reflection, in part, of the degree of civility it is able to achieve. For example, if enough people in any society refuse, for whatever reason, to act in a civil manner toward their fellow man, order descends to anarchy and society is harmed, perhaps irreparably. Society is based on rules, on norms that must be oberved. Without standards of right and wrong, each person does as he pleases, following the dictates of his interests and passions. Civility ceases to exist and chaos reigns. Freedom is ruled out for everyone.

Community is important for two reasons: it is the key to social well-being and psychological health. Both society and the individual will fall apart unless some measure of community is achieved. Community is the essence of the social bond: it binds one person to another, transforming aggregates of individuals into coherent social groups. It is also the staple ingredient of a well-balanced person, that is, psychological health is to a large extent a function of social relations; the more social supports an individual possesses, the less likely he is to exhibit psychological disorders.

When the English philosopher Thomas Hobbes wondered how society was possible, he had in mind how it could come to pass that men would live together in some semblance of civility and community, since their natural wont was to follow their own interests. The great French sociologist, Emile Durkheim, was struck by a similar observation: man naturally inclines toward the pursuit of his own interests, yet cannot live except in society, and that demands that he yield to the interests of others. The trick is to find the most palatable way of making society possible.

Society can be created either through coercion or consensus. The former being unacceptable to a people who have chosen freedom as their paramount want, we are consigned to adopt the latter. Consensus, however, demands constraints. There's the rub. By defining freedom as the liberation of all constraints, we have undermined the ability of society to cohere, thereby depreciating both wants and needs. It's a no-win proposition.

Man can live without freedom, but he cannot live without civility and community. If in the pursuit of freedom he destroys civility and community (and with them, all prospects for freedom), a chorus of demands will quickly surface: All of them will be directed at restoring order, none of them will insist on freedom. As Plato first warned, an excess of liberty would lead directly to tyranny. The choices, then, should be clear: (1) we can maximize order and dispense with liberty, or (2) we can have some freedom and some order. Our problem has been in thinking there's a third way: maximizing freedom while neglecting order. It's a sociological impossibility.

By defining rights as the sine qua non of liberty, we have been driven to conclude that the more rights an individual has, the freer he is. So the pattern has been to pile one right on top of the other, as if the higher the stack, the greater the degree of freedom. It is precisely this logic that motivates civil libertarians to lobby for a new round of rights each time they score a victory in the courts. To them, rights are a sufficient cause of freedom.

Ironic as it might seem to some, a value is not enhanced when maximized. It is corrupted. Take rights. Push one person's rights too far and the result is the emasculation of someone else's rights. Elevate rights to the status of an absolute and the result is the destruction of other values. Expand the definition of rights to include all desirable ends and the result is a diminution of interest in the rights that really matter. Extend the idea of rights to every conceivable animate and inanimate subject and the result is a depreciation of human rights. In short, attempts to maximize rights insure their minimization.

Another problem with the freedom-as-rights equation is that the social bond short-circuits when there is a rights overload. When every individual interprets his quotient of freedom by dividing the number of claims he's made against others by the number of claims against himself, the end product is a disinterest in the rights of others and a lack of concern for the common good. Individual responsibility cannot help but diminish in such an environment. Indeed, a society that makes a fetish of individual rights will inevitably view individual responsibilities as an unfair burden, to be disposed of as quickly as possible.

When freedom is seen only in terms of rights, a blind spot develops with regard to other competing values. It becomes difficult to see that negative social consequences emerge as a direct result of pushing individual rights to extremes. Yet this is precisely what has happened, especially in big cities. Newly won individual rights have been brazenly and defiantly exercised to the detriment of the public good. In this context, unreflecting citizens may be forgiven for concluding that rights have become the enemy of freedom; the quality of public life seems to be eviscerated with the awarding of additional individual rights.

The public good is further undermined when the freedom-as-rights mentality is conjoined with a belief in the doctrine of moral neutrality. Once again we have taken a good idea, in this case pluralism, and run it to extremes, thereby corrupting its value. When moral pluralism is pushed to extremes, there is no such thing as the public good—there are only private goods. When people abandon a concern for the public interest in favor of a preference for

strictly personal matters, the quality of public life suffers as society fraction-
ates into disparate and conflicting spheres. This is a world in which people
pretend to be totally unaffected by the values of their neighbor. More significant, it is a world in which people pretend to be free.

"Different strokes for different folks." "Do your own thing." "If it feels
good, do it." These have become the standard cultural cliches of our time,
accurately expressing the reigning conception of freedom. Freedom is purely
an individualistic exercise, one that celebrates autonomy and castigates compliance. On a scale of 1 to 10, with 10 as the maximum degree of freedom,
those who rate a 10 are individuals who experience the fewest social constraints, while those at the bottom of the scale experience the most. The road
to freedom, then, is paved by distancing oneself from the norms and values of
others. It is a solitary road, one without comfort or relief.

In *Habits of the Heart*, Robert Bellah and associates outlined two sets of
traditions that are evident in American history. On one side, there are the
biblical and republican strands; on the other, there are the utilitarian and
expressive varieties. The biblical tradition, epitomized by John Winthrop,
represents the contribution that religious beliefs and institutions have made to
the dominant culture. Thomas Jefferson symbolizes the republican strand; a
consensus about the public interest, to be achieved via the active participation
of the citizenry, is the key to this tradition.

At the other end of the spectrum lay individualism. Benjamin Franklin is
identified with utilitarianism, reflecting as he did the quest for self-
improvement, measured largely in material ways. Expressive individualism,
as seen in the work of Walt Whitman, places a priority on feelings, on the
ability to experience life without limits.

It is the utilitarian and expressive tradition that clearly dominates contemporary American culture. As Bellah sees it, "Utility replaces duty; self-
expression unseats authority. 'Being good' becomes 'feeling good.' "[7] This is
a society that firmly rejects the appeal of John F. Kennedy: "Ask not what
your country can do for you, ask what you can do for your country." In
today's milieu, the republican notion of doing good for one's country is
practically incoherent: the public good has no meaning.

The utilitarian and expressive individualism that characterizes American
society goes hand in hand with the popular belief in moral neutrality. To be
morally neutral about the values, beliefs, and sentiments of others is seen as a
badge of open-mindedness. Better not pass judgment on the ideas, even the
conduct, of others, lest one be labeled close-minded. Those who truly believe
in freedom never indulge in value judgments. They simply "let it be."

To profess a belief in moral neutrality is to profess a contempt for tradition.
It is to say that all that came before us is without value, and that nothing is in
need of preservation. Tradition, of course, is anything but valueless; it is the

accumulation of values that constitutes tradition. By turning our backs on tradition, by casting off the trappings of social and cultural conventions, we seek to free ourselves of moral sanctions, to propel ourselves toward self-liberation. It is as though freedom can be achieved by running from society. Strange thing is, though, the faster we run, the less good we feel about ourselves. This is a race without a finish line.

"Tolerance" has become the ruling mantra of the new freedom. Everywhere we are told to be tolerant of others, tolerant of diversity and tolerant of change. Scholars tell us how respectful we are of civil liberties by measuring how tolerant we are of the beliefs and life-styles of others. Psychotherapists advise us to practice tolerance in dealing with loved ones, counseling that conflict can be avoided when concessions are granted. And peace activists propose we be more tolerant in understanding the rhetoric and behavior of our adversaries. There is virtually no aspect of living that can't benefit by adding a bit more tolerance to it.

The idea of a moral hierarchy is positively repulsive to the ethos of the new freedom. Different but equal is the usual response to inquiries concerning deviance. There are some behaviorial patterns that are "bizarre," but none that are abnormal. If someone says that a person who defecates in public is engaged in abnormal behavior, he will be quickly answered by some contemporary sage, of open mind and nothing else, that such judgments reflect middle-class values. (Are lower-class values to be preferred?) This is to be read as an indictment, the purpose of which is to close the discussion. In one swoop, middle-class values have been emptied of significance and assigned a purely sectarian role.

Social observers are often ecstatic when they read that a new survey reveals Americans to be more tolerant than they were ten or twenty years ago. They interpret such findings as confirmation of the dawning of a new day, a day in which individual liberties can be maximized. It seldom occurs to them that beneath the veneer of tolerance lies exhaustion, a total collapse of caring about what others do to themselves. Scratch tolerance hard enough and indifference will surface. Not always, but in many more cases than we are willing to admit.

For example, when sociologist Theodore Caplow and associates examined Muncie, Indiana, they boasted that there was a significant increase in tolerance in the fifty years that separated their study from the earlier ones conducted by Robert and Helen Lynd. The Middletown researchers also noted a stark increase in divorce, illegitimacy, drugs, and pornography.[8] They were largely reticent about the possibility that the increase in moral decay was occasioned by the increase in tolerance. Tolerance, in the modern worldview, has only good effects.

That tolerance might signify something negative—a retreat from commitment—seems to be understood by Bellah. But he is unsure and, given his faith in the positive effects of tolerance, is unable to find much fault with growing levels of tolerance. He applauds the "new atmosphere" of tolerance for creating "more sensitive, more open, more intense, more loving relationships . . . it is an achievement of which Americans can justly be proud." But wait, tolerance is a double-edged sword: He adds: "To the extent that the new atmosphere renders those same relationships fragile and vulnerable, it threatens to undermine those very achievements."[9] Well said, but the implications are generally ignored.

The upshot of all this is not that rights, pluralism, or tolerance is undesirable. On the contrary, no society can claim to be free without a great deal of all three. But that doesn't mean that a society achieves maximum freedom by maximizing these values. That would be true only if there were no competing values that mattered. But since that is not the case, since social well-being counts for something, as does public order, it cannot be said that the more rights, pluralism, and tolerance we have, the more freedom we have.

American society has been operating under the opposite assumption: we have taken it as an article of faith that "the more, the better." But just as having too much good food sours the stomach, too much individualism sours society. George Will once said that the four most important words in politics are "up to a point." Lots of things are good, "up to a point." But drawing the line, even acknowledging the need to draw one somewhere, is not an idea that registers well with those who have embraced the new freedom.

Notes

1. Quoted in " 'Casualties of Adolescence' to Be Examined," *New York Times*, June 30, 1986, p. A15.
2. Robert Nisbet, *Prejudices* (Cambridge: Harvard University Press, 1982), p. 214.
3. Harry V. Jaffa, "On the Nature of Civil and Religious Liberty," in William F. Buckley, Jr., and Charles R. Kesler, eds. *Keeping the Tablets: Modern American Conservative Thought* (New York: Harper and Row, 1988), p. 153.
4. Sigmund Freud, *Civilization and Its Discontents* (New York: W. W. Norton, 1961), pp. 62, 87.
5. *The Works of Aristotle*, trans. J. A. Smith and W. D. Ross, vol. 10, *Politica* (Oxford, 1921), p. 1318b.
6. Edmund Burke in *Burke's Politics*, ed. Ross J. S. Hoffman and Paul Levack (New York: Knopf, 1967), p. 109.
7. Robert Bellah et al., *Habits of the Heart* (Berkeley: University of California Press, 1985), p. 77.
8. Theodore Caplow et al., *Middletown Families: Fifty Years of Change and Continuity* (Minneapolis: University of Minnesota Press, 1982), chaps. 1, 6, 8.
9. Bellah, *Habits of the Heart*, p. 110.

PART II

ORIGINS OF
THE NEW FREEDOM

2

The Unburdening of the Individual

The contemporary idea of freedom was not born in a vacuum. It is the result of a long series of political, economic, social, and cultural changes, all of which have worked to erode restraint and weaken civility and community. Those changes, which broke out into a rage in the 1960s, made the new freedom what it is today: a socially reckless force standing in the way of true liberty.

If a moderate level of social constraints is necessary to personal and social well-being, and to ordered liberty as well, then it is clear that the depth and range of today's psychological and social disorders will not substantially decline until the dynamics of the new freedom are understood. Those dynamics spring largely from the fact that restraint in the late twentieth century has for the first time in history become a social achievement.

In the past, restraint was born of necessity; it was a precondition of survival. Throughout most of human history, men and women were burdened with so many demands and responsibilities that they hardly had time to cast restraint aside. That is no longer true. To an unprecedented extent, we have freed ourselves of the burdens of the past, leaving more room for individual pursuits than ever before. Of this we can be justly proud. But the flip side of this achievement is that we have also freed ourselves of the necessity of exercising restraint. That's the problem: without a measure of restraint, the interests of the individual turn inward, resulting in behavior that is increasingly narcissistic and antisocial in nature.

Consider what the burdens of the past were. Economic constraints were felt so severely that none but the elite managed to escape the discipline of subsistence. It wasn't as though the individual was forced to pull his own weight. No, it would be accurate to say that individuals, embedded in families, collectively pulled one another's weight.

Today we live in a society where family burdens have lessened to an unbelievable extent. Until fairly recently it was a societal expectation that

15

each person assume responsibility for his parents, siblings, spouse, and children. The idea that somehow the individual was not responsible for his family's well-being would have been considered bizarre by previous generations. Families were large and that meant that older siblings were responsible for their younger brothers and sisters. Children, upon reaching maturity, were obliged to provide for their parents, as their parents had provided for them. Reciprocal obligations were a requirement, not an option.

Family relations were given sustenance by the certain knowledge that mutual reliance was a fact of life. The near-absence of governmental programs for the aged and the infirm meant it was the duty of family members to provide for those in need. Interdependence was also furthered by the fact that parents lived with their children throughout a large part of their lives; life expectancy was short and marriage was generally postponed until relatively late in life. The social bond was tight but it wasn't due to naturally affective relations. It was due to the constraints of a developing economy.

The economic independence of the elderly has been one of the most striking phenomena of the twentieth century and one of the most visible indications of the decline of family burdens. From time immemorial, the elderly have been as dependent on their next of kin as a child is on his parents. But today most have achieved a state of independence that is the envy of young couples. The vast majority of the elderly live in homes, pay no mortgage, and receive property tax relief. More elderly are covered by private pension plans today than ever before (half the corporate stock is owned by pension funds). Not only do they not live on a fixed income, but they have the assurance that their Social Security checks will be indexed to inflation. The poor among the elderly, a segment that has declined dramatically in the past few decades, are eligible for Supplementary Security Income, a guaranteed minimum-income program available in all fifty states.

Another factor that has reduced family burdens has been the declining size of the family. Since the time of the American Revolution, the trajectory of the birth rate has been pointing downward. There have been some major blips, typically following a war or in times of unusual prosperity, but the spiral has been descending for the past two hundred years. With fewer siblings to take responsibility for while growing up, and fewer children to provide for later in life, most men and women can escape the extent and degree of traditional family obligations. The effect of this demographic pattern has been to allow more freedom for the individual. But it has also resulted in a contracting orbit of primary relations.

The reduction of family burdens has had a profound impact on our culture. "The major historical change in family values," writes sociologist Tamara Hareven, "has been a change from a collective view of the family to one of individualism and sentiment." What she means by this is the shift from the

nineteenth-century family of mutual obligations to the twentieth-century vari-
ant of individual priorities and preferences. This shift, she maintains, has
seen family economic and social needs give way to the "liberation of individuals."[1]

The contraction of the family has been mirrored by a contraction in the
community. The late anthropologist Philippe Aries argued that from the
Middle Ages to the eighteenth century, it was the community, not the family,
that was the most important social unit in Western societies. "Every individual grew up," he contended, "in a community made up of relatives, neighbors, friends, enemies, and other people with whom he had interdependent
relationships." "Feelings," he added, "were diffuse, spread out over numerous natural and supernatural objects, including God, saints, parents, children,
friends, horses, dogs, orchards, and gardens."[2]

The extensiveness of the social web described by Aries is a thing of the
past. Social and geographic mobility, coupled with increasing economic
independence, has diminished the central role that community relations once
played. Feelings, it is evident, have collapsed inward, making self-absorption
a style of life for millions of Americans. The result is a shrinking nucleus of
relationships, none of which has the permanency of past ties.

What has happened, in essence, has been a steady release of the individual
from traditional family obligations and community constraints. As the twentieth century has progressed, it has become easier and easier for men and
women to escape family burdens and the reach of social sanctions. Less
accountable to fewer people, they have less reason to practice individual
responsibility, and less need to exercise restraint.

Many of today's best social observers blame capitalism for the erosion of
individual responsibility and restraint. Sociologist Daniel Bell, for instance,
maintains that our society comprises two conflicting sets of values. On the
one hand, there are the values of the Puritan ethic: hard work, thriftiness, and
sobriety, these are the values upon which capitalism was built. On the other
hand, there are the values of hedonism: immediate gratification, personal
pleasure, and expressiveness, these are the values of corporate capitalism,
working to undermine the very values that made capitalism a success.[3]

Two astute left-wing critics, Christopher Lasch and Michael Harrington,
blame capitalism for the deracination of our culture. Lasch contends that the
rugged individualism of our dog-eat-dog capitalist society has descended into
a sea of narcissism. Individualism has become so extreme that nothing short
of self-absorption satisfies in this culture of decay.[4] Michael Harrington
laments the lack of transcendent values, blames "late capitalism" for creating
this condition, and prescribes socialism as the cure.[5]

Sociologist Robert Bellah also blames capitalism.[6] It used to be that the
Protestant ethic ruled the land, holding society together. Capitalism, with its

"get-ahead" individualism, destroyed the social fabric by releasing the individual from the grasp of kinship, community, and inherited status. Bellah feels that the government should take the lead and put an end to "the inordinate rewards of ambition" that make for excessive individualism. In other words, the government should put a lid on the maximum amount of money anyone can earn or win. That presumably would lessen the social distance between classes and give way to a greater sense of harmony.

The critics' emphasis on capitalism is misplaced. If there were some inherent feature of the capitalist system that accounts for social disorganization, then why would it appear during "late" capitalism and not earlier? The late nineteenth century was a far better approximation of pure capitalism than today. A hundred years ago, laissez-faire capitalism was at its peak, as businessmen went about their business unencumbered by government regulations and constraints. Yet the age of the robber barons was an age of greater social solidarity than the degree we enjoy today.

If anything, nascent capitalism strengthened the demand for individual responsibility and restraint. Harvard social scientist James Q. Wilson contends that industrialization accentuated accountability "by replacing the lost discipline of the small community with the new discipline of the factory and the public school." The burgeoning manufacturing sector of the economy insured responsibility: "Economic efficiency required punctuality, industriousness, and habits of cooperative effort; failure to abide by this new regimen condemned the urban worker to destitution or to an inhospitable almshouse."[7] The minuscule role of government reinforced this reality.

Perhaps the biggest mistake that capitalism's critics make is in assuming that other modern economic systems are not as nakedly individualistic as capitalism. It is true that capitalism possesses no "transcendant ethic," no ultimate end that binds the community together. But stripped of its rhetoric—and that is all it is—what exactly does socialism have to offer? Is there anyone who wants to argue, on the basis of the evidence, that is, on the basis of the actual historical record, that socialism advances a moral end? Considering the extent to which atomized relations characterize Soviet society (the Swedes are not much better), what with the high rates of divorce, alcoholism, and delinquency, there is little reason to believe that socialism induces a sense of community.

Of course, it is true that capitalism, stripped of the Protestant ethic, has no moral underpinning. But that is like saying that a man without morals is immoral. Strip the moral base from any system of exchange—economic or otherwise—and the result will be the same. It is morality, grounded in religion, that makes for community. Yes, it is more difficult for morality to assert itself in a society that prizes individual liberty, but it is not impossible.

If capitalism leads to a weaker social bond, then why haven't the Japanese succumbed to the same fate? They are, after all, every bit as capitalistic as we are. Yet judging from the degree of social cohesion evident in their society, it is apparent that capitalism, per se, doesn't foster social decay. There must be some other factor that's been discounted. That factor is culture.

For different historical reasons, the cultures of America and Japan are wildly different. In America, the individual has always reigned supreme; in Japan, the group. In Japan, unlike America, the social bond has always commanded the utmost attention, never being taken for granted. The Japanese have repeatedly shown far more interest than we have in nurturing a highly structured society. The result is a tightly knit society, one that effectively checks rampant individualism.

The critics of capitalism are getting warmer when they hint that there might be something negative that advanced capitalism does to society, rather than any systemic flaw it has. There is a link, but it is one of consequence, not design: the affluence that capitalism produces tends to make superfluous the need to practice restraint. This is particularly true in a society like ours where individual liberty is almost a religion. Affluence unburdens the individual, lifts his load, and eases his responsibilities. Most important, it awakens in the individual a desire for freedom from burdens of any kind. Hence, burdens that previously were seen as unavoidable and comparatively light in load are now interpreted as intrusive and overbearing. They must go.

The reason that affluence hasn't had the same effect in Japan as it has in the United States is due to the many sources of social constraints that operate there. The "we-ness" that characterizes Japanese culture is a product of the values distilled in the home, reinforced at school, and demanded on the job. The Japanese, though economically modern, have managed to preserve their cultural heritage far better than the Americans or the Europeans. The Japanese work hard at creating social cohesion; it doesn't come "naturally" to them. Children are taught to subordinate their interests to the needs of the group. Workers are taught to subordinate their interests to the needs of the corporation. The Japanese value loyalty, authority, tradition, and custom. We value individualism and have never shown much respect for authority, tradition, and custom.

Affluence solves some problems, most of them material in nature, while creating new ones, most of them social in nature. What it does best is to lessen the need for toil, effort, and burden. That being the dream of mankind throughout the ages, it deserves to be said that capitalism has done more to make life easier than any economic system ever devised. But success has whetted the appetite for more freedom from toil, effort, and burden. We have created the world's first truly effortless society.

It takes hard work, sustained effort, sacrifice, and compromise to make a relationship a good one. These are values that in our material world have been made obsolete. But they are just as necessary today as ever before when it comes to social relationships. We may be modern in terms of our technological achievements and standard of living, but we are no different from the ancients in terms of human needs.

There is another factor, besides declining family and economic constraints, that has contributed to the unburdening of the individual: the socialization of responsibility. The twentieth century has experienced a massive redistribution of responsibility from the individual to the institution. As individual responsibility has declined, so too has the urgency of practicing restraint. Nothing channels an individual's energy more toward the best interests of society than individual responsibility. Individuals who accept responsibility for their actions are a social asset. Those who do not are a liability.

The degree of individual responsibility that inheres in any society is a function of demand. American society in the late twentieth century exhibits little in the way of individual responsibility precisely because little is demanded. Institutions have replaced individuals as the prime agents of responsibility. We expect institutions to take care of our financial planning. We expect institutions to pick up the tab for our education, training, and retraining. We expect institutions to provide us with an income in our old age. And most important, we expect institutions to accept the lion's share of the blame whenever anything goes wrong in our lives.

The popular refrain goes like this: society is to blame; our culture conditioned it; the corporations made it happen; government is the culprit; we're all guilty. Everyone is responsible but the individual. Rare is the person who "owns up," who believes in accountability and admits fault. It is no wonder that so many people fail in school, work, and marriage. Few are willing to accept a measure of responsibility for their behavior.

State paternalism has something to with the decline of individual responsibility. The New Deal of Franklin Roosevelt and the Great Society of Lyndon Johnson did as much to unburden the individual as anything. Today, half the households in the United States receive some kind of benefit from the government. Government programs include Social Security, disability insurance, unemployment compensation, railroad retirement benefits, veteran's pensions, Medicare, Medicaid, food stamps, housing subsidies, civil service pensions, educational assistance, energy assistance, school meals, Supplemental Security Income, and Aid to Families with Dependent Children. For some, indeed for millions, their entire livelihood is due to government money and in-kind relief.

The more institutions do for individuals, the less individuals do for themselves, and there's no getting around it. It used to be that when someone was sick or disabled or simply down on his luck, he'd turn to his next of kin for support, or possibly to a neighbor. Now no one in his right mind would ask a cousin for a loan. He'd quickly be told to take a hike to the nearest bank or welfare office. And asking a neighbor for a little assistance is about as likely to result in a loan as asking Scrooge for a Christmas donation. Only the dumb would bother to ask.

Big government undermines individual responsibility in several ways. Our civic muscles atrophy unless occasionally flexed. What happens when the government becomes all-encompassing is that individuals lose the resolve to attend to the needs of their community. As taxes increase, so does the expectation that community responsibilities are the duty of government, not citizens. Self-government loses its appeal and citizen participation dwindles. Needless to say, the democratic process itself becomes jeopardized.

Another way the growth of government enervates civic virtue is by inducing a sense of impotence in individuals. The bigger government grows, the harder it is to convince men and women that they should get involved. Take education. Not too long ago if a parent had a complaint with the curriculum, or textbooks, or whatever, he or she could get the matter resolved by paying a visit to the teacher or principal. Now parents are directed to the school board, which in turn refers them to local officials, who recommend they visit the state education office, which asserts that Washington makes the decisions. And in Washington, no one is sure who makes what decision. So why get involved?

Given this reality, those who do get involved tend to serve very narrow, partisan interests. The increase in single-issue politics in this country, while often deplored, is little understood. People who feel powerless to change society, due to the omnipotence of government, will gravitate toward whatever issue is of the single most importance to them. Mustering enough energy to rally around one issue or cause is about the extent of most people's commitment. The conviction that it is possible to change a part of the system, but not the system itself, is alluring to those who feel that most decisions are beyond their reach.

As the size of government has increased, so too have the demands made on it. No longer is the government expected to simply provide a bit of social insurance for those who might need it. Increasingly, we have come to see government as an insurer against risks. In the words of Israeli professor Yair Aharoni, we have become "the no-risk society."[8]

Aharoni notes that over the past few decades there has been a large shift of risks from the individual to the government. Examples are legion. We are insured against earthquakes, floods, storms, unemployment, poor health, hazardous products—just to name a few. Safety in the workplace, guaranteed working hours, pollution abatement, Social Security benefits, and no-fault workers' compensation offer other examples of the shift in responsibilities. Ailing firms and ailing cities receive support, even when it is clear that they have no one to blame but themselves. Research and development are subsidized by guarantees and grants, loans are guaranteed, quality is controlled, information and social insurance supplied, foreign competition checked, and even social status is protected. Much of this is undertaken by what Aharoni aptly calls "the invisible government," that is, a combination of regulations, laws (for example, licensing laws), and changes in institutional setting.[9]

In recent years, the government has done more than just protect individuals from risk, it's protected corporations as well as cities. Chrysler, Lockheed, Continental Illinois, and New York City are the most obvious examples. With so many cushions to fall back on, market discipline has gone the way of self-discipline: it's a rare commodity. Not for nothing does John Kenneth Galbraith cynically call the rash of government bailouts the "new socialism."[10]

Aharoni is correct in his analysis that a "new social order" is emerging. The shift in burdens away from the individual and onto "society" represents a profound philosophical and political change. The displacement of responsibilities affects our conceptions of justice and the balance of political power. A great deal is at stake, much more than we are willing to admit.

Perhaps nowhere is the "new social order" more evident than in the field of tort law. It sometimes seems as though virtually anyone but the wrongdoer can and will be held responsible for an act of negligence. Our no-fault society has made it increasingly popular to blame the "environment" or "society" or some other faceless entity for the delinquency of specific individuals. When culpability is stretched to cover almost anyone who might have had anything at all to do with someone else's misfortune, lines of individual responsibility blur and lose their visibility. The cost to society is manifold.

Beginning in the 1960s, a move away from a standard of negligence to a rule of strict liability took place. Caveat emptor ("let the buyer beware") was discarded as a relic of the age of rugged individualism, holding little credibility in an age that saw the consumer in an unequal power relationship with manufacturers. Consumers' rights became the rallying call and strict liability the weapon: anyone who sells a potentially dangerous product that is defective is liable for any injury that the buyer may incur. The result has been a gigantic increase in product liability cases since the 1960s.

It is no coincidence that this expansion of civil liability took place in the 1960s. It was in the sixties when freedom became defined as freedom from restraint. It was in the sixties when the redistribution of responsibility from the individual to the institution reached unprecedented levels. It was in the sixties when the idea of no-fault was broached.

In 1965 two law school professors, Jeffrey O'Connell and Robert Keeton, proposed a solution to climbing auto insurance rates: they recommended that a no-fault plan replace the negligent standard of liability. Less than ten years later, O'Connell was arguing that his no-fault idea be adopted universally to include all nonauto insurance as well. Heavyweights from law, industry, and insurance companies lined up on both sides of the issue, producing arguments based on reason, emotion, and propaganda. At stake was more than money; whether responsibility should be individualized or collectivized was the central philosophical issue, though regrettably it was not always perceived that way.

Under the traditional tort liability system governing auto insurance, the party that was innocent had to prove the wrongdoing of the negligent driver. This system had the virtue of holding the negligent driver responsible for his behavior, but it had the drawback of creating considerable delay, insofar as determination of guilt and the amount to be awarded for alleged pain and suffering were often the subject of endless disputes. The proposed no-fault system simply switched the trade-offs: proving fault was scratched altogether (each party would be compensated for out-of-pocket losses only), thereby eliminating the necessity for time-consuming legal battles.

The record on no-fault since the 1970s has been mixed. Whether it "works" or not (usually measured in terms of time and money) is important, but of secondary significance. What matters most, at least in terms of its cultural import, is whether it contributes to, or erodes, a sense of individual responsibility. On this count, no-fault must be judged a failure.

No-fault goes beyond strict liability by doing away with the concept of fault. Under strict liability, a person who is injured by a nondefective product cannot hold the manufacturer liable. Under no-fault, he can. Legal scholar Jethro Lieberman put his finger on the problem: "This is a radical concept in a free society that is uneasy about collective or communitarian responsibilities toward the individual."[11] It leads to what law professor Alfred F. Conrad has called the "socialization of injury."[12]

No-fault abandons once and for all the notion that the guilty must pay for their indiscretions. It sends a message to all individuals that the law will not seek to restrain or deter their wrongdoing. It invites carelessness instead of carefulness. Justice, in the words of Professor Conrad, becomes "macro-justice," that is, it turns on a cost-benefit, utilitarian analysis.[13] And responsibility becomes collectivized, thereby freeing the individual of yet another burden.

The changes in liability law that started in the 1960s reflected more than an attempt to socialize responsibility. They symbolized a growing hostility toward institutions. The individual was fighting back, asserting his rights against the megastructures of government, corporations, and large-scale organizations that towered over him. Martin Luther King and Ralph Nader led the way, demonstrating that the lone individual could fight city hall and the board room and win. They inspired others to do the same.

The antipathy displayed toward institutions was populist in spirit. The individual, who had always been king in America, felt threatened by the enormousness of the institutions that engulfed him. It was David against Goliath, the individual against the institution, with the courtroom as battle-field. Suing was a way of getting even, providing a chance to tame the institutions that disparaged the individual. Suing also represented the failure to resolve disputes informally: it meant the social bond was in a state of disrepair.

Nothing illustrates the individual's vindictiveness against institutions better than the munificent awards that have been sought for an array of alleged damages. Punitive damages, as well as damages for pain, suffering, and mental anguish, have escalated in recent years, as more and more people have become convinced that they are entitled to more than just normal compensa-tion for their misfortunes. Punitive damages, which are applied in excess of actual compensatory damages, are awarded primarily to punish and deter someone who has acted either recklessly or maliciously. Such awards were initially applied sparingly, but no more. *New Republic* writer Michael Kinsley knows why: "Courts have become far more imaginative in their definitions of actual harm, awarding large sums for emotional distress, fear of getting cancer (as opposed to actually getting cancer), and so on."[14]

The big money that people go after, and that the courts award, comes from institutions, not individuals. Municipalities and corporations are the favorite targets; they supposedly have "deep pockets" and can afford to divvy up the big bucks. What is particularly striking about this view is the extent to which institutions are conceived as abstract entities, as though people have nothing to do with them. It is sometimes forgotten that people pay bills, not abstract entities. But such is the no-fault mentality, a direct consequence of no-fault legislation and the new freedom that it expresses.

This ethos is so prevalent and so strong that it characterizes the personality makeup of a growing number of Americans. One in fifteen now files suit each year, and the rate is growing. Tamar Lewin of the *New York Times* studied the skyrocketing awards being sought and concluded that "almost anyone with a grievance or an injury considers taking it to court, knowing that even if the complaint is frivolous, the defendant and his insurer might find it cheaper to settle out of court than to defend themselves."[15]

Even when no-fault legislation is not the bait that lures the "get-the-deep-pockets crowd," the pursuit of inflated awards mounts nonetheless. The misuse of the principle of joint and several liability is a case in point. As an old common law idea, this principle at one time had the merit of holding all parties to an injury accountable for their contribution. Now it has evolved into a weapon to extract as much as possible from the richest party involved, independent of the role that said party played in contributing to the injury.

In fact, it no longer matters whether the plaintiff himself was responsible for his own injury. The City of Los Angeles was held liable in a case where a sixteen-year-old girl was injured when the drunk driver of the car she was in ran a stop sign and crashed into another motorist. The city was found to be 22 percent liable due to poor visibility of the street lane lines. That it was raining the evening of the accident didn't matter: the girl was awarded over $2 million. Her drunk friend, it turned out, had very little insurance. Hence, he was judgment free.

Jethro Lieberman believes that people sue because they're unhappy,[16] not because of changes in liability laws. But if unhappiness is the issue, then are we to believe that beginning in the 1960s there was a sudden and sizable increase in personal unhappiness? Was it simply a matter of unhappiness that inspired the father of a thirteen-year-old boy to sue school officials in Milford, Connecticut, after he found his son had committed suicide *in his home*? (Teachers and administrators were blamed for not knowing the boy was troubled.)

Lieberman refuses to believe that legal changes have behavioral consequences. "In the final analysis," he says, "supposing that liberal tort laws are the cause of litigation is like arguing that liberal constitutional rights for criminal defendants prompt crime."[17] It is true that liberal tort laws do not give rise to injury, any more than liberal constitutional rights for criminal defendants cause crime. But both inexorably provide an incentive for irresponsible people to practice their irresponsibility. Once the tone is set by law, it is picked up very quickly by those who seek to exploit it. That is why those who shape the law must take responsibility for the kind of signals the law delivers.

The onslaught of litigiousness has created problems for virtually every segment of society. Particularly hard hit have been doctors, dentists, drug companies, day-care operators, small businessmen, accountants, contractors, architects, real estate brokers, and bar owners. Even the clergy, teachers, and parents have proved vulnerable. Lawsuits against municipalities doubled in just three years, between 1982 and 1985. Local police departments have shut down and insurance companies have refused coverage to a growing number of municipalities. Almost 10 percent of obstetrician-gynecologist specialists quit their jobs in 1983 alone.

There are now two companies that make football helmets; there used to be eighteen. New York City paid $700,000 to insure the Roosevelt Island Train in 1985; the next year it paid $10,000,000. The Boy Scouts have slapped a fee on every troop and Cub Scout pack in the country to help cover insurance costs. Little League teams in one area of Queens, New York, were told to come up with $25,000,000 in coverage if they wanted to play ball. Customers can no longer sample wine, or beer, at a number of wineries and breweries.

Adding to the fun has been a sharp increase in insurance premiums for beaches, resorts, restaurants, and bars. Ice skating and skiing have been devastated. And the famous Cyclone roller coaster at Coney Island had to shut down for half the season in 1986 for failure to come up with the $3,000,000 it needed to operate.

Even more serious has been the intimidating effect that rising insurance costs have had on the publishing industry. Some publishers are so scared of a large lawsuit that they are flatly refusing to publish controversial books. It never seems to end. We have defensive medicine and defensive architecture. There is the specter of Coca-Cola bottlers suing Coca-Cola over the price they're charged for Diet Coke syrup. Lawyers are suing lawyers, and obstetricians in Georgia are refusing to care for pregnant lawyers, law clerks, and wives of lawyers whose firms sue doctors for malpractice. It's no wonder that Lloyds of London says the U.S. court system is breaking the bank.

It all started in the 1960s. The litigation explosion is directly traceable to the liberalization of tort law that began after 1960. By expanding civil liability to the extent that it has reached today—so that a mental patient who jumps in front of a subway in a failed attempt at suicide is allowed to collect $650,000 in damages (the driver should have stopped sooner!)—it is clear that we're heading down the wrong road.

It is folly to think that law has no effect on values, ethics, beliefs, sentiments, and ideas. It is the very idea of no-fault that makes such legislation ominous. Such a concept would have been unthinkable in a different day and age. But not today. Today rights mania defines freedom as the absence of any and all responsibilities and restraints. Push the responsibilities of the individual onto institutions and set him free! Let someone else—some rich guy or corporation—pay the bill. We're entitled to it.

This, then, is the climate in which the new freedom was born. Our longing for freedom without restraint is a natural outgrowth of a society geared toward the unburdening of the individual. Declining family obligations, increasing affluence, and a redistribution of responsibility from the individual to institutions have lessened the need for restraint and ignited a demand for freedom from every conceivable limitation in our lives. The new freedom tolerates no abridgments of liberty and regards appeals to the common good as unconscionable infringements on the rights of the individual. Duty is a chore not worth exercising. Freedom means having it all, now and forever.

Notes

1. Tamara Hareven, "American Families in Transition: Historical Perspectives on Change," in Arlene and Jerome Skolnick, eds., *Family in Transition* (Boston: Little Brown, 1986), p. 49.
2. Philippe Aries, "The Family and the City," *Daedalus* (Spring 1977): 227–29.

3. Daniel Bell, *The Cultural Contradictions of Capitalism* (New York: Basic Books, 1976).
4. Christopher Lasch, *The Culture of Narcissism* (New York: Norton, 1978).
5. Michael Harrington, *The Politics at God's Funeral* (New York: Holt, Rinehart and Winston, 1983).
6. Robert Bellah, *Habits of the Heart* (Berkeley: University of California Press, 1985); see especially the last chapter.
7. James Q. Wilson, "Crime and the American Culture," *Public Interest* (Winter 1983): 25.
8. Yair Aharoni, *The No-Risk Society* (Chatham, N.J.: Chatham House, 1981).
9. Ibid., pp. 1–2, 110, 135.
10. John Kenneth Galbraith, "Taking the Sting out of Capitalism," *New York Times*, May 26, 1985, sec. 3, p.1.
11. Jethro K. Lieberman, *The Litigious Society* (New York: Basic Books, 1981), p.52.
12. Quoted by Peter Vanderwicken, "Toward the Socialization of Injury," *Fortune* (November 1971): 161.
13. Ibid., p. 177.
14. Michael Kinsley, "Torts and Courts," *Pittsburgh Post-Gazette*, November 6, 1985, p. 11.
15. Tamar Lewin, "Insurance a Liability for Some," *New York Times*, March 8, 1986, p. 35.
16. Lieberman, *The Litigious Society*, p. 10.
17. Ibid., p. 64.

3

Rights Mania

It would be hard to find a man, woman, or child in America who isn't aware of his or her rights, real and contrived. And it would be equally hard to find anyone who can recite his responsibilities as quickly as his rights. The severance of rights from responsibilities is a twentieth-century phenomenon, having no counterpart in history.

Responsibilities without rights has been far more typical of societal arrangements than its obverse. When rights did exist, they were tied to responsibilities. More than that, they were limited, specific, and widely understood. Not today. Rights flourish while responsibilities flounder. As Rutgers sociologist Irving Louis Horowitz has said, the central mark of the twentieth century "is that a world in which obligations were taken for granted has been transformed to one in which rights are presumed to be inalienable."[1]

It's not hard to understand why there's been an inversion in the equation between rights and responsibilities. Rights are directed inward, that is, they serve the interests of those who exercise them. Responsibilities are directed outward, that is, they serve the interests of others. Rights liberate; responsibilities constrict. In a society that defines freedom as the abandonment of constraint, it is no wonder that rights are celebrated while responsibilities are shunned.

Rights and responsibilities have historically been determined by one's status. Ascribed status, that is, status inherited at birth, was the social imprint that defined one's station in society. Age, sex, and order of birth fixed a person's position in society, important as they were in determining one's privileges and obligations. With mutual dependence on family members the rule, rights and responsibilities were exercised within the bounds of kinship.

As societies progressed, the individual became detached from the family and assumed newly created responsibilities. Society was now bound by contractual agreements between free individuals, enforced by the state. This, at least, is the account offered by the erudite nineteenth-century British sociologist Sir Henry Maine.[2]

The process that Maine observed has since been taken one step further: the individual's detachment from the family (and other social units) has accelerated, this time accompanied by a sharp decline in responsibilities of any kind. It is to the rights revolution of the 1960s and 1970s that one must turn in order to make sense of these social changes.

The rights revolution experienced two waves. In the 1960s social reform was popular, as protest and demonstration marked the events surrounding the war in Vietnam. In the 1970s personal reform was fashionable, as a preoccupation with the self colored the cultural landscape. The 1960s witnessed an explosion of "we-orientedness"; the 1970s underwent an implosion of "me-orientedness." It was the rights of others that mobilized people in the 1960s. It was the rights of oneself that charged the 1970s.

The common ground of both waves was an unabiding hostility to existing social conditions. Authority, tradition, and custom were pinpointed as the enemy of freedom. To be free meant to be liberated from the traditional figureheads of authority: parents, teachers, clergymen, policemen, judges, employers—anyone who upheld the status quo—came under a full-scale attack. The damage done is still with us, even as a move to restore a measure of authority has gained ground.

Rights mania began once liberty was seen as rights alone and freedom from responsibility became respectable. The behavior of government had a lot to do with both. The creation of new rights for the individual, many of them long overdue, had the unanticipated effect of raising the ante for yet more rights, many of them unwarranted. This occurred at the same time that government was redistributing responsibilities from the individual to institutions. It was the interaction between the two—more individual rights and fewer individual responsibilities—that proved to be decisive.

The rights revolution, which is still running at fever pitch, is a recent phenomenon. But the motor force behind the various movements—the idea of rights—is much older. From the beginning of the Republic, liberty has been cast as the nation's most prized value; the individual our most treasured resource. Initially, individual liberty was seen as more a promise than a reality, as the existence of slavery and other forms of institutional denial made abundantly clear. But it was a promise so firmly embedded in our culture, so repeatedly proclaimed by presidents and preachers alike, that the lack of anything short of complete emancipation for all would remain visible, troubling, and consuming. History in America was on the side of liberty.

The treatment of blacks, first as indentured servants, then as slaves, and then as second-class citizens, left the pledge of freedom unfulfilled. Yet from the end of slavery to today, blacks have been included in the promise of individual liberty. The struggle to make the promise good constitutes the resolution of what the late Swedish economist Gunnar Myrdal once called the "American Dilemma," that is, the inconsistency between a creed that sports a belief in individual liberty and equal opportunity and the reality of racism and discrimination against blacks. The creed was so strong, Myrdal wrote in the 1940s, that the dilemma would be resolved favorably for blacks.

Exactly ten years after Myrdal's book appeared, the Supreme Court, in *Brown v. Board of Education*, gave sustenance to Myrdal's thesis: the gap between the American Creed and the treatment of blacks was going to be slammed shut. What no one knew in 1954 was that much more was happening than the finding that "separate but equal" was unconstitutional. Looking back at it now, it is evident that *Brown* effectively launched the rights revolution.

Exactly ten years after *Brown*, the Civil Rights Act of 1964 was passed. It was, without doubt, the most comprehensive antidiscrimination legislation ever written. Although the legislation was primarily designed to rectify the injustice that had been done to blacks, others took note of the sweep of the law. Among them were women, Indians, Asians, Hispanics, teachers, tenants, migrant farm workers, aliens, the handicapped, the elderly, employees, students, servicemen, prisoners, homosexuals, and lawyers. Especially lawyers.

Group rights became the rage of the 1960s as ethnic groups organized as interest groups. Sociologists Nathan Glazer and Daniel Patrick Moynihan were among the first to note that ethnic groups were behaving as interest groups.[3] They attributed this phenomenon, which they saw as a worldwide trend, to the unprecedented growth of government in the twentieth century. The more government largess grew, in the form of jobs, licenses, contracts, services, and programs of every kind, the more citizens competed for their fair share of public goods. Unable to build effective allegiances on the basis of something as unwieldly and impersonal as class, citizens turned to their ethnic affiliation as an appropriate source of mobilization.

Whatever the cause, the rights revolution would not have been possible without the role played by the courts, the most independent branch of government. It was to the courts that rights activists turned for redress of grievances. Beginning with *Brown*, unpopular minorities learned that unelected judges were the least beholden to public sentiment and the most likely officials to take an activist approach in addressing controversial social issues. It was to the federal courts, in particular, that rights activists turned. "The last quarter century," writes Circuit Judge Richard Posner, "has seen much legislative and particularly judicial creation of federal rights."[4]

Posner's observation is easily verified. Decisions affecting school desegregation, busing, affirmative action, abortion, capital punishment, civil liability, prayer in the schools, rights of the accused, the homeless, pornography, prisoners, mental patients, and students have been rendered by the federal courts, often to the wonderment of those who still believe that it is the duty of the courts to interpret law, not make it.

The reach of judges has been extended, in part due to the more expansive role of government in the postwar period, but it is also true that activist lawyers have made a major contribution. Having failed in the court of public opinion, and having failed in convincing congressmen of the rightness of their causes, public interest lawyers have sought to make an end run around the legislature by taking their agenda straight to the courts. Class-action suits, another product of the 1960s, are the preferred tactic, an approach declared illegal in every other part of the world.

Law professor Richard Morgan has aptly dubbed the array of interest group advocates, law professors, activist judges, and publicists who seek to redo America as "the rights industry." Imbued with a missionary spirit, these unelected spokesmen of the public are convinced that the road to freedom is marked by simply securing more rights for individuals. "They have increasingly ignored or distorted important aspects of the American tradition," says Morgan, "which bear on the adjustment of liberty and fairness claims."[5] In doing so they have disabled key American institutions, all the while declaring that they were liberating those in need of liberation.

Ralph Nader epitomizes what the rights movement is all about. "The ultimate goal of this movement," explains Nader, "is to give all citizens more rights and remedies for resolving their grievances and for achieving a better society."[6] The underlying assumption is that society is better off when each of its members is armed to the hilt with rights, prepared to do battle in the arena of law. This militaristic mentality does not allow for consensus to emerge from the give-and-take of human relations. Rights industry specialists preempt this process by casting disputes, often inchoate in nature, into the domain of jurisprudence. It is not surprising that relations are often strained beyond repair once the law succeeds in imposing a resolution to everyday quarrels, as well as to more serious matters.

It was the rights industry that acted as a catalyst for rights mania. Rights mania represents the rights revolution gone berserk. The rights industry popularized the idea that most of us are victims, or at least potential victims. Our fellow man did the victimizing, so we had better defend ourselves with a cache of rights lest we lose the battle. A competitive war of all against all was in store and no one could afford to be without legal armaments. It was this kind of thinking that turned a noble and decent movement—the quest for liberty, equality, and justice for all—into a gluttonous and self-serving romp undeserving of admiration.

The transmutation of the rights revolution from a crusade for justice into a crude outburst of individualism has resulted in a noticeable decline in both loyalty and standards of conduct. The single-minded pursuit of rights has jettisoned an interest in serving the common good. The prevailing attitude, one that borders on paranoia, seems to be a variation on the theme that the best defense is a good offense, viz., better move fast to get everything that's coming to us and more, lest someone else come along and take our fair share first.

We have come to think of rights as nothing more than a weapon of self-interest. It is this idea that buttresses the popular ethic of entitlement and, its close cousin, the public-be-damned conception of the common good. A "gimme" kind of attitude has triumphed as more and more people come to the joint conclusion that someone else owes them everything and they owe no one anything. It is a disastrous mix, one that eats away at the social fabric.

The welfare rights movement of the 1960s contributed heavily to the establishment of a "gimme"-type attitude. The welfare explosion was a response by public officials to a growing demand for public assistance. Welfare activists such as Richard Cloward and Frances Fox Piven like to blame public officials for initiating welfare as a means toward "regulating the poor." But they've got it backward: it was people like them to whom politicians responded, giving in to the clamor for welfare. It was radical ideology, not political manipulation, that launched the welfare rights movement.

In the midsixties, Cloward and Piven led the demand for welfare by insisting on a strategy specifically designed to disable local institutions, bankrupt the cities, and force the nationalization of welfare. The strategy they proposed was "a massive drive to recruit the poor *onto* the welfare rolls." Every person who was even remotely eligible for public assistance had to be found and then convinced as to the wisdom of becoming a welfare recipient. "Advocacy must be supplemented," they added, "by organized demonstrations to create a climate of militancy that will overcome the invidious and immobilizing attitudes which many potential recipients hold toward being 'on welfare.' "[7]

The middle class took note of what was happening. An "if-them-why-not-us" attitude was born, a sentiment that still marks American culture today. John Lindsay may have been the first public official in the country to see this attitude in action. At the stroke of midnight, January 1, 1966, Lindsay became the mayor of New York City, and at precisely that time he was met with a transit strike, organized by Mike Quill, president of the transit workers' union. Quill reasoned that if New York had plenty of money to pay people for not working, surely it could afford to give a raise to those who did work. Lindsay was forced to concede. Then the sanitation workers struck, followed by doctors, nurses, police, and firemen.[8]

Going on strike is one of most popular ways of exercising rights mania. Many respected professionals have amply demonstrated just whose interests they're really serving. Teachers, for example, were once regarded as pillars of the community, professionals deserving of the highest respect. When they occasionally went on strike to secure better wages or benefits, it was a painful experience for everyone, including themselves. Today it is common to see a "Back to School" ad on television followed by an evening-news story on striking teachers—teachers who struck only a few years ago. With characteristic aplomb, teachers violate the public trust by beginning the school year with a carefully planned walkout.

The breakdown in loyalty that rights mania fostered has by now spread to virtually every sector of society. Those in the public eye, such as professional athletes and public office-holders, provide visible evidence of a declining sense of loyalty to anyone save themselves. In sports, loyalty to fans is almost nonexistent as owners shuffle players and entire teams from city to city. Free agency did much to grant autonomy to ballplayers, but in doing so, it also cut player-fan loyalty. The effect of constantly traded players is to weaken allegiances; the same is true of constantly hired and fired managers.

Players have unionized, gone on strike, and generally thumbed their nose at the fans. Barely qualified infielders demand a share of the gate each time attendance tops fifty thousand, though no one came to see them play. Overweight outfielders come to spring training late, exhibiting neither shame nor embarrassment, and then demand a bonus if they report fit next season. Players who spend as much on drugs as most fans spend on mortgage payments are quick to portray themselves as victims. And college pups, who never set foot on a professional playing field, demand six figures, plus a fat bonus just for signing.

The same callousness is evident in party politics. It used to be that party loyalty was a given, and that office-seeking candidates would reflexively support the party, holding infighting to a minimum. But all that has changed in the age of the new freedom, as allegiances are perceived as a drawback, a hoop that no one need jump through. As with the other fruit of the new freedom, the breakdown of party politics ripened in the 1960s.

The decline of political parties is a textbook example of the consequences of rights mania, especially as reflected in the Democratic party. Until 1972 no one could hope to become the nominee of either party without the support of party regulars. Clubhouse politics prevailed as prospective candidates spent most of their time trying to curry favor with the party hierarchy. Characterized by inbreeding, this procedure nonetheless provided for a sense of community and made loyalty an absolute must for success. But this method of candidate selection was rent by the events of 1968.

After Eugene McCarthy saw how difficult it was to win delegates at the

1968 Democratic convention, some members of the party sought to change the delegate rules so that in the future party outsiders like McCarthy might have an easier time beating party insiders like Hubert Humphrey. They succeeded. Led by George McGovern, they radically changed the primary system. No more would voters choose delegates to the convention (who were mostly party regulars), they would now choose candidates, thus undercutting the power of party officials to influence the selection of the ultimate nominee.

On paper the changes sounded democratic: open the party to everyone, not just the party loyalists, and watch participatory democracy in action. But the irony is the parties are less democratic now than ever before because political opportunists have come out of the woodwork to leapfrog over the party regulars right into the center of attention. An elite corps of well-educated activists has supplanted grass-roots party workers, especially in the Democratic party. The rhetoric is democratic, but that's all.

By opening the primary system up to every Tom, Dick, and Harry who has enough money to spend his way into notoriety, party loyalty has gone by the wayside, a relic of a different era. Those who can't afford to buy television space have sought the organized support of the most ideologically committed men and women in the country. But the problem is, the politically gung ho tend to be extremists, hence the relative success of Lyndon La Rouche's followers in local Democratic parties; they would never have amounted to anything under the old rules.

It is much more difficult for political parties to achieve consensus now than ever before. And for good reason: once rights mania became a strain in the dominant culture, it was only a matter of time before rampant individualism would find its way into party politics. With the moral authority of the party hierarchy challenged, the same chaos evident in society at large turned up within the parties. Brooklyn Congressman Charles E. Schumer said it best: "Congress is atomistic now. We are 435 or 100 atoms bouncing off each other and colliding. There used to be more structure, but the old glue that tied atoms into molecules has greatly weakened."[9]

The guiding spirit of the rights revolution has always been equality. Hierarchy, reflective of inequality, has been the object of destruction by rights activists. In the field of politics this has meant an attack on party leaders and the traditional coalitions of power. In economic affairs the unequal distribution of wealth has given rise to novel attempts at leveling. The social sphere has seen many and varied strategies at equalizing status differences, as between men and women, or adults and children. And in the area of culture, it is the existence of a moral hierarchy that has come under persistent assault by rights enthusiasts.

The idea of a moral hierarchy is anathema to anyone who takes an egalitarian approach to morality. The very existence of a cultural ordering of values is interpreted as unfair and elitist because the final selection represents the triumph of one set of values over another. To those who worship at the altar of equality, and there are millions who do so, this is too much.

We are now left with the doctrine of moral neutrality, with the belief that no cluster of values is morally superior to any other. We are also left with its progeny, that is, with the notion that nothing matters, that anything goes. Of course, those who promote moral relativism deny loudly that they are in any way responsible for the moral crisis that exists. They assume, against all evidence, that a society that sanctions a moral menu of norms and values can still provide for acceptable levels of civility and community.

The social fallout that has resulted in the attack on a moral hierarchy can be seen quite clearly in declining standards of excellence. That standards should decline as moral neutrality asserts itself is to be expected. Standards are, by their very nature, constricting, exclusionary, and emblematic of hierarchy. They are, therefore, representative of all that moral egalitarians find intolerable. That is why we hear so much about how subjective and really meaningless the whole discussion of merit is. Curiously, it never seems to occur to those who make such pronouncements that there is no reason that anyone should accept anything they say as meritorious, including their judgment that merit is meaningless.

The decline of standards has meant a decline in effort, and, ultimately, a decline in performance. Effort and performance, inextricably linked, have typically been a function of demand, so it is only natural that they should wither as standards lose their rigor. Standards have fallen in entrance examinations and in hiring, in the boardroom and in the bedroom, on the ballfield and on the battlefield, in schools and in playgrounds. Simple acts of courtesy are found less today than ever before, and gentlemanliness is scorned as atavistic. There has even been a noticeable decline in table manners.

There have always been people, in any age, who flouted the standards of the day. What makes our age different is the rejection of the very existence of standards. In the 1960s, Will Herberg accurately referred to this accomplishment as "the moral crisis of our time."[10] Standards, we are told, are "subjective," as if that were to deprive them of any value. So we are left with a situation in which each person picks and chooses exactly which standards, if any, he or she elects to follow, making social cohesion a virtual impossibility. This is the sociology of the new freedom, and the cause of moral unrest.

In his revealing portrait of Americans, Daniel Yankelovich commented that his research disclosed a strong increase in aimlessness and hedonism in recent years, especially among young people. He identified the cause: "Once people begin to question social rules, they find it difficult to draw the line."[11] Robert Bellah explained the prevalence of anomie the same way: "In the absence of any objectifiable criteria of right and wrong, good or evil, the self and its feelings become our only moral guide."[12]

The evidence is mounting that the new freedom, whether expressed in its freedom-as-rights form, or tendered as the doctrine of moral neutrality, is incompatible with the social and cultural bases of a free society. That individuals are deserving of rights is not the issue; no friend of liberty would ever suggest otherwise. The issue at hand is whether a free society can be expected to exist when individuals become so preoccupied with salvaging their rights that they lose interest in assuming their responsibilities. At stake is a respectable level of civility and community, without which pursuits of freedom cannot exist at all.

Notes

1. Irving Louis Horowitz, "Human Rights, Foreign Policy and the Social Sciences," in *Rights and Responsibilities* (Los Angeles: University of Southern California Press, 1978), p. 171.
2. Sir Henry Maine, *Ancient Law* (Gloucester, Mass.: Peter Smith, 1970), pp. 163–65.
3. Nathan Glazer and Daniel Patrick Moynihan, "Why Ethnicity," *Commentary* (October 1974): 33–39.
4. Richard A. Posner, *The Federal Courts* (Cambridge: Harvard University Press, 1985), p. 80.
5. Richard Morgan, *Disabling America* (New York: Basic Books, 1984), p. 4.
6. Quoted by Michael Kinsley, "Saint Ralph," *Pittsburgh Post-Gazette*, November 27, 1985, p. 9.
7. Richard Cloward and Frances Fox Piven, "A Strategy to End Poverty," *Nation*, May 2, 1966, pp. 510–17.
8. For a good account of what happened to New York, see Charles R. Morris, *The Cost of Good Intentions* (New York: Norton, 1980).
9. Quoted by Steven Roberts, "Phil Gramm's Crusade against the Deficit," *New York Times Magazine*, March 30, 1986, p. 23.
10. Herberg's 1968 article, "What Is the Moral Crisis of Our Time?" was republished in *Intercollegiate Review* (Fall 1986): 7–12.
11. Daniel Yankelovich, *New Rules* (New York: Bantam Books, 1982), p. 90.
12. Robert Bellah et al., *Habits of the Heart* (Berkeley: University of California Press, 1985), p. 76.

4

The Revolt against the Human Condition

Thus far we have seen how the success of capitalism and the socialization of responsibility have combined to unburden the individual, leaving him impatient with all that limits or in any way encumbers him. Also noted have been the effects of the rights revolution, as both a social and moral phenomenon. To understand the genesis of the new freedom, one other factor must be added: the cultural contribution of new-freedom artists and writers. It is they who led the charge, preparing the culture for further assaults on the limitations of the human condition.

If there was one area of culture that witnessed the full force of the new freedom, it was music. In the 1960s, Jimi Hendrix tested the outer limits by making a frontal assault on harmony, attacking the very idea of what passed as "good taste." Janis Joplin, who like Hendrix overdosed on drugs, accurately described the essence of the new freedom by offering the refrain "Freedom is just another word for nothing else to lose." It was left to the heavy metalists to knock down the remaining cultural ordinates, trashing the very idea of harmony altogether. And by glorifying sex and violence, today's performers have mobilized parents to demand that the recording industry label records the way the movie industry rates films.

Jazz has been particularly hard hit by the new freedom. The path-breaking creativity of John Coltrane has been poorly imitated by a generation of musicians who know neither style nor substance. Calling it "avant-garde" seems enough to grant it legitimacy, though much of what has been produced is indistinguishable from the cacophony of sounds found in a mental ward. Fortunately, talented musicians like Wynton Marsalis and David Murray have helped to restore a measure of order and structure to jazz, demonstrating once again that improvization and spontaneity work best within defined parameters of expression.

The theater has succumbed to the same fate. Avant-garde has become synonomous with the latest mind-blowing techniques of light and sound, running the gamut from lasers to electronic gimmicks of the wildest sort. The National Endowment for the Arts and the Kennedy Center in Washington have contributed to the barrage, funding new theater companies that take direct aim at traditional norms and values. Never before have more people been able to make a living—and a good one at that—by tearing down the culture that supports them.

Literary analysis has trumpeted the new freedom by condemning outright any attempt to maintain critical standards of evaluation. We are told by some that poems and novels have no meaning, save what the reader gives them. We are free to import whatever we want, selectively choosing and discarding from the text at will. No one's interpretation is any better than anyone else's; this is moral neutrality at its stark naked best.

Authors, we are taught, don't reveal themselves to us. We decide what is revealed. Social reality is an ongoing enterprise, and how it is interpreted by society's actors is what exists, nothing more. This perspective, which is grounded in social psychology, depreciates history just as much as it delegitimatizes the authority of those who sponsor it. If everything is up for grabs, what is the point of criticism? And when everything is said and done, and the text has been deconstructed out of existence, what do we do with the carcass?

Perhaps no medium of communication has celebrated the new freedom more than art. Modernism, the no-holds-barred free-for-all revolt against bourgeois culture, expresses a raging desire to trample, mutilate, and destroy the norms, values, beliefs, and sentiments of established culture. Accordingly, freedom can be achieved only by annihilating every vestige of constraint. All that constitutes the status quo has to be swept aside if true freedom is to be realized.

Modern art has no social function, except of course to stimulate the dissolution of society. The idea of social obligations is repugnant to the modernist, for it is the very idea of subordinating the individual to society that gives rise to man's enslavement. Unlike the Renaissance artist who was driven out of commitment to civil or clerical authority, today's artist has no social function or mission. If the avant-garde symbolizes anything, it symbolizes the absurdity of those who portray the human condition.

Much of the nihilistic quality of modern art is rooted in Dada, a term that, appropriately, has no meaning. Dada art, which flourished in New York, Paris, Zurich, Berlin, and Cologne at the time of the First World War, was born out a need for total independence and emancipation. "Everything had to be demolished," proclaimed Marcel Janco in 1916. "We would begin again after the tabula rasa." As Janco made clear, Dadas would stop at nothing, making war on the bourgeois "idea of art, attacking common sense, public opinion, education, institutions, museums, good taste, in short, the whole prevailing order."[1]

Surrealism, which thrived in the 1920s and 1930s, turned to the Marquis de Sade for inspiration. Once again, the conviction surfaced that only by going to battle against existing social and cultural conditions could man hope to be free. "The destruction of traditional human relations," wrote surrealism's greatest chronicler, Maurice Nadeau, "leads to the construction of new ones, and of a new type of man."[2] The new man, of course, would be purged of greed and self-interest, thus giving hope to the dream of reconstructing the human condition. Surrealism, like its predecessor, Dada, was a movement of unmistakable twentieth century character: it represented the apotheosis of individualism and the ardor of despair.

The very idea of "good taste," and all that constituted it, came under heavy attack in the 1950s. Jasper Johns and Robert Rauschenberg led the way, making cynical statements about the products of bourgeois culture. Modernism delights in parodying the superficiality of contemporary culture and positively luxuriates in promoting disdain for the content of accepted mores. There is no form of expression that is too blasphemous for the avant-garde. Indeed, the more blasphemous, the better.

Abstract art soared to new heights in the 1960s, attracting the attention of a new generation of rebellious artists. By wrapping oneself in the banner of abstraction, it was possible to garner the admiration and applause of critics and patrons alike. It did not seem to matter that much of what was produced was junk, pure unadulterated junk. In 1959, *New York Times* critic John Canaday stunned the avant-garde set by suggesting that "freaks, charlatans and the misled" had surrounded the truly creative, thereby granting legitimacy to the work of phonies. "Let us admit," he wrote, "that the nature of abstract expressionism allows exceptional tolerance for incompetence and deception." Canaday aptly concluded, "We have been had."[3]

Should abstract art be judged by the same high standards that Western art has historically been subjected to? The very question would have been inconceivable twenty years ago. But now Frank Stella, one of the most gifted abstract painters of the century, demands that the question must be answered, and answered affirmatively at that.[4] After flouting the etiquette of the bourgeoisie for decades, this about-face may be coming a little too late. "Many divergent claims to authority have begun by now to undermine and weaken art's integrity and plausibility," explains art critic and social observer Suzi Gablik, "since what pluralism really means is that the lines between what is acceptable as art and what is unacceptable no longer exist."[5] It remains to be seen whether the yardsticks of culture can be resurrected. After all, the avant-garde has been busy burying them for the past hundred years.

Gablik has put her finger on the real crisis of modernism: "If the great modern enterprise has been freedom, the modern hubris is, finally, the refusal to accept any limits." In a telling commentary on how far we have progressed, Gablik wryly notes that "our one common belief at this point seems to be that no one can be made accountable: any form of limitation is experienced as a prison."[6] The new freedom has spent itself, and with nothing left to challenge, the avant-garde has boxed itself into a corner from which it cannot escape. Having succeeded in anesthetizing the public's capacity to be shocked, modernism has wrung itself dry.

"The great ages of genius, starting with the fifth century B.C. in Athens," notes sociologist Robert Nisbet, "have never been calculatedly revolutionary, contemptuous of the past, in avid search for originality."[7] That is why the present age will not be counted among the best: it wallows in negativism and thinks iconoclasm is proof positive of creativity. The truly creative have always been well steeped in tradition, mastering the masters before building their own portfolios. Why this should come as a surprise to many aspiring young artists is testimony to their collapse of intellect.

To be sure, creativity is conditioned on freedom. Where individual liberty is absent, creativity cannot be found. But the opposite is also true: the apogee of freedom (defined as the abandonment of constraint) is the nadir of creativity. Creativity flourishes when there is a healthy tension between individualism and community. When the individual emerges from the grip of community, the potential for creativity—in the arts and sciences—is great. But when individualism runs wild, the result is not more creativity but incoherence disguised as creativity. The Bauhaus notion "Start from zero" is both unattainable and unwise; it makes more sense to start where others have left off.

Public sculptor Scott Burton understands that creative freedom is meaningless when conceived in isolation. Unlike the studio artist who removes himself from social constraints, Burton finds that creativity is achieved by learning to deal successfully with constraint: "If you can deal with the restrictions, you get a heightened sense of freedom and power."[8] Burton's finding has been shared by all the masters, and succinctly explains the triumph of the Renaissance. But quite unlike the artists who made the Renaissance what it was, today's artists must decide to impose some restrictions on themselves, for few will be forthcoming from society.

To understand the thinking of new freedom-writers in the postwar period, it is important to recognize that their real animus was directed not so much against American society (though they surely were not supportive of it) as against the very idea of society itself. Though they would not admit to this charge, it is evident in their writings that they were profoundly alienated from all that is constitutive of society. Their belief in a society of total, uninhibited expressions of individuality is a contradiction in terms: society demands at least *some* subordination of the individual to the social.

Many new-freedom writers were reacting to the stability of the 1950s. For them, stability was synonymous with sterility. New Left inspirator Paul Goodman, for example, was among the first to complain about the halcyon days of the fifties. "When time, clothes, opinions, and goals become so regulated that people feel they cannot be 'themselves' or create something new," he predicted, "they bolt and look for fringes and margins, loopholes, holes in the wall, or they just run."[9] Legions of young people did exactly that—they bolted and hit the fringes and margins, pushing them back to a point that even Goodman did not anticipate.

Goodman's observation was characteristically American. Individualism, as history informs, is not so much a human want as it is a cultural product, one that resonates well with the American experience. Freedom in the West, and in the United States in particular, reserves a special place for the individual, a mantel so high that it towers over all its competitors. No place else is the idiosyncratic welcomed so uncritically as in the United States; it is as though new ground is broken each time someone departs from the norm. In such an environment, the nihilistic is often confused with the creative. When Goodman's expressions became operative in the 1960s, what emerged was a full-blown assault on the very meaning of society. Marriage, the family, sex roles, tradition, custom, religion—all the institutions, norms, and values that are the stuff of society—were attacked as instruments of repression. Liberation was conditioned on the emancipation of the individual from all that constrained him. The new freedom had taken hold.

The vision of freedom that is entertained by new-freedom writers is pre-political, that is, it conceives freedom as a property prior to man's existence in the body politic. It is a purely philosophical construct, having little bearing on the human imperatives that make man a social animal. Thus it has a hard time understanding that much of what makes society possible is necessarily restrictive of individual pursuits. It imagines chains where there are none, and hopes to sever those social harnesses that restrain the individual and allow him to conform to the common good.

If there was one writer who represented what the new freedom was all about even better than Goodman, it was the much-vaunted hero to the New Left, Herbert Marcuse. Addressing the Congress of the Dialectics of Liberation in 1967, Marcuse maintained that liberation meant the creation of a new person, one who "rejects the performance principles governing the established societies; a type of man who has rid himself of the aggressiveness and brutality that are inherent in the organization of established society, and their hypocritical, puritan morality; a type of man who is biologically incapable of fighting wars and creating suffering; a type of man who has a good conscience of joy and pleasure, and who works collectively and individually for a social and natural environment in which such an existence becomes possible."[10]

Marcuse's utopia is a place where the residue of history is unrecognizable.

All that is characteristic of man—his deeds, foibles, and proclivities—is strangely missing. So totally dissatisfied was Marcuse with what man had wrought that he could not envision any demonstrable improvement in the human condition short of a complete remake of the species. It was this fantasy, the hope of creating a world without unhappiness, that prevented him from utter despair.

Marcuse was a dreamer. He sincerely believed that we could create a society shorn of all but the most essential social strictures. The idea of a "non-repressive civilization," he said, could be discussed "not as an abstract and utopian speculation" but as a realistic possibility.[11] To that end, we need to commit ourselves to the struggle and break away from all reigning orthodoxies. Liberation required new paradigms as well as new strategies.

Marcuse cut directly to the marrow of the issue by confronting the Freudian proposition that civilization is based on repression. For Freud, as civilization advanced, so too did the need to subjugate human instincts; the former was conditioned on the latter. This pessimistic projection had to be defeated if the prospect of a nonrepressive civilization were to succeed. Marcuse set out to challenge the master and provide an elixir. His response helped launch a redefinition of the meaning of freedom.

Freud argued that man was, at bottom, guided by the "pleasure principle," by which he meant animal drives, passions, and impulses. Because no society could exist unless man's primordial appetites were checked, the need for a socially constructive "reality principle" was a never-ending process that knew of no exceptions in history. It was scarcity, maintained Freud, that accounted for the need to tame the animal in us and made possible the production of the human being.

Marcuse took umbrage at the idea that restraints on human instincts were necessitated by "the brute *fact* of scarcity"; scarcity was actually "the consequence of a specific *organization* of scarcity," that is, it was socially produced.[12] By maintaining that scarcity was in reality the result of conscious design, Marcuse challenged the fundamental Freudian proposition that repression is a staple characteristic of civilization. Such thinking, he contended, served only to rationalize the privileged position of the ruling class.

Marcuse believed that the distribution of scarcity that existed in contemporary society was the product of a particular mode of the reality principle, one he tagged the "performance principle." Ours was an acquisitive society, the kind that is predicated on the manipulation of labor and the thwarting of libido. A nonrepressive society, he held, would dispense with such historically induced patterns of inequality, providing for libidinal, as well as social, liberation.

Though he was willing to concede the impossibility of absolute freedom, the degree that he thought was attainable came close to approximating total liberation. There was a level of "basic repression" that could not be avoided, he yielded, but anything over and above what was absolutely necessary to conduct human associations was "surplus repression," the type based on domination, not rational authority. As he made clear, virtually all the alleged repression in society was surplus.

The rational mind-set exhibited by Marcuse is illustrative of new-freedom thinking. Unless a given social institution, norm, value, or custom makes sense according to the calculus of rationality, it has no legitimate role to play in the organization of society. This perspective cannot help but trash tradition, for it necessarily holds in contempt the very stuff that is the legacy of human behavior. It is not so much critical of any given type of society as it is critical of all that the term *society* conveys.

Marcuse saw "surplus repression" everywhere. The bourgeois family, the hierarchial division of labor, the entertainment industry[13]—virtually anything associated with the trappings of modern society—was treated with scorn. We were all oppressed, yet few knew it.

We were so oppressed in America that even the existence of a Bill of Rights didn't matter. In point of fact, Marcuse argued that civil liberties were the enemy of freedom in our society, operating as they were as yet another form of social control.[14] The choices that people exercised in the market were also seen as repressive; we didn't realize it, but "alien needs" were being imposed on us. In sum, the individual had been claimed by the forces of modernity. Obviously, there were exceptions: like his mentor, Marx, Marcuse was somehow able to rise above the conditioning forces that were ubiquitous for the rest of us.

Marcuse held out the hope that "the progress of civilization" eventually would undermine the reality principle based on scarcity. A level of *"abundance"* would somehow make moot the kinds of restraints that have historically been seen as functional to the best interests of society. A merging of instinct and reason would characterize a new reality principle in the non-repressive society.[15]

What would the new society—the nonrepressive one—look like? Here is where Marcuse exposes his antipathy toward the human condition best, for it is in his fancical society that he renders himself hostile to all that marks civilization.

To begin with, economic freedom would not mean individual choice, it would mean nothing less than "freedom *from* the economy —from being controlled by economic forces and relationships; freedom from the daily struggle for existence, from earning a living."[16] In short, freedom from the kinds of exchanges that make intelligible what it is to be a human being.

Political and intellectual freedom would similarly mean an end to life as usual. Marcuse envisioned a world wherein each individual had complete autonomy over every idea he entertained and everything he did. For example, there would be no such thing as our thinking being influenced by "public opinion."[17] This is a world where people interact but have no effect, where associations are made but have no impact, where exchanges are held but have no consequence, where decisions are rendered but have no outcome.

To those who scoffed at these projections, Marcuse replied that "the unrealistic sound of these propositions is indicative, not of their utopian character, but of the strength of the forces which prevent their realization." Furthermore, "All liberation depends on the consciousness of servitude," meaning that the first step toward the emancipation of the individual is recognition of the forces of oppression.[18] And that means that hostility to the existing social order is a natural predicate of liberation. Once again, shades of Marx. Those who accept his reasoning can see clearly; those who cannot, suffer from "false consciousness."

The message that Marcuse was sending was similar, in the end, to that of Fritz Perls and the Gestalt school of psychology: reject restraint; don't conform; repression is for neurotics; change society. Above all, let nothing stand in the way of total self-actualization.

The Counterculture

By the late 1960s, it was evident that the existing social order was being challenged, in many cases ravished, by those who saw adjusting to the dominant culture's norms and values as tantamount to "selling out." Freedom was interpreted as action—action taken in defiance of the most elementary rules of social discourse. Before the new social order was to appear, the old one had to go. This was, and still is, a cardinal principle in the thinking of the new freedom. It was a defining characteristic of what came to be known as the "counterculture."

Two social observers who both chronicled the changes that were occurring, and who by their immense popularity helped to inspire even more changes, were Philip Slater and Charles Reich. Their contributions were as reflective of the triumph of new-freedom thinking as any writers of their day. They were convinced that American society was at a threshold, Slater saying that we had reached "a breaking point," and Reich maintaining that a "revolution was coming." Both sought to push the process along.

Slater detailed the emergence of a new culture, one that was in every way contradictory to the culture of old. Because these cultures were fundamentally contrary to each other, there was no basis for a merger, only the possibility of an eclipse, of the old by the new. Those who huddled in the center of these two opposing cultures would be devoured at both ends; there was no room for fence sitters in this environment.

Like a model Utopian, Slater assigned a negative connotation to all that totaled the old culture, and gave uniformly high marks to the burgeoning new culture. The old culture—the still-dominant but clearly receding one—was based on competition, not cooperation. It denied sensual pleasure instead of celebrating it. It basked in privacy, as opposed to openness. It served the producer but not the consumer. It was tight, as oppposed to loose. Above all, it was cold and artificial, not warm and genuine.

Like Marcuse, Slater contended that it was scarcity that was responsible for the existence of the dominant value pattern in society. And like the German philosopher, he maintained that scarcity was a passing phenomenon, one that promised to alter the nexus upon which contemporary society was ordered.[19] Ironically, radicals seem to observe the end to scarcity only in those societies that have practiced the very values they have come to hate. Indeed, the communally oriented societies they seem to adore are strikingly impoverished.

As with other new-freedom writers, Slater wants it both ways. He wants efficiency as an outcome, but not the competitiveness from which it grows. He wants community, but not social compliance. He wants the removal of restraint, but not the antisocial consequences it entails. He wants human feelings to be freely expressed, but not the kind that hurt others. He wants people to be free to associate, but not the status differentiation that inevitably results. He wants it *his* way. Who doesn't?

The attack that Slater launched against American society—and it was launched with seething hatred against every aspect of it—evinced an enormous alienation from the bureaucratic-technological world of the twentieth century. This is not at all surprising because new-freedom consciousness finds disconcerting the kinds of elaborate structures of organization that the modern world requires. Devotees of the new freedom prefer spontaneity to order, and there is nothing spontaneous about life in megasized, high-tech organizations.

The misfit as hero is the theme of Charles Reich's *Greening of America*. Were it not for "people who were unhappy or maladjusted for personal reasons,"[20] America would have no hope. Our salvation lay in the hands of the most disaffected segment of the population. They were the bearers of the new freedom.

Reich's book provides the best inside look at the consciousness of the new freedom. Though he glorifies the wonders of the new day that was upon us, and is patently absurd in his romantic picture of youth, he does offer a valuable casebook analysis of new-freedom thought. Although the magnificent results he predicted never materialized, the adoption of a radically different set of norms and values did take place. They are the norms and values of the new freedom. And they are the principal cause of our psychological and social disorders.

What energized the thinking of the new freedom, and the thought of new-freedom guru Reich, was a two-pronged conviction: (a) America was in a state of crisis, culturally killing its own people, and (b) a revolution was on its way to undo the mess and literally create utopia. The revolution "promises a higher reason, a more human community, and a new and liberated individual. Its ultimate creation will be a new and enduring wholeness and beauty—a renewed relationship of man to himself, to other men, to society, to nature, and to the land." Begun by youthful misfits, it would in time include "all people in America."[21]

Reich saw the new freedom (he literally called it that)[22] as first and foremost a change of consciousness. Two modes of consciousness had characterized the American past; a third, that of the new freedom, was just developing. Consciousness I represented early American history, with its imagery of the hardworking farmer, small businessman, and God-fearing individual struggling against adversity. Centered on self-interest, the competitiveness and inequality that it produced worked to its demise. It ended with robber barons, corruption, and failure.

Consciousness II also collapsed of its own dead weight. Ushered in by the needs of a growing industrial order, this mind-set places a premium on everything and anything that serves the interests of the corporate state. The prototype carrier of this vision is a reform liberal, dedicated to the proposition that science and technology can be used to control experience. Ensconced in institutions, this sophisticated yet shallow creature of modernity has wrought a world of meaninglessness, hypocrisy, and injustice. Having sacrificed basic human feelings in exchange for material gain, he finds himself empty, exhausted, and defeated.

The alarm having been sounded, Consciousness III came to the rescue. Consciousness III began "with a few individuals in the mid-nineteen-sixties," and was, as of the late sixties, "the greatest secret in America."[23] A secret no more (not, at least, since Reich divulged its existence), the consciousness of the new freedom represents a new age—America's greening.

"The foundation of Consciousness III," says Reich, "is liberation." It is the kind of liberation that "starts with self," that is, it allows the individual to be "free to build his own philosophy and values, his own life-style, and his own culture from a new beginning."[24] It is the most novel, yet promising, form of consciousness ever to develop. It will set us free.

Reich's definition of liberation, according to the postulates of Consciousness III, is the new freedom defined. It imagines a world where everyone is free to create his own norms and values, de novo. There is no need for consensus in this amalgamation, just the appropriate dose of tolerance that is necessary to enable everyone to "create his own culture." This is a form of liberation that lies outside the scope of what is generally known as society.

The idea that each person is capable of creating his own culture is not an understandable proposition for human beings. To be exact, it does violence to the term *culture* to speak about it in such solitary terms.

As with Slater's picture of new-freedom consciousness, Reich emphasizes that competitiveness is unacceptable; he even holds that "the whole concept of excellence and comparative merit" is taboo. The flat rejection of standards of excellence (expressed, interestingly, by a Yale professor) stems from the conviction that to compete is to divide, and there can be no division in the world of the new freedom. The "world is a community,"[25] proclaims Reich, and that means that everyone is included.

One of Reich's most revealing insights into Consciousness III is his observation that the dictum "No one judges anyone else"[26] is nothing less than a "commandment" in the ethics of the new freedom. There are no deviants, outcasts, or pariahs allowed. Nothing that anyone does will be considered good or bad, wise or foolish. There will be no labeling, no conferring of honor, no stigma. What people do, accomplish, or produce makes little, if any, difference in how they will be received. Everyone is equal, whether provider or parasite, doer or dreg, champion or chump. This is a society without winners or losers. It is also a society without humans, for no such society has ever existed, or is capable of existing.

The revolt against society that is indicative of the new freedom finds expression in its abhorrence of such societal staples as authority, obligations, and roles. To say that no society can exist without these fundamentals is to state the obvious, yet it is precisely the obvious that has escaped new-age students of liberty. No one could get through the day if people proceeded willy-nilly to do as they pleased, abandoning their roles and behavioral expectations. Without some measure of authority, or legitimate power, rules would prove unenforceable and social discord would flourish. And without obligations to others, self-interest would prevail and the bonds that make for community would shatter.

The new freedom hates the idea that roles exist, and that is because roles are seen as constraining. Roles do constrain, and much the same can be said of institutions, norms, and values, but to imagine a society without them is to imagine a bird without wings: it is a self-contradictory proposition. Roles, institutions, norms, and values confer on human interaction the kinds of patterned behaviors that make society possible. That is why role differentiation based on sex, age, and occupation has existed in every known society, bar none. But new-freedom intellectuals think roles are dispensable artifacts, the kind of cultural lineament that is peculiar to a given episode of history. They always seem to think that they are on the cutting edge of a new sociological breakthrough. Until reality conquers once again.

When Reich speaks of the "role-prison"[27] that we are forced to live in, he has in mind the idea that somehow our true "self" is not allowed to emerge in contemporary society. He imagines that in his society—the free one—we will all be able to discover the uniqueness that is our own true self and proceed according to our own internal engine. This formulation depicts what might be called an aggregate of automatons—surely not a society of human beings. It is one thing to say that some people are enslaved in their roles, quite another to maintain that roles, per se, enslave.

Reich began his book with the prediction that the new consciousness that was arriving would require a " 'new head'—a new way of living—a new man."[28] He ended his work by saying that the new freedom will go beyond the release of man's instincts that Marcuse spoke of, and actually "augment and inspire" it. Underlying the new freedom was, as he said, "an exalted vision of man."[29] More than that, it was a vision of man so wholly at odds with everything we know about the species that it lay squarely in the realm of science fiction.

The new freedom was not designed for men and women living in society. It was designed for imaginary beings living in an imaginary world. Trying to implement its logic has wrecked havoc in the social fabric, while not advancing the cause of human freedom. Our gravest mistake has been in thinking that the structures, patterns, and institutions that constitute society are antiquated and expendable baggage. They are not. They are the meat of society, the only context in which the struggle for freedom can take place. They are the properties upon which ordered liberty must be built.

Notes

1. Marco Janco, "Dada at Two Speeds," in Lucy R. Lippard, ed., *Dadas on Art* (Englewood Cliffs, N.J.: Prentice-Hall, 1971), p. 36.
2. Maurice Nadeau, *The History of Surrealism*, trans. Richard Howard (New York: Macmillan, 1985), pp. 50–51.
3. John Canaday, *Embattled Critic* (New York: Noonday Press, 1959), pp. 31–33.
4. Frank Stella, *Working Space* (Cambridge: Harvard University Press, 1986).
5. Suzi Gablik, *Has Modernism Failed?* (New York: Thames and Hudson, 1984), p. 75.
6. Ibid., pp. 30–32.
7. Robert Nisbet, *Prejudices* (Cambridge: Harvard University Press, 1982), p. 140.
8. Quoted by Douglas C. McGill, "Sculpture Goes Public," *New York Times Magazine*, April 27, 1986, p. 68.
9. Paul Goodman, *Growing up Absurd* (New York: Random House, 1956), p. 129.
10. Quoted by Dennis Altman, *Homosexual* (New York: Avon Books, 1971), p. 102.
11. Herbert Marcuse, *Eros and Civilization* (Boston: Beacon Press, 1955), p. 5.
12. Ibid., p. 33.
13. Ibid., pp. 34, 205.
14. Herbert Marcuse, *One Dimensional Man* (Boston: Beacon Press, 1964), p. 1.
15. Marcuse, *Eros and Civilization*, pp. 137, 177, and ch. 10.
16. Marcuse, *One Dimensional Man*, p. 4.

17. Ibid.
18. Ibid., pp. 4, 7.
19. See the last two chapters of his book for the discussion of the old and new culture and the prospect for utopia. Philip Slater, *The Pursuit of Loneliness* (Boston: Beacon Press, 1970).
20. Charles Reich, *The Greening of America* (New York: Random House, 1970), p. 268.
21. Ibid., p. 4.
22. Ibid., p. 332.
23. Ibid., pp. 217–18.
24. Ibid., p. 225.
25. Ibid., p. 227.
26. Ibid., p. 226.
27. Ibid., pp. 139–40.
28. Ibid., p. 5.
29. Ibid., pp. 390–91.

PART III

THE RIGHTS OF MEN, WOMEN, AND CHILDREN

5

The Quest for Autonomy

If there is one theme that is pervasive in American culture, it is that of the lone individual who struggles against adversity and wins. The hero in America has always been the superman, and now superwoman, the person who rises above the masses and strikes a victory for independence. Our heroes, and they include the Davy Crocketts, John Waynes, Clint Eastwoods, and Sylvester Stallones, are much more than men of violence—they are men who possess an iron will, a determination to do it their way, and a ferocious optimism to beat the odds. They inspire.

We have never really liked the Babbitts of Main Street, and that explains why Yuppies are found contemptible: there is little to admire in those who bask in mediocrity, adore wealth, prize status, and wallow in nothingness. We have no use for sycophants, those unprincipled, spineless, obsequious flatterers who seek to get ahead by using others as a means to their ends. Who excites Americans is the iconoclast, the do-it-yourself individualist. Our fantasies revolve around daring, not complacency.

It is against this background that we are able to make sense of the cultural divide that separates the 1950s from the 1960s. Although the new freedom burst on the scene in the 1960s, its roots were watered in the social soil of the 1950s. In the 1950s, millions found happiness and security in suburbia. But members of an important minority felt unhappy because they were secure, unsettled because they were settled. They were the initial sponsors of the new freedom, men and women raised in comfort and tutored by conformity. What they wanted was freedom, pure and uncut, the kind that could be gotten only by going off-limits.

As feminist writer Barbara Ehrenreich has perceptively noted,[1] it was the men, not the women, who rebelled first. Led by *Playboy* founder Hugh Hefner, middle-class men began to assess and openly question the virtue of conformity. The social regimentation of the 1950s, complete with its cultural

baggage of a breadwinner's ethic, made for security all right. But it also made for sterility.

What *Playboy* promised was release. It painted a picture of men absorbed in mundane pursuits, in need of a release from the routine and familiar. It was women—no, wives—who saddled men with appointments. Freedom could be had by escaping from the constraints of the male sex role. It was pleasure that Hefner sold, the fruit long forbidden by a culture bent on self-denial. A new day was dawning, and only those hopelessly blinded by middle-class dogma could fail to acknowledge it.

So the men started first. They were the original bearers of the new freedom. But while a growing number of men were acting out their fantasies—speeding along the road to freedom in their flashy Corvettes—a small but increasingly important part of the female population was beginning to question the victory of affluence. If "that's all there is," those women wondered, "then where do we go from here?" "Follow me," answered Betty Friedan. Many did.

Women, Friedan said, were trapped. They were locked into a role that gave them no identity, no sense of achievement. They were merely an appendage, a pretty figurine that was displayed on request. Stapled to their husbands' status, women clung to their men, thus foregoing prospects for autonomy. "She becomes a parasite," Friedan remarked of the housewife, "not only because the things she needs for status come ultimately from her husband's work, but because she must dominate him, own him, for the lack of an identity of her own."[2] Many men agreed.

"Progressive dehumanization" was how Friedan characterized the life-course of women, a condition she said amounted to a "comfortable concentration camp." Women were infantile, passive, dependent, and listless. "The feminine mystique," Friedan maintained, "has succeeded in burying millions of American women alive."[3] Self-fulfillment was what women needed, the kind born of independence and forged with purpose. It was not to be had mending clothes, scrubbing floors, and making dinner.

Influenced by the proponents of humanistic psychology, Friedan argued that only by realizing one's potential could freedom be achieved. Self-realization, of course, was exactly what women had been denied, subsumed as they were in their role of housewife. It was this belief—the idea that women were incomplete—that attracted a sizable audience and laid the groundwork for the new freedom. To be free meant to be liberated from the shackles of sex-role socialization. It meant an end to the self-destructive path that had been neatly carved out for them. It meant a radical break with the past.

The conception of freedom offered by Friedan was pure 1960s vintage. It would have been unrecognizable to most nineteenth-century women. Freedom for women in the nineteenth century meant greater inclusion in society,

greater opportunities in education and employment, and greater participation in society in general. Women in the early twentieth century focused their energies on the franchise, hoping for political inclusion, and continued the fight for equal opportunity. The thrust of their efforts was clear: it was toward greater inclusion.

So much progress had been made to empower women that in 1949 anthropologist Ruth Benedict was able to declare, "The family in the United States has become democratic."[4] Even Friedan acknowledged that by the start of the 1960s it was possible to cheer "the removal of all the legal, political, economic and educational barriers that once kept woman from being man's equal. . . ."[5] It appeared as though the traditional goals of women had finally been realized.

Then it happened: no sooner had the obstacles to advancement been knocked down then freedom was redefined. To be free no longer meant to be included in society. It meant to be totally, 100 percent autonomous. The new freedom had arrived.

Those who were affected by the vision of the new freedom came to loathe traditional social arrangements and the contentment they offered. Hence the hatred of the 1950s evident in the writings of feminist Shulamith Firestone: "The fifties was the bleakest decade of all, perhaps the bleakest decade in some centuries for women."[6] There is no way to understand such an observation other than referencing the effect of the new freedom on her thinking. By any objective index, women in the 1950s were less burdened than ever before, a fact known to Firestone as well as everyone else. What caused her to despair was the extent to which millions of American women had accustomed themselves to the settled life of suburban living. From the vantage of the new freedom, such complacency was positively disastrous.

Women who found a comfortable niche in their marriage and family were excoriated by those who adopted the mantle of the new freedom. Friedan, for example, was ill-tempered with women who professed satisfaction with their lives. She had something to say about those carefree housewives who enjoyed playing bridge and hosting lunches: "Staring uneasily at this image, I wonder if a few problems are not somehow better than this smiling empty passivity." It was "the miserable, frustrated ones," reckoned Friedan, "who still [had] some hope."[7]

Sociologist Jesse Bernard was struck by the same phenomenon. "It is true," she admitted, "that a considerable proportion of married women judge themselves as happy." Then she unloaded with *the* question: "But how happy is the happy housewife?" Bernard was convinced that happiness was not what women experienced when they reported themselves happy. They were "reconciled" or, worse still, "mentally ill." She then pondered, "Could it be that marriage itself is 'sick'?"[8]

Bernard was by no means alone in questioning the legitimacy of marriage. In the late 1960s–early 1970s, the question of marriage's inherent sickness was on the minds of every radical feminist. No one was more explicit than Germaine Greer: "If independence is a necessary concomitant of freedom, women must not marry."[9] Marriage, according to this perspective, oppresses both men and women, leaving them unfulfilled and shortchanged. It stifles human creativity and provides for a sclerotic existence. Only those hopelessly brainwashed by society could fail to recognize this reality.

Notice that Greer's rejection of the institution of marriage is unqualified. To be free is to be autonomous and to be autonomous is to live unburdened by rule and regulation. Self-actualization is to be realized solely through one's own doings. There is no need to bind oneself over to another, for where there is a merging of interests there is the specter of subordination. Liberated persons are free from one another; that is why they are free.

But if liberated persons are totally autonomous, is love possible? The new freedom maintains that yes, love is possible, but only in those relationships that are completely equal. Because few relationships meet this acid test, love is a chimera. "Total love," maintain new-freedom enthusiasts Sidney Abbott and Barbara Love, "is total vulnerability and unselfishness and should allow both parties to receive maximum pleasure." And who in society is best suited to experience "total love"? Lesbians. "The lesbian," according to Abbott and Love, "both expands and curtails her activities to work things out so that both partners have maximum opportunities."[10] They are a role model for the rest of us.

According to the vision of the new freedom, the love that is said to take place in most heterosexual relationships is really a form of social control. Kate Millett, for example, maintains that the idea of romantic love "affords a means of emotional manipulation which the male is free to exploit";[11] love is basically a technique of patriarchy.

No one defined the new freedom conception of love better than Firestone. The problem with love, she said, was that it bestowed legitimacy on a fundamentally unequal power relationship. It made a woman's life "hell," turning the experience of love into nothing less than a "holocaust." We've been fooled into thinking that love is altruistic when in fact it represents "the height of selfishness." Women who think themselves free once they marry are being deceived. They have simply been promoted to "housenigger"; they have been transformed from "Blushing Bride to Bitch."[12]

There is a humorless quality evident in the writings of new-freedom feminists. To say that they are unhappy with society would be an understatement. Firestone, in particular, is red hot over the fact that many women smile. She, herself, admitted that while growing up she rarely smiled, having nothing to smile about. "My 'dream' action for the women's liberation movement," she confessed, would be to stage "*a smile boycott*, at which declaration all women would instantly abandon their 'pleasing' smiles, henceforth smiling only when something pleased *them*."[13]

It is impossible to understand the depth of Firestone's despair without appreciating just how far-reaching is the source of women's oppression: "Feminists have to question, not just all of *Western* culture, but the organization of culture itself, and further, even the very organization of nature."[14] There is no better description of what the new freedom is all about than this. Firestone takes first prize.

With the enemy of freedom being a function of both nature and nurture, women had their work cut out for them. They had to destroy what existed and start all over again from scratch. But where to begin? In the bedroom, counseled Firestone: "A revolutionary in every bedroom cannot fail to shake up the status quo."[15] The isolation of women from one another could now be transformed into a strategic asset. The men wouldn't know what hit them.

The sense of total dissatisfaction with existing social conditions was shared by the founding members of the National Organization for Women. In their 1966 statement of goals, they listed "a sex role revolution for men and women which will restructure all our institutions: childrearing, education, marriage, the family, medicine, work, politics, the economy, religion, psychological theory, human sexuality, morality and the very evolution of the race."[16] Nothing was worth saving.

The message of the new freedom was clear: there could be no real progress toward freedom until and unless a hole was cut deep into society, excising both the institution of marriage and the family. The problem with past efforts at liberation was that they were blinded as to the true nucleus of oppression: the family. "*The failure of the Russian Revolution*," advised Firestone, "*is directly traceable to the failure of its attempts to eliminate the family and sexual repression*."[17] Germaine Greer went even further, attributing to the destruction of the family a dynamic, self-propelling force: "Women's liberation, if it abolishes the patriarchal family, will abolish a necessary substructure of the authoritarian state, and once that withers away Marx will have come true willy-nilly, so let's get on with it."[18]

The idea that a Marxist revolution is conditioned on total sexual liberation antedates the rise of the new freedom in the 1960s. Decades earlier, Freudian scholar Wilhelm Reich argued the necessity of tying sexual emancipation to social revolution. But it wasn't until the Age of Aquarius that the idea became culturally rooted. Reich would have been pleased to learn that by the 1970s, women in Boston had organized for the purpose of disseminating their collective thoughts on the subject of their bodies. Writing *Our Bodies, Our*

Selves proved to be an exhilarating experience, so much so that "body education" had been recommended to others as a "starting point for the liberation of many other women."[19]

In the mind-set of the new freedom, sexual liberation must be total if it is to be successful. And that means that everything goes, including the taboo against incest. From Byron and Shelley, who spoke glowingly of the wonders of incest, to Freud, who held that the taboo against it was "perhaps the most drastic mutilation which man's erotic life has in all time experienced,"[20] there has never been any shortage of intellectuals prepared to defend the indefensible. The idea of "positive incest" is now being circulated at scholary symposia as well as by the proponents of the North American Man/Boy Love Association. As one contemporary sage put it, incest is a game "every family can play."[21]

Feminist Firestone also promotes the abolition of the incest taboo. Indeed, she sees it as important as anything to be done in the cause of absolute freedom. Only when the family and the incest taboo are destroyed would sexuality "be released from its straightjacket to eroticize our whole culture, changing its very definition." With the incest taboo gone for good, we could return "within a few generations to a more natural polymorphous sexuality." And what exactly would that mean? It would mean that "relations with children would include as much genital sex as the child was capable of," and that "nonsexual friendships" would be a thing of the past.[22] Everyone would be getting it on.

Sexual liberation is not complete once Sodom and Gomorrah lose their stigma. Total freedom means rejecting nature as well society. "Nature," testifies Firestone, "produced the fundamental inequality—half the human race must bear and rear the children," making women hostage to "the tyranny of their reproductive biology." So it is nature, after all, that is to blame. With de Beauvoir, Firestone concludes that "it was woman's reproductive biology that accounted for her original and continued oppression, and not some sudden patriarchal revolution, the origins of which Freud himself was at a loss to explain."[23]

Firestone's view that "pregnancy is barbaric"[24] is certainly demonstrable of new-freedom extremism. But it is more than that. It is a clear-cut statement of the outer limits of our culture. To be sure, it is an exaggeration of the prevailing ethos, but that is all it is. It accurately portrays, in extended fashion, what new-freedom consciousness has wrought. All that constrains is bad, and pregnancy constrains badly, as well as unequally.

When the idea that pregnancy constrains is coupled with the idea that unwanted pregnancies constrain absolutely, support for abortion grows commensurately. In a culture that thinks that to be burdened is to be oppressed, an unwanted pregnancy is tantamount to enslavement. Pro-choice organizations like the ACLU have long made it clear that their sole interest is in securing the "reproductive freedom" rights of women, thereby liberating half the population from the inequities that nature has imposed. And that is why it is fair to say that Firestone's thinking has found its way into the dominant culture. The new freedom confirms it.

In a society in which every new increment in rights is accompanied by a proportionate decrease in individual responsibility, it is to be expected that the phenomenon of "abortion repeaters" would become a commonplace. It is estimated that 40 percent of the women who undergo an abortion in New York City have had at least one before. When a nineteen-year-old was asked why she was coming back for her third abortion, she told her inquisitors that yes, she knows about the pill, and even keeps some in her home. "But I forget to take them," she said. "After all, I don't take vitamins or anything else every day so there's nothing to remind me."[25]

The kind of thinking that is exemplified by this teenager would have been branded irresponsible by nearly everyone in the 1940s and 1950s. But since the 1960s, we have developed a novel form of compassion for those who choose to be irresponsible: being open-minded, we exercise tolerance and refuse to succumb to "value judgments" regarding untoward behavior. So instead of being chastized, the young girl is "understood." And what is understood is that she is not responsible for her behavior. She may even be a victim. One thing is sure: under no circumstances should she be made to feel guilty—we wouldn't want to "lay that trip" on her.

The new freedom is tolerant not only of abortion on demand but of parents who sue doctors for delivering "defective" infants. By 1985 George Annas, a professor of law and medicine at Boston University's School of Medicine, was able to declare that the concept of "wrongful birth is very firmly established."[26] Doctors subject themselves to malpractice suits if they don't apprise pregnant women of possible complications and allow them enough lead time to gut the baby before the third trimester. The idea that a birth could be pronounced "wrongful" by the courts is part of the cultural value train that began once freedom from unwanted pregnancies become legal.

The pro-choice movement is as emblematic of the new freedom as any contemporary social current. It definitively represents the quest for autonomy, perfectly expresses the belief in rights without responsibilities, and vividly illustrates the meaning of moral neutrality. When freedom from constraint is defined as the ultimate liberty, then all that constrains—as children surely do—becomes the enemy of freedom. It is as logical as it is certain.

The pro-choice movement is now in transition to the next phase. Having secured the right of a woman to rid herself of her pregnancy, the battlefield is now set to give women the right to choose whether they are satisfied with what they've delivered. Characteristic of the new freedom, rights activists want to up the ante again, this time by extending the limits of sex-without-consequences to its furthest point. If we don't like what we have wrought, we don't have to keep him or her. Infanticide is rights without responsibilities taken to its ultimate end.

Joseph Fletcher is a theologian, a man who has won the Humanist of the Year award. His speciality is ethics. He believes that infants may properly be killed if they don't measure up to his fifteen "indicators of personhood." Newborns, he wants us to understand, are not "persons," only "human lives." Should disabled infants be treated? Not unless the prognosis for attaining a satisfactory quality of life is good.[27]

Fletcher is not a freak among rights enthusiasts. From distinguished law schools to influential departments of philosophy, religion, and biology, the demand for a right to infanticide has come forth. Although many pro-choice advocates are themselves alarmed by this new wave of rights, they shouldn't be surprised. For years pro-life groups have maintained that there is no logical moral difference between feticide and infanticide. Now the sponsors of the new freedom have come full circle, with a twist: if it's legal to kill a child before birth, it should be legal to do so after birth.

Perhaps the most curious aspect of this whole area of new-freedom consciousness is the spectacle of declining respect for human life coexisting with a marked increase in respect for animal life. As the right to kill infants gains intellectual respect, the right to kill animals loses ground.

In 1984 Australian philosopher Peter Singer said that is makes no sense to say we can kill a baby before he or she is born, but can't do so afterward. "The solution," he said, was "to abandon the idea that all human life is of equal worth."[28] The same Peter Singer wrote a book in the 1970s, *Animal Liberation*, wherein he argued against animal experimentation, holding that vertebrate animals are entitled to a higher moral status; some of them, he contended, are more self-aware than human infants.[29] We have entered a new day when some scholars think that pets should have more rights than children.

The latest round of pro-choice demands includes the right to choose the qualities one wants in a child with as much freedom and certainty as is exercised in choosing the options on a new car. With the advent of wombs for sale have come cloning mechanics trained to meet all specifications. The freezing and thawing of embryos is becoming more accepted, as the high-tech baby business gears up to satisfy the choices of virtually everyone. And if one isn't happy with the product, it can always be exchanged—or simply discarded—for another one.

The quest for autonomy has already led to a broadening of the right to reproductive freedom. It has, quite deliberately, cast unwanted and undesirable children into a precarious position. Whether others will be considered expendable is not known. But those who are currently a burden to others have the most to fear. The new freedom has shown that new rights for some may be bought at the expense of all rights for others. That's an unsettling prospect, at least for some.

Notes

1. Barbara Ehrenreich, *The Hearts of Men* (Garden City, N.Y.: Anchor Press, 1983), chap. 4.
2. Betty Friedan, *The Feminine Mystique* (New York: Norton, 1963), p. 271.
3. Ibid., p. 336.
4. Ruth Benedict, "The Family: Genus Americanum," in Ruth Nanda Anshen, ed., *The Family: Its Function and Destiny* (New York: Harper, 1949), p. 165.
5. Friedan, *The Feminine Mystique*, p. 68.
6. Shulamith Firestone, *The Dialectic of Sex* (New York: Bantam Books, 1971), p. 27.
7. Friedan, *The Feminine Mystique*, pp. 64, 311.
8. Jesse Bernard, "The Paradox of the Happy Marriage," in Vivian Gornick and Barbara Moran, eds., *Women in Sexist Society* (New York: Mentor Books, 1972), pp. 150, 158.
9. Germaine Greer, *The Female Eunuch* (New York: McGraw-Hill, 1970), p. 11.
10. Sidney Abbott and Barbara Love, "Is Women's Liberation a Lesbian Plot?" in Vivian Gornick and Barbara Moran, eds., *Women in Sexist Society* (New York: McGraw-Hill, 1970), p. 619.
11. Kate Millett, *Sexual Politics* (Garden City, N.Y.: Doubleday, 1970), p. 37.
12. Firestone, *The Dialectic of Sex*, pp. 128, 132–33, 142.
13. Ibid., p. 90. Though Firestone's dream of a "smile boycott" did not come true, she was not alone in voicing displeasure at women's smiling. Witness this comment by a woman from Cambridge, Massachusetts, regarding the Statue of Liberty at the time of its centennial celebration: "What I love about her is that she is not smiling, and she has a clear don't-mess-with-me look on that wonderful face." Letter to the editor by Gabrielle Bernard, *New York Times*, July 15, 1986, p. A28.
14. Ibid., p. 2.
15. Ibid., p. 38.
16. Quoted by Betty Friedan, "Up from the Kitchen Floor," *New York Times Magazine*, March 4, 1973, p. 30.
17. Firestone, *The Dialectic of Sex*, p. 212.
18. Greer, *The Female Eunuch*, p. 326.
19. Boston Women's Health Book Collective, 2d ed., *Our Bodies, Our Selves* (New York: Simon and Schuster, 1976), p. 12.
20. Sigmund Freud, *Civilization and Its Discontents* (New York: Norton, 1961), p. 51.
21. See James B. Twitchell, *Forbidden Partners* (New York: Columbia University Press, 1987), pp. 15–17.
22. Firestone, *The Dialectic of Sex*, pp. 60, 240.
23. Ibid., pp. 73–74 and 205–6.
24. Ibid., p. 198.
25. Quoted by Nadine Brozan, "The Abortion Repeaters," *New York Times*, September 19, 1979. p. C10.

26. Quoted by Alan Otten, "Parents and Newborns Win New Legal Rights to Sue for Malpractice," *Wall Street Journal,* June 7, 1985, p. 10.
27. Quoted by David Cannon, "Abortion and Infanticide," *Policy Review* (Spring 1985): 13. See also Robert F. Weir, *Selective Non-treatment of Handicapped Newborns* (New York: Oxford University Press, 1984).
28. Quoted by Cannon, "Abortion and Infanticide," pp. 12–13.
29. Peter Singer, *Animal Liberation* (New York: Avon Books, 1977).

6

The New Man and the New Woman

By the mid-1980s, it was generally agreed that the women's movement had entered a second stage. With many of the legal battles won, and with progress on the job moving along at a record pace, feminists began to appraise what they had achieved and draw up an agenda for the next round. Not surprisingly, many of them turned their attention to the private side of women's lives, questioning whether the gains they had made outside the home were worth the price they had paid inside the home. They had succeeded, to some extent, in forging a new man and a new woman. But were they satisfied with the new model?

The problem wasn't with her—it was with him. To be sure, the new man (new middle-class man; working-class man remained unchanged) was somewhat of an improvement over traditional man. The new man was more sensitive, empathic, considerate, and helpful. But he was also more detached. Women's lib had left its mark and the results were not all that endearing. While she became more assertive, he became more aloof.

Feminists, nonfeminists, and antifeminists alike, all agreed that the new man was undependable, rudderless, and above all, lacking in commitment. Indeed, by the late eighties there must have been more magazine articles and radio talk shows devoted to this topic than to any other issue confronting the sexes. Somewhere along the line, the connecting link between men and women came unhinged.

The popular explanation was as follows: everyone feels the effects of widespread social changes, and no one feels it more acutely than those who lose power during the transformation. Men, it was argued, were the beneficiaries of centuries of unearned power, status, and prestige. Now the tide was changing and some couldn't handle the drift. A temporary period of adjustment was to be expected, given the entrenched patterns of past institutional inequalties. Progress always entails risks, but given past history, it was high time to take a chance.

The analysis was incomplete. True, social change is most painful for those who have the most to lose. True, it was the men who had the most to lose. But women had something to lose as well: men.

By seeing the relations between the sexes purely in terms of power, contemporary students of social change blinded themselves to other realities. Namely, the degree to which men and women had historically depended on each other for love, comfort, and sustenance. That he made the decisions outside the home was true. But that they were mutually dependent on each other for psychic reward was also true.

There is nothing inherently contradictory about a love relationship that is as unequal as it is strong. The love of parent for child is one obvious example. And who is prepared to argue that because men and women have typically held unequal positions in society, true love has never existed? Only the most extreme dogmatist would make such an assertion.

Love does not require inequality, but neither does it demand equality; it is quite independent of both. It does require, at a minimum, some degree of dependence (preferably, one that is mutual); that is not an option to be discarded at will. What love cannot tolerate, under any circumstances, is complete independence. That would close the relationship and leave both parties in the lurch.

There is much confusion in this area. Where there is a dependent relationship, there can be love, but there can also be exploitation. Where there is interdependence, there can be love, with no possibility of exploitation. Where there is total independence, there can be no love, though exploitation is negated. The problem for many women is that they went from being totally dependent to totally independent, without ever really experiencing interdependence. As a result, relationships dissolved under the chilling effect of absolute independence.

A man and woman can be socially and economically independent of each other and still be in love; there are many such examples. What they can't be is psychologically independent of each other. That would mean total independence, a state characteristic of relationships between strangers, not spouses. He needs to need her; and she him. Otherwise, they can each go their own way without remorse or regret. And that is exactly what has happened to millions.

So why does the new man lack commitment? Because he is under no social pressure to exercise it. What comes naturally to most of us is to look out for our own interests. Looking out for the interests of others requires a reason. Two totally independent individuals do not provide a context in which commitment is likely to be manifested. There needs to be some genuine reason for making the effort. People must need one another before a departure from self-interest can take place.

Individuals are less likely to be committed to one another when cultural support for commitment is lacking. And that is why demonstrations of commitment are in short supply: our culture supports the new-freedom ideal of unbounded individual liberty, not commitment. Total independence wrecks the prospects for commitment by casting sacrifice, without which there can be no real commitment, as the enemy of freedom. We want the ends but are not prepared to accept the means. So we lose.

When independence is defined as freedom, it follows that the more independent two people are of each other, the freer they are. The flip side to this arrangement, however, is that the more independent two people are of each other, the more carefree they become regarding each other's legitimate needs. It cannot be denied that any relationship worth having will not last long if and when both parties come to the conclusion that the other is a dispensable item. For when he or she has served his or her purpose, the relationship is over.

What do people say when they want to describe a best friend? "He'd give you the shirt off his back," or "He'd go to the wall for you." They don't talk about how autonomous or sovereign or independent he is. To do so wouldn't make any sense. When people say, "A friend in need is a friend indeed," they are expressing the degree to which people can depend on one another. People who can depend on one another are committed to one another; they are not independent of one another.

Nothing is more necessary to psychological well-being than a sense of belongingness. In fact, there is a growing body of evidence that shows that healthy social relationships are tied to good physical health as well.[1] But establishing a good, sound relationship is not easy, as countless millions will testify. It doesn't take a Ph.D. in sociology or psychology to know that bonding does not evolve naturally when self-actualization takes center stage in a nation's cultural priorities. Tragically, those who should know better, namely, students of human behavior, often provide advice that makes the situation worse.

When commitment is seen as an obstacle to personal self-growth, when sacrifice is cast as a hang-up, and when responsibility is defined as guilt, it should come as no surprise that such thinking finds a resonant chord in the hearts of millions; this is especially true of young people. Men, in particular, surveyed the new landscape and saw something in it for them. Beneath all the talk about liberation for women was the appealing proposition that men could get out from under once and for all. They could sit back and relax, and leave the responsibilities behind. Emancipation was a game two could play.

To find out what makes the new man and new woman tick, much can be gained by examining the phenomenon of cohabitation—what used to be called "shacking up." It is estimated that the number of unwed couples living together tripled between 1960 and 1986 to more than two million. Its prevalence has been duly registered by both social scientists and lawyers: there is a "Cohabitation Research Newsletter" and an American Bar Association Family Law Section on Marriage and Cohabitation.

It is agreed by nearly everyone that the women's movement played a major role in contributing to the popularity of cohabitation. Cohabitation was seen as an advance for women because they were now free to demolish the double standard and freely engage in as much premarital sex as men. It is interesting to note that the collapse of the double standard meant more sexual liberty for women, not less sexual liberty for men. The strength of the new freedom ensured that women would become more like men, and not vice versa.

Research on cohabitation shows some significant differences between men and women who cohabit and those who don't. Far and away the biggest difference is the role that religion plays: those who cohabit are much more likely to report no religious affiliation.[2] With the external constraint of religion's playing little or no role, it is not surprising to learn that those who cohabit report themselves more liberated from conventional moral standards and more liberal in their values than their noncohabiting counterparts.[3]

Those who cohabit are descriptive of the new man and the new woman. Cohabiting women report themselves more aggressive, competitive, autonomous, and managerial than their noncohabiting peers. Men who cohabit describe themselves as less competitive and managerial; they also assert that they are warmer and more emotionally supportive than their friends who haven't adopted the new freedom.[4] This is the kind of androgynous outcome that feminists have struggled to attain.

Gloria Steinem sees the movement toward androgyny as a goal that everyone should experience. "We want to make the whole human experience available to everybody," she says. "The goal now is to complete ourselves," by which she means making women more assertive and men more compassionate.[5] But although the research shows that women are indeed becoming more assertive, it also shows that men have been pulling back, displaying their newly acquired sense of compassion at selective intervals.

There is no doubting the fact that men and women who cohabit are experiencing a sex-role evolution: equality is what colors the near-institution of cohabitation. But there is a coldness to this contemporary form of equality, and it is a condition that pleases no one. What is lacking is spontaneity, and what is evident is a kind of programmed response characteristic of commercial transactions. Everything from household chores to the rules regarding foreplay must be agreed to up front, just to make sure that no one is being exploited. The end result is a fully rational, calculated approach to human relationships, one devoid of warmth, giving, and love.

A cohabitation agreement is the quintessential contractual agreement: nothing is done for anyone unless spelled out in advance. This is the type of association that sociologists call a secondary relationship: it is role specific (excepting that in this case the roles are always being worked out) and lacking in the kind of emotion-laden features that describe a primary relationship. Only this is *supposed* to be a primary relationship!

It is one of the well-understood laws of cohabitation that neither party is responsible, in any way, for the welfare of the other. This is a boon for the men, in particular, because they have traditionally been ascribed the role of provider. But provide no more, he learns, this is a new day—the day of self-sufficiency. Such a condition explains why there has been so little organized resistance on the part of men to the feminist agenda. Her liberation has meant his as well. Perhaps more so.

When men and women enter into a self-sufficient relationship, it rarely has the kind of egalitarian outcome that women expect. Because he typically earns more than she, it's a net plus for him to split the costs fifty-fifty. Going dutch has always been an attractive feature for men, it's just that until recently, most men were embarrassed even to suggest it. Now they can offer to go dutch and appear to be respectful of the woman's status.

In their comprehensive study of men and women in the 1980s, Philip Blumstein and Pepper Schwartz found that many married men wished they no longer were financially responsible for their partner. "Looking at the cohabitors," they added, "we can see that when relationships between men and women are less scripted, men can, and indeed do, cast off that responsibility."[6] If cohabitation is a victory for women, it is clearly not the men who are the vanquished. Whether society as a whole is better off is another matter altogether.

The empirical research that has been done on cohabitation lends support to Blumstein and Schwartz's observation. Those who cohabit are significantly less committed to each other than married couples are.[7] They seem to have adopted what sociologist Robert Bellah calls "the contractual ethic." As a therapist told Bellah, "Commitments take work, and we're tired of working."[8] Well said.

The most revealing research comes from comparative studies done on those who engaged in cohabitation before marriage and those who did not. For a long time we have been treated with anecdotal impressions that suggest that cohabitation makes marriage easier; couples who live together before marriage get a chance to know each other better and work the bugs out of their relationship. When cohabitation functions as a "trial marriage," we are told, it serves to provide a more solid platform upon which to build a more permanent relationship.

The problem with the common folklore is that it is not borne out by the research. Canadian sociologist Roy E.L. Watson conducted a study of eighty-four couples, some of whom cohabited before marriage and some of whom did not, seeking a measure of adjustment in the first year of marriage. He unexpectedly found that those who did not cohabit actually had a significantly higher level of adjustment than their new-freedom counterparts. Watson concluded that those who did not cohabit looked forward to marriage as a time of new possibilities; those who lived together before saying, "I do," were struck by newfound responsibilities.[9] Apparently, that's not something they bargained for when they tied the knot.

Watson's study adds to the earlier findings of Clatworthy and Scheid. Comparing couples who had and had not lived together before marriage, they found that those who had cohabited were (a) less likely to acquiesce in disagreements, (b) more likely to disagree over matters such as finances, household chores, and recreation, (c) more independent of their spouses, (d) less likely to consider marriage an intrinsic part of their life, (e) more likely to have broken up, and (f) more likely to have sought a marriage counselor.[10] The failure of cohabitation is not unique to America; In Sweden, couples who live together before marriage have an 80 percent higher divorce rate than those who do not.[11]

Why is the common wisdom wrong on this subject? Midge Decter offers a convincing explanation: "Their household [of couples who cohabit] is in its very inception and definition conditional. Neither will be forced, by convention and circumstance, to put up with very much from the other."[12] It makes sense. The independence that characterizes cohabitation is decidedly *not* the best platform to launch a permanent relationship. Those who have lived the life of the new freedom are clearly not prepared to handle the burdens that marriage entails.

Despite the problems associated with cohabitation, social scientists have been reluctant to criticize it. This is due less to scientific neutrality than to ideological preference: most social scientists are themselves accepting of the new freedom. What is interesting to note here is that despite the profeminist leanings of academicians in general, most scholars continue to refrain from criticizing an institution that the research shows has ill-served women, who are the ones most likely to lose out in cohabitation arrangements.[13]

The new-freedom emphasis on open-mindedness is so strong that those who study cohabitation typically either endorse it outright or complain about how the participants are stigmatized by a closed-minded society. Eleanor Macklin, for instance, is troubled by the fact that fornication is still a crime in some states. She sees fornication as being nothing more than a privacy issue, and is critical of landlords and employers who allegedly discriminate against cohabitors. Inequities in the tax structure is another problem area cited by Macklin.

"The only problems that seem unique to cohabitation," exclaims Macklin, "are those which grow out of the lack of general societal support for this lifestyle, and the hassles some cohabitants experience when dealing with our legal, economic, and religious institutions.''[14] Blumstein and Schwartz are just as frank about their priorities. It is the institution of marriage that creates the biggest problems for those who cohabit, acting as it does, as a lure. "If cohabitation is to be a unique institution," they maintain, "it must be perceived as different from marriage, and *marriage cannot be allowed to be seen as a better or next step in the relationship.*''[15]

If new-freedom thinking is anything, it is predictable. Support will always be forthcoming for anything that challenges the status quo and allows the individual to live by his own rules. Thumbing one's nose at society is the mark of the new freedom, and those who sanction cohabitation do just that. Whenever a new-freedom exhibition fails to satisfy, it is a sure thing that fault will be found not with the design but with society.

Blumstein and Schwartz's comment is all the more remarkable given their stated belief that "marriage is an institution that seems to be in danger of collapse.''[16] As model sociologists, they refrain from actively supporting cohabitation, but speak with such neutrality regarding the subject that it is clear where their sympathies lie. They want to impress upon us that if we are to give cohabitation a break, we need first to dethrone marriage from its present status. They are absolutely right. If society wants to sanction cohabitation, it must equalize its status with that of the institution of marriage. The real question is why it should.

Those who defend cohabitation, as well as those who pose as "nonjudgmental" observers, help to contribute to the contemporary flouting of traditional moral standards by extending legitimacy to "alternative life-styles." More than that, they inspire changes in the mores, which result in changes in the legal code. When the time came for California judges to rule on the legality of the "palimony" suit brought by Michelle Marvin against actor Lee Marvin, they concluded that "the mores of the society have indeed changed so radically in regard to cohabitation that we cannot impose a standard based on alleged moral considerations that have apparently been so widely abandoned by so many.''[17] The causal sequence is readily apparent.

It is distinctive of the extreme individualist character of the new freedom that those who write approvingly on the subject of cohabitation rarely, if ever, mention children. It is as though they don't have any role to play. Defenders of cohabitation are so worried about constraint that they don't even want to think about the problems that children pose. But if many who cohabit eventually marry and have kids, then it is an issue of direct concern to society, and not just the participants of procreation.

If cohabitation has the effect of weakening responsibility, and if those who cohabit are less inclined to work things out, then the prospects for children are ominous. The values and behavioral patterns associated with living together in defiance of public support cannot be shaken at will. There is a reason that those who marry without first cohabiting find it easier to adjust in their first year of marriage than their more progressive cohorts: they enter marriage without the negative, self-fulfillment conditioning that cohabitation produces. Marriage, for them, has obligations as well as privileges. And that is why they are better suited to the duties of parenthood.

But even in the most auspicious of circumstances, marriage in the late twentieth century is proving to be problematic for an increasing number of men and women. Statistics on divorce are not encouraging, though perhaps not as bad as some have said. A statistic that has been widely quoted, though infrequently checked, is the divorce rate figure of 50 percent. Pollster Lou Harris shed some light on the record by pointing out that this popular misperception stems from a 1981 report of the U.S. National Center for Health Statistics wherein it stated that there had been 2.4 million new marriages and 1.2 million divorces during the year. While not disputing these figures, Harris contends that what was not emphasized was the fact that 54 million other marriages remained intact during the same period.

Harris maintains that the idea that half of American marriages are doomed is "one of the most specious pieces of statistical nonsense ever perpetrated in modern times."[18] But Harris's prognosis is not shared by other demographers. Andrew Cherlin and Frank Furstenberg flatly predict, "At current rates, half of all American marriages begun in the early 1980s will end in divorce."[19] Arizona State sociologist Paul Glick studied the data and concluded that "49 percent of persons aged 25 to 34 in 1980 had either ended their first marriage in divorce by 1980 or may be expected to do so before the age of 75."[20] One thing no one disputes is that divorce has markedly increased since the 1960s, making the United States first in that category among nations.

Divorce has become a multibillion-dollar-a-year business as lawyers, mediators, and therapists weigh in to collect their due; real estate, travel, and insurance agents have also profited from broken marriages. Indeed, divorce has become so common that social scientists who study marriage and the family now find that couples who remain together are often asked to explain to their friends why they have chosen to do so.[21] The number of television shows depicting one-parent families has also increased. It is clear that divorce has become an integral part of our culture.

Though divorce is a painful experience for the individuals involved, and is socially disruptive as well, it is not at all uncommon for social scientists to downplay these negative features and emphasize the good that has been done. Many of today's chroniclers of social change are themselves carriers of the new freedom; they do not want to give ammunition to those who think a less permissive attitude toward divorce is warranted. Family sociologist Tamara Hareven, for instance, has done excellent work on the family, but when it comes to assessing the moral worth of divorce, she succumbs to the popular ethos. She says "the increase in divorce statistics as such is no proof of family breakdown." [22]

It needs to be asked why an increase in divorce could be seen as anything other than proof that the family has fallen on hard times. Surely it could not be reasoned that an increase in divorce is indicative of stronger families, and surely it could not be inferred that it has no bearing at all on the quality of family relations, so what else could it be a sign of other than family discord? The fact that some people are better off after they divorce is true but not relevant. It is relevant only to the particular individuals involved, and not to more general interests of society. It is typical of new-freedom thinkers to cast a discussion on the status of a social institution in purely individualistic terms.

One area where the new freedom has clearly asserted itself is in the area of divorce law. No-fault divorce has radically changed the way we've come to think about divorce, and has had demonstable effect on both men and women. Begun in California in 1970, the purpose of no-fault divorce was to eliminate the need for spouses to file charges and countercharges, complete with personal testimony and statements from witnesses. The thinking was that this was not the state's business, that if either party wanted out—for any reason— it should be granted. Simply asserting "irreconcilable differences" ought to be sufficient.

Though there are many different variants of no-fault divorce legislation available throughout the country, the California model proved to be the basic reference for the other states. The California model best expressed the feminist objective of freeing women from the economic dependence of their husbands. What that meant, however, was that upon divorce his legal obligations to her ceased, leaving him in a more advantageous position. Stanford sociologist Lenore Weitzman calculated the harm done to women by their purported representatives: one year after the divorce law changed, the standard of living for women declined by 73 percent; that of men rose 42 percent. [23]

Why this should have come as a big surprise to many feminists—and there is no doubt that it did—is revealing. Common sense, one might have thought, would have indicated that if (a) women typically earn less than men, and (b) they continue to keep the kids, then (c) they will go backward as he goes forward. But no, the idea of equality was embraced in such a pure form as to make trivial almost any question about the consequences of no-fault legislation. If misogynists had attempted to pass a law setting back the cause of women's liberation, they simply could not have achieved a better result than what radical feminists succeeded in creating.

Although no-fault divorce clearly hurt women, its effect on the dominant culture was even more dramatic. What no-fault divorce did was to transform the core set of values upon which traditional divorce law had long been based to a morally neutral set of procedures. No longer was fidelity a matter of striking importance. "The no-fault law," notes Lenore Weitzman and Ruth Dixon, "ignores both moral character and moral history as a basis for awards."[24] And that is precisely what the proponents of the new freedom want to do.

It is difficult, if not impossible, to measure the effect that a change in law has on the tissue of society. But that should not stop us from analyzing the quality of the change. In the case of no-fault divorce, what has changed is the symbolic role that society has traditionally played in divorce proceedings. By denying society a role, the new law reduces divorce to a purely individual exchange. It makes a statement loud and clear regarding the intrinsic moral content of divorce: accountability is limited to the interests of the two parties involved. Hence the purview of society has been rent.

How much no-fault divorce has contributed to the sharp increase in divorce that has occurred since 1970 is not known, though there is information, like the 70 percent increase in divorce cases filed in New Jersey in the year following the switch to no-fault,[25] that is suggestive. Even if the exact proportion were known, the more important fact remains the timing, context, and acceptability of no-fault. That such a change in law occurred in 1970 in California is instructive: that was when the new freedom was taking off, and nowhere did it take off quicker than in California. The fact that so many other states followed suit shows the influence of the new cultural ethos.

The new freedom had impact in other areas of law as well. In the 1980s there was a sizable increase in the number of fathers who were falsely charged with molesting their children. This social occurrence is traceable to the growing interest that fathers have had in securing custody of their children upon divorce. Dr. Diane Schetky, a child psychiatrist from Maine, explains the link between the two phenomena as stemming from a change in both custody laws and moral values: mothers have learned that they have "to get a little more vicious and come up with something better than adultery" if they expect to defeat their spouses' efforts at securing custody.[26]

The fact that mothers have to "come up with something better than adultery" to win in court shows quite clearly the waning social significance of infidelity. It is, of course, anything but insignificant to the party that has been burned, to say nothing about its effect on children. But the change in mores, and in law, is toward a more relaxed and relativized policy regarding sexual misconduct.

The declining stigma attached to divorce is as good an example as any of the willingness of society to drop its guard against social deviance. Indeed, calling divorce social deviance rings as an outdated expression, one that is likely to be greeted with bewilderment, if not derision. And that is because marriage is no longer considered first and foremost a *social* institution. It is an agreement between two solitary individuals; they may exit the relationship with as much ease as they entered.

The desocialization of marriage represents a glacial shift in values. From time immemorial, marriage was viewed throughout the world as the joining together not of two individuals but of two families; it often joined two clans or tribes as well. The individuals were merely the symbols of convergence. They did not fall in love and then marry: they were told whom to marry and when. Arranged marriages were based on duty—duty to one's family and ancestors. It was the lineage that was important.

The modern conception of marriage, a union of two individuals based on love, is not as stable as the traditional model, but it is by no means as inherently vulnerable as it might seem. Marriage is besieged today largely because husbands and wives find themselves without external societal support. And yet such support is absolutely necessary to lasting relationships. By focusing on the removal of stigma from divorcees, instead of finding ways to augment existing marriages, we have established a curious set of priorities.

We are caught in a dilemma. No one but the most cruel would want to inflict psychological distress on men and women who are in the process of divorce; they deserve our understanding, not imprecations. It therefore seems compassionate to do everything we can to remove the last vestiges of stigma from divorce. But the rub is this: by weakening the social penalties attached to divorce, we necessarily occasion more of it. One of the main reasons that the divorce rate was so low throughout history was the severity of penalties prescribed by society. Once they are removed, there is little societal deterrent left.

In point of fact we are not really in a dilemma anymore; we have resolved the impasse in favor of weaker stigma and weakened marriages. The new freedom accords greater weight to what pleases the individual than to what is in the best interests of society. Ironically, though, it is only the individuals who are currently facing divorce who are helped by reducing stigma. By lowering the social cost of divorce, we have unwittingly made it a more attractive option for prospective spouses. It is hard to understand how this can be scored a victory.

Certainly the affluence of our age has contributed to a rising level of divorce. Economic need is what kept marriages together for centuries, not love or even duty. He couldn't make it without her and vice versa, to say nothing about the children and the elderly. Growing economic opportunities for women has also made it easier for spouses to call it quits when trouble strikes: she doesn't *need* him anymore. Such observations are confirmed by the fact that the divorce rate lessened during the depression, then quickened during the recovery of the forties.

Economic affluence, however, is not alone capable of explaining the high rate of divorce. Japan is an affluent country but has a low divorce rate. What Japan doesn't have, but we do, is a conception of freedom that is purely individualistic. The Japanese recognize a different type of freedom, an inner freedom, one that is not defined in terms of freedom from society. The Japanese woman who exhibits *gaman*, or silent suffering, is showing signs of moral strength.[27] To accede to her family's interests is considered a virtue. The new freedom sees it as a vice.

It would be undesirable and impractical to try to import Japanese family values; they are not suited to the American way. But there is a lesson to be learned. Pushing individual liberty to excess tears at the social fabric, leaving behind a desolate freedom. As Midge Decter has observed, a number of young women with children have "liberated themselves straight into total abandonment."[28] She's right: a majority of fathers who are under court orders to give full child support fail to do so; the figures for those who pay alimony are worse. Men have liberated themselves right out of their responsibilities.

Psychologist Maxine Schnall has succinctly captured the essence of the problem: "In pursuing liberation without understanding the need for limits, we wind up with *less* freedom than we had before."[29] But like so many other social scientists who are good at identifying and diagnosing personal and social disorders, Schnall is not prepared to recommend a strong tonic. Though she knows that unbridled liberty is destructive, she is not willing to rein in the individual. That would violate the precepts of the new freedom.

Schnall thinks we are embarking on something called "rational love," what she says is nothing less than "the love of the future." Rational love fuses "tenderness and genital satisfaction" and allows for "the autonomy of the partners as well as the bonds of attachment."[30] It promises to be all things to all people. It combines the commitment of traditional relationships with the choices of modern arrangements.

Unfortunately, Schnall's hope remains an abstract idea: it does not describe empirical reality. We are left with relationships that succeed or fail, depending on the degree of duty, obligation, and sacrifice that is observed. In other words, we are left with relationships imbued with traditional values and those of the new freedom.

The quest for a third way continues. We want the genuineness of traditional relationships and the freedom of modern ones—all at the same time. "How to preserve the warmth and closeness while at the same time holding onto the new freedom to choose?—this is the preeminent question the culture confronts on the domestic scene," comments social tracker Daniel Yankelovich.[31] Few are prepared to say that such a quest is futile, but that is exactly what it is. This is not to say that we are left with choosing between two extremes. We are not. But we are left with choosing a point that falls within the two extremes.

Despite the hoopla surrounding the much-heralded new man and new woman, he and she are very much the same as their predecessors. They have the same emotional need to bond and the same desire to be a part of something larger than themselves. What is different is the extent to which individual freedom is prized. This quest for freedom is not entirely inappropriate, and can be successfully incorporated into a good relationship, just so long as full recognition is given to the fact that no one can ever have it all. If this is done, problems can be mitigated. If not, they will mount. Needlessly.

Notes

1. For the most recent evidence, see James S. House, Karl R. Landis, and Debra Umberson, "Social Relationships and Health," *Science*, July 29, 1988, pp. 540–45.
2. B. Yorburg and I. Arafat, "On Living Together without Marriage," *Journal of Sex Research* 9 (1973): 97–106; L. F. Henze and J. W. Hudson, "Personal and Family Characteristics of Non-Cohabiting and Cohabiting College Students," *Journal of Marriage and the Family* 36 (1974): 722–26; E. D. Macklin, "Unmarried Heterosexual Cohabitation on the University Campus," in J. P. Wiseman, ed., *The Social Psychology of Sex* (New York: Harper and Row, 1976); D. J. Peterman, C. A. Ridley, and S. M. Anderson, " A Comparison of Cohabiting and Non-Cohabiting College Students," *Journal of Marriage and the Family* 36 (1974): 344–54; Roy E. L. Watson, "Premarital Cohabitation vs. Traditional Courtship," *Family Relations* 32 (1983): 139–47.
3. E. D. Macklin, "Nonmarital Heterosexual Cohabitation," *Marriage and Family Review* 1 (1978): 1–12.
4. Ibid.
5. Quoted by Betsy Carter, "Liberation's Next Wave, According to Gloria Steinem," *Esquire* (June 1984): 205.
6. Philip Blumstein and Pepper Schwartz, *American Couples* (New York: Morrow, 1983), p. 325.
7. M. P. Johnson, "Commitment: A Conceptual Structure and Empirical Application," *Sociological Quarterly* 14 (1973): 395–406.
8. Quoted by Robert Bellah in *Habits of the Heart* (Berkeley: University of California Press, 1985), p. 130.
9. Watson, "Premarital Cohabitation vs. Traditional Courtship."
10. The unpublished 1977 Ohio State manuscript by N. M. Clatworthy and L. Scheid was cited by Macklin in "Nonmarital Heterosexual Cohabitation."
11. See the report on cohabitation prepared by Neil Bennett, David Bloom, and Ann Blanc, published by the National Bureau of Economic Research, Cambridge, Massachusetts, 1987.
12. Midge Decter, "Liberating Women: Who Benefits?" *Commentary* (March 1984): 33.
13. Macklin, "Nonmarital Heterosexual Cohabitation."
14. Ibid.
15. Blumstein and Schwartz, *American Couples*, pp. 321–22.
16. Ibid., pp. 318–19.
17. Quoted by Macklin in "Nonmarital Heterosexual Cohabitation."

18. Quoted by Raymond Pike, "New Poll Finds Marriage Stable," *Pittsburgh Post-Gazette*, June 29, 1987, p. 1.
19. Andrew Cherlin and Frank Furstenberg, "The American Family in the Year 2000," *Futurist* (June 1983).
20. Paul C. Glick, "How American Families Are Changing," *American Demographics* (January 1984): 21–25.
21. Blumstein and Schwartz, p. 46.
22. Tamara Hareven, "American Families in Transition: Historical Perspectives on Change," in Arlene and Jerome Skolnick, eds., *Family in Transition* (Boston: Little, Brown, 1986), p. 55.
23. Lenore Weitzman, *The Divorce Revolution* (New York: Free Press, 1985).
24. Lenore Weitzman and Ruth Dixon, "The Transformation of Legal Marriage through No-Fault Divorce," in Arlene Skolnick and Jerome Skolnick, eds., *Family in Transition* (Boston: Little, Brown, 1986), p. 348.
25. Jethro Lieberman, *The Litigious Society* (New York: Basic Books, 1981), p. 173.
26. "Molestation Charges in Divorces," *New York Times*, October 22, 1986, p. A24.
27. See Susan Chira, "Against the Japanese Grain," *New York Times*, June 20, 1982, p. 36.
28. Decter, "Liberating Women: Who Benefits?" p. 35.
29. Maxine Schnall, *Limits: A Search for New Values* (New York: Clarkson Potter, 1981), p. 7.
30. Ibid., pp. 270–72.
31. Daniel Yankelovich, *New Rules* (New York: Bantam Books, 1981), p. 103.

7

Children's Rights

In the past few decades, quality-of-life surveys have proliferated, reflecting the interest that social scientists have in measuring life satisfaction. The results depend as much on what is being measured as on the instrument of measurement itself. For example, measuring health is one thing; gauging happiness is another. We know, for instance, that infant mortality rates declined steadily in the 1980s, for both whites and blacks, despite fears in some quarters that the Reagan budget cuts would impair progress. The health of the average child continues to improve, by almost any yardstick, as advancements in nutrition and medical care spread throughout the population. However, reports on the emotional state of youngsters do not yield the same optimistic picture.

The late twentieth century may be remembered as a time when the physical condition of children improved while their psychological well-being deteriorated. It is a sign of the times that more people today owe their livelihood to serving children in distress than ever before in history. They constitute a large portion of the service sector of the economy, working in special education, foster homes, runaway shelters, school counseling, therapy, delinquent treatment centers, suicide prevention clinics, and the like. The number of volunteer support groups, from Big Brothers to crisis-hot-line staffers, is also impressive. As a societal response, the results are encouraging. As an indication of social health, the data are damning.

It is one of the great tragedies of our day that those who professionally say they represent the best interests of children—the self-described child advocates—often do more to contribute to the problem than resolve it. Specifically, it is the children's rights advocates who have pushed for positive rights (as opposed to those who seek to stem child abuse) that have done, and are continuing to do, great damage to the psychological well-being of children. Their motives may be benign, but that is of little consequence in the end. They think the number-one problem facing children is a lack of freedom.

Having made the wrong diagnosis, they double their mistake by holding a flawed definition of freedom. Strike three is their solution to the problem.

Like so many other liberationist movements, the children's rights movement began in the 1960s and gained additional ground in the decades that followed. According to two of the leading children's rights advocates, Beatrice and Ronald Gross, the movement was launched "to rectify the shameful conditions that lead to the damage and death of so many children." What prompted this assessment was the Grosses' perception that "young people are the most oppressed of all minorities. They are discriminated against on the basis of age in everything from movie admissions to sex. They are traditionally the subjects of ridicule, humiliation, and mental torture in homes, schools, and other institutions."[1]

It would be inaccurate to suggest that most people accept the rendering of children painted by the Grosses. But it would be equally inaccurate to conclude that no one of any importance would be inclined to agree with them. Lawmakers, judges, administrative compliance personnel, and school officials, as well as much of what constitutes the human services industry, have been receptive to the general notion that more rights for children are long overdue. They firmly believe that giving children more rights is a humanitarian and progressive thing to do. While many would not be prepared to go as far as the Grosses, they have nonetheless been persuaded that change in a more libertarian direction is a good thing.

The children's rights advocates are right about one thing: today's kids are faced with unprecedented problems. But it is not a lack of freedom that they suffer from—it is a lack of roots. The evidence culled from psychological and social statistics reads like a litany of pathological disorders. If there is one thing that today's kids don't need, it's another dose of individualism to "set them free"; they are emotionally starved enough without abandoning them any further. They need to be fastened *to*, and not broken from, the social web.

Children's rights advocates are second to none in their commitment to the new freedom. They proceed on the assumption that the welfare of children is best advanced by unshackling them from every conceivable constraint. Nowhere in their writings is there the slightest reservation concerning the psychological and social consequences of their agenda. Individual freedom is good; children are individuals; the more freedom they have, the better off they are. Social status, as well as context, means nothing; all that matters is the promise of an abstract idea.

It seems logical that those who profess a professional interest in the well-being of children would want to take their cues from the findings of child psychologists. But do advocates of children's rights actually listen to what psychologists say is necessary for healthy child development? The evidence on this point is not encouraging, raising doubts about their entire agenda.

Child psychologists do not speak with one voice any more than economists do, but there are areas where consensus exists. Perhaps the most noncontroversial thing that can be said regarding the psychological health of children is that they need love, and lots of it. One does not have to be a Freudian to acknowledge that the first years of life are crucial to the psychological maturation of human beings. Deprive a child of love, of an opportunity to set anchor, and the consequences are likely to be disastrous.

Child psychoanalyst and University of Michigan professor Selma Fraiberg has done as exhaustive a search of the literature on child development as anyone, and it is her conclusion that psychological development is inextricably tied to the degree of attachment that a child experiences; maternal deprivation can have deadly consequences. The boys and girls who, for whatever reason, do not establish a strong bond with their parents (their mother, in particular) are prime candidates for mental institutions, prisons, urban slums, and other such places. Bondless men, women, and children, she maintains, "constitute one of the largest aberrant populations in the world today, contributing far beyond their numbers to social disease and disorder."[2]

Fraiberg's account of individuals who suffer from "the disease of nonattachment" is instructive: we should not expect anything positive to result if children are denied an opportunity to develop roots. Although it is true that those who are the most disabled are a minority, it is also true that there are millions of others who experience hardship because they are less than adequately integrated into family and community; they have more than their fair share of personal problems. Insofar as this is common knowledge among students of human behavior, it is all the more troublesome to learn how widely ignored the accumulated research is by those who should know better.

Children's rights advocates add to the problem when they propose that the road to freedom is paved by removing children from the reach of their parents. They not only slight the findings of social science in this regard but summarily dismiss the accumulated wisdom of tradition. Nor is this accidental; children's rights advocates typically see tradition as the enemy of human liberty. To those who hold the vision of the new freedom, children have historically been the most oppressed persons: a constellation of restrictive traditions has worked to deny them an autonomous condition. This is what children's rights advocates seek to redress.

It is true that children have historically been denied equal rights, but it does not follow that they have therefore been oppressed. It makes no sense to make a blanket statement that anyone who does not have as many rights as the next person is somehow persecuted. Prisoners and the insane, for example, do not have the same rights as others, yet few think this unjust. We need to know, among other things, whether the deprived person is deserving of equal rights. Children, it can be argued, are not deserving of equal rights, and this is because they lack the requisite resources to exercise rights in a fashion that liberates. That they deserve *some* rights is incontestable. But it is unfair to grant equal rights to those for whom the bestowal is a burden. For instance, because children cannot support themselves, it makes no sense to give them equal economic rights. In fact, because to do so is cruel since it cannot help but lead to their exploitation. Children in pursuit of equal economic rights is a travesty, for it needlessly misleads them into thinking that they are as capable of shouldering responsibilities. It sets them up for failure.

Viewed historically, the concept of children's rights is an oxymoron. In Western civilization it is well known that the Hebrews allowed children to be put to death for reviling their parents. Moreover, Hebrew fathers exercised virtually complete control over the labor and marriages of their children. Greek children, in preclassical Athens before the reforms of Solon (ca. 640– ca. 558 B.C.), lacked rights and were without recourse if their fathers were forced to sell them because of indebtedness. Ancient Roman fathers determined if a newborn infant was accepted as a member of the family or abandoned. Infanticide was practiced throughout much of Western history and even more so in Eastern civilizations. (However, except perhaps during famines, ancient infanticide was probably not more common than modern abortions.) A harsh environment for children continued during the Middle Ages, though some scholars have overstated the plight of children in the premodern world.[3]

As rough as matters were for children, it needs to be said that most adults did not fare any better. Economic hardship was the norm, for every family member, and appeals made on the basis of individual rights were virtually nonexistent; the very idea of political rights was so foreign to daily reality that it was rarely voiced at all. As bad as things were, however, children still managed to acquire an occasional right or two, though the process was erratic.

Oftentimes children were distributed rights unintentionally, as by-products of conflicts between the state and patriarch. For example, when ruling elites sought to strengthen their hand, they typically moved to lessen the power of local potentates, and this meant a diminution of authority exercised by the father. Less power for the father meant more power for the son. War, too, had the effect of loosening the rein on sons, as they freed themselves from the purview of their fathers and experienced life on their own.

But it wasn't until the intervention of the church that real protection was given to children. The Jesuits, in particular, played a critical role in fostering the innocence of childhood, shielding children from the corrupting influences of adult living. Further progress attended the rise of capitalism, as fathers went to work in factories, allowing mothers to stay at home caring for the children. With the advent of women working in the home, children's physical and mental health improved markedly over feudal conditions. Contrary to much ideological cant, children's quality of life increased—in virtually every respect—as the social effects of a market economy became manifest.

Considering how austere life was for children throughout the ages, and given the lack of legal protection they had, it is with some relief that respect for the rights of children should be greeted. Almost everyone today is in agreement that children (those who are born, at least) are entitled to be free from physical abuse and wanton neglect. However, once the discussion proceeds beyond the serious, clear-cut cases of maltreatment, controversy arises. There is even less consensus with regard to awarding positive rights to children.

It is often difficult to get good data on child maltreatment, even when those who generate the research are themselves beyond reproach. For example, in defining the overall level of violence that children are submitted to in the home, a 1985 study by the renowned National Institute for Mental Health included everything from a slap to murder. The study also failed to consider the motivation for violence, so we have no way of knowing whether a child was slapped for playing with a knife or playing with a kite. The National Family Violence Surveys are just as prone to abuse with interpretation, as demonstrated by the practice of collapsing data on children who are "pushed" by their parents with data where a gun or knife has been used; the overall level of violence that such a research technique produces is suspect.[4]

It is even more difficult to determine the level of emotional child abuse that occurs. What constitutes emotional abuse is variable and lacks wide agreement by the experts. But no one doubts that serious emotional damage is inflicted on some children, leaving effects that long surpass most physical abuse. Indeed as Douglas Besharov has shown, approximately 80 percent of all substantiated child maltreatment cases involve forms of emotional or developmental harm, not physical abuse.[5] As to be expected, the controversial cases are the ones where no easy determination of harm, or guilt, can be established.

Does calling a fat child "fatso" constitute emotional child abuse? Some experts think so.[6] Their willingness to seek legal remedies for such cases is the heart of the controversy. By calling on the state to intervene in these everyday matters (should there be a law against ostracism?), child advocates display a mind-set that is both naive and dangerous. It is naive to think that the state can regulate human sentiment and dangerous to even try; privacy rights would never survive such intense scrutiny.

It is in the area of positive rights for children that child advocates often ill-serve their clients, proposing agenda that, if adopted wholesale, would demonstrably make matters worse for everyone. That children's rights activists have not succeeded thus far in achieving all of what they want is no reason not to take them seriously. Their specific goals haven't been realized, but the vector of their thinking has been followed by many upper-middle-class people, including those in the child care professional ranks and family-law professors. They are helping to define the parameters of the debate. They deserve a response, not a dismissive rejoinder.

According to Jan H. Blits, three major groups of child advocates can be identified. One group maintains a strong belief in total equality, and nothing less than an end to adult-child distinctions in law and practice is morally acceptable. A second group is convinced that the hierarchial patterns associated with the nuclear family are the cause of much repression, leading to an authoritarian existence, enslaved libido, and other nefarious outcomes. A third group wants to replace the alleged failure of conventional child-protective measures with the supposedly more effective approach of arming children with equal rights against adults.

The unifying principle behind all three factions is a passionate belief in equality. "Driven largely by a desire to establish a fully egalitarian society," contends Blits, "the children's rights movement takes aim at the last bastion of traditional inequality in America—paternalism within the family."[7] This is where the interests of rights extremists intersect: they hate the family. "We must include the oppression of children in any program for feminist revolution," counseled Shulamith Firestone.[8] The reason for doing so has nothing to do with protecting the best interests of children. It has everything to do with securing the ambitions of the new freedom—the desire to remake the human condition *de novo*.

To many child advocates, justice demands that children be given equal rights. Influenced by philosopher John Rawls, Lyla H. O'Driscoll posits that justice requires "that each person is entitled to the most extensive liberty compatible with a like liberty for all." What this means is that "both parent and child are seen as bearers of rights—fundamentally, the right to maximal equal liberty."[9] It should be noted that this position goes way beyond anything John Stuart Mill had in mind when he was thinking about the advancement of liberty: he specifically exempted children from experiencing the fruits of his "one very simple principle."

It is perfectly logical that any child advocate who would adopt a Rawlsian conception of justice would be led to conclude that "maximal equal liberty" ought to rule family relations. The driving force behind Rawls's theory is equality, and there is no better way to infuse that element into family relations than by appeal to equal rights. Intellectually seductive though it may be, this example highlights the problems that occur when philosophy is not grounded in experience. When philosophy divorces itself from reality, it no longer speaks to human needs and capabilities: it speaks to figments of the imagination.

A theory of justice or liberty that does not consider the limits of childhood yields neither justice nor liberty; it may very well yield the obverse. A meaningful exercise of rights presupposes a level of maturation that most children have not reached. Self-discipline is a property that is absolutely indispensable to any conception of freedom, yet we hear very little about it from contemporary children's liberationists. They are too preoccupied with scouring the legal code for inequalities to care about such matters. Yet without self-discipline, liberty becomes license and destroys justice.

Two authors who offer case examples of the "maximal-equal-liberty" school of thought are John Holt and Richard Farson. One of the nice things about their writings is that they are crystal clear in their prescription for liberation: one doesn't have to infer anything from their work. Holt is a respected author on education and Farson is a wellknown psychologist. Both are convinced that we need a bill of rights for children. Nothing less will do.

Holt wants young people to have the right to vote. So as to be understood without confusion, Holt flatly argues that "I am talking not just about the sixteen-year-old vote but about the six-year-old vote." Indeed, he cites the example of a six-year-old who worked in the McGovern presidential campaign of 1972 as testimony to his idea.[10] He also wants to do away with child-labor laws and give children of all ages the right to work, earn a living, own property, and travel independent of their parents. To those who say that children traveling alone might get lost, Holt replies, "Yes, they might. Adults get lost right now. It may be a nuisance, but not a tragedy or disaster."[11]

Holt, who has taught graduate students at Harvard University, wants to extend to children other rights as well. He wants them to be able to choose their own guardian, thus freeing them from the lock their parents now have on them. What will they do for money? Holt wants a guaranteed income for every man, woman, and child. Leaving no stone unturned, he recommends that we abolish compulsory education, permitting every child to decide whether he wants to attend school. What about legalizing drugs for everyone, including children? Or allowing kids to drive? Or have sex? Holt wants it all. Nothing is to be denied.

Psychologist Farson concurs. He wants to end what he sees as the double standard, obliterating all distinctions in law between child and adult. Children should have the right to live where they want, and with whom, including residences operated by other children. Whether a child ought to be educated is no one's business but the child's, and, not to be outdone, Farson proposes that if the child wants to go to school, he should determine the curriculum. The right to vote and work for a living must also be observed. The right to sexual freedom is another must.[12]

If someone were to set out to destroy the family, it is not likely that he could do a better job than to follow the advice of child experts Holt and Farson. By granting children rights identical to those of adults, the very seat of parental authority would collapse. Absent that social base, all the individual attributes that freedom is predicated on would never develop. Society, and the liberty that inheres in it, would self-destruct.

It is testimony to the grip that the new freedom has on many thinking people that a rebuttal to Holt and Farson is required. The real problem, of course, is not with Holt and Farson; they represent the outer limit of the new freedom. The real problem is with those who are prepared to go a long way down the liberationist road, stopping short of the final destination, but not before great social damage has been done. There are literally millions of parents and teachers who think that children are free to the extent that they are free from constraint. They associate freedom with rights.

To make the point more plainly, consider two children, Frank and John. Frank is under strict adult supervision, both at home and in school. He is told when to go to school, what clothes to wear, when to speak in class, when to study, when to play, when to come home, when to go to bed, and so forth. John chooses if and when to go school, wears whatever he wants when he goes, does exactly as he pleases in class, decides if and when to study, stays out late, and generally sets his own standards. Who is freer, Frank or John?

If the lack of constraints is what counts, John is freer. Now ask yourself who will be freer when he's twenty-one, John or Frank? Frank, of course. But why? Because while John at twenty-one will be hostage to his passions, Frank will more than likely have developed his resources to at least a satisfactory level, leaving him freer to choose among society's options. His freedom is a function of the constraints placed on him while growing up, limitations imposed on him by responsible adults. Freedom, then, is not anathema to discipline. Rather, freedom is conditioned on discipline.

To discipline a child is not to tyrannize him; it is to enable him to become what he is capable of becoming. Success in any field, whether it be in music, athletics, science, or whatever, is dependent on the ability of the individual to practice self-restraint. Self-restraint alone doesn't insure anything, but its absence guarantees failure.

Advocates of the new freedom see things differently. Their alienation from society has led them to assault the middle-class value structure that undergirds the social order. For them, imposing such values is restrictive of real human liberty. That is why so many of them look upon the lower class with a strange sense of envy; they are regretful of having missed the opportunity to experience primal freedom. Stripped of conventional cultural dress, so goes the argument, the poor are closer to their primordial baseline, and better situated to experience the promise of the new freedom.

Listen to Firestone's lament. She deplores in no uncertain terms the degree to which middle-class children are supervised. But not all youngsters have succumbed to this "supervised nightmare," for there are "children of the ghettos and the working class where the medieval conception of open community— living on the street—still lingers.'' This is it. The totally open and free community is found on the streets, where everyone harmonizes and rhapsodizes. This is where freedom and community meet: in the streets of urban America—uptown.

Having gone this far, it was inevitable that she'd take the next, and last, step. ''Sexually, too, ghetto kids are freer. One fellow told me that he can't remember an age when he didn't have sexual intercourse with other kids as a natural thing; everyone was doing it.'' Sex is so ''groovy'' for ghetto kids that ''they do it on the stairs.'' According to Firestone, this is why ''free childhood'' exists only in the lower class.[13] The rest of us, one supposes, are too encumbered with social constraints to experience such freedoms.

Sweden is another place where unbounded liberty exists. It is fair to say that Sweden has become the Shangri-la for many new-freedom thinkers, this notwithstanding the high levels of suicide, illegitimacy, and drug and alcohol abuse that it sports. But the kind of moral destitution that royal commissions in Sweden have found is no deterrent to champions of the new freedom. When they look at Sweden, they see individual liberty, pure and simple, with none of the moral hang-ups that still plague the puritans at home. They are especially taken by the extent to which children have been granted nearly total legal rights.

Klaus A. Ziegert is an Australian law professor who is convinced that ''the dream of any child of ideal parents will come true, if at all, for all the children in Sweden sooner than in any other industrialized society.''[14] The source of his enthusiasm is the degree to which Swedish society has already achieved what he calls ''the normative stabilization of indifference,'' which in simpler terms means the extent to which legal distinctions between children and adults have all but vanished. To those who think there is no higher virtue than equality, such an achievement is a tremendous victory. But to those who think the law should take due consideration of children's legitimate needs and special interests, such legislation is a social and moral disaster.

The new freedom in Sweden is much more than a cultural celebration; it is the font of public policy. The Swedish government provides for abortion on demand, comprehensive day care, parental leave, 270 days of paid sick leave per family (not counting unlimited sick leave for either parent to be with a sick child), social security (advances are given, if needed), guaranteed family income, child allowances, housing allowances, student loans, retraining programs, and so forth.

Has it worked? The low infant mortality rates that Sweden has achieved are unfortunately matched by its high rates of death before birth and later in life. It is the paradox of paradoxes that Swedish society proportionately kills many of its own people before they are born, then keeps most of those alive who manage to get born, and finally watches an exceptionally high proportion of its adults kill themselves off. A high abortion rate, low infant mortality rate, and high suicide rate (especially among the elderly) is not exactly many people's picture of Shangri-la. But it evidently is for some.

Then there is the children's ombudsman, an official whose job it is to preserve children's rights. There is much to preserve. No corporal punishment is allowed anywhere in Sweden, and this has come to mean that a child can sue his parents if he is either spanked or "humiliated"; his parents pick up the bill for the lawyer's services in their taxes. Every child has a legal voice in family decision making, and is entitled to be heard and *not overruled* in divorce proceedings. The right to "divorce" one's parents is another new freedom victory for Swedish youngsters.[15]

The Swedish experience dramatically weakens the argument that extremists like Holt and Farson can't possibly carry the day. Sweden is a society where it is illegal for a father to slap his daughter, but not to have intercourse with her.[16] The point to be made is not that legalizing incest leads to an increase in it; no doubt it doesn't. But the law's erasure is not without meaning: it symbolically represents the moral priorities of Swedish society.

The fundamental problem with the new freedom as it applies to children is that it denies them childhood. It thrusts upon them the conditions, situations, experiences, responsibilities, challenges, and expectations that are properly the reserve of adulthood. Children are a protected class in our society, and with good reason: they need to be protected. They do not possess the faculties of mind, emotional development, and experience that adults do. Obviously, there are children who are infinitely brighter and more mature than some adults, including, on occasion, their parents. But no sane social policy can be based upon rare exceptions.

The new freedom is at odds with social reality. Society consists of men, women, and children who take their identity from family, religion, custom, tradition, and social convention, and who respond to one another on the basis of role and status. No society can exist without these cultural characteristics.

It is often said that what exists is nothing more than a social construct, the product of a given historical episode. The deduction is then made that what exists is dispensable, because anthropology has taught that there are many different ways of living. Therefore, some conclude that our conception of what is good for children is only one of series of ways in which childhood can be conceived. The new freedom, it is argued, will surely change things, but in the long run we'll be glad it did.

Although it is true that there are tremendous differences among societies, it does not follow that any given society is capable of entertaining tremendous differences within its own normative structure. Cultural diversity is real, but many available possibilities are quite incompatible with one another. The important question is not whether many social arrangements are possible—that much is beyond dispute—the key is whether a particular arrangement fosters healthy communities and individuals.

The wisdom of any social order is evident, at least in part, in how people treat themselves and others. A society plagued by increasing psychological and social disorders is one that bears watching. More than that, it demands an inquiry as to what went wrong. If the number of people who self-destruct is increasing, as judged by rates of suicide, and alcohol and drug abuse, there is a reason, grounded in culture, for that phenomenon. The reason obviously has much to do with the way in which people are socialized, the kinds of norms and values they hold, and the types of experiences that are open to them.

It is a serious mistake to regard the values that inhere in the new freedom as things distinct and separate from the psychological and social disorders that they engender. The human desire for freedom stretches beyond individual and social needs, but those needs cannot be ignored in the pursuit of a specious freedom. Children, especially, need to be coached before they can participate in the quest for freedom. They need coaching in developing their potential, the kind that someday will allow them the freedom to take good advantage of whatever liberties inhere in society. And that means discipline before liberty, not liberty before all else.

Children are affected by the kind and degree of social nourishment they are afforded. To remove constraints from their diet is tantamount to emotional starvation. They need structure, predictability, and stability in their lives. That is one of the central lessons of child psychology. Unfortunately, it is not a lesson that many children's advocates seem to have mastered.

Notes

1. Beatrice and Ronald Gross, eds., *The Children's Rights Movement* (Garden City, N.Y.: Anchor Press/Doubleday, 1977), p. 1.
2. Selma Fraiberg, *Every Child's Birthright: In Defense of Mothering* (New York: Basic Books, 1977), p. 62.
3. The dismal condition of medieval childhood, as portrayed by Philippe Aries, Edward Shorter, and Lloyd DeMause has been challenged by John Demos, *Past, Present and Personal: The Family and the Life Course in American History* (Oxford: Oxford University Press, 1986), and Frances and Joseph Gies, *Marriage and the Family in the Middle Ages* (New York: Harper and Row, 1988). I am indebted to Bryce Christensen for bringing this to my attention. See his review of the Gies volume in *Chronicles* (July 1988): 33–34.
4. For a report on the studies, see Ronald Sullivan, "Admissions of Child Abuse Found to Drop Sharply," *New York Times*, November 11, 1985, p. A13.
5. Douglas J. Besharov, "The Child-Abuse Numbers Game," *Wall Street Journal*, August 4, 1988, p. 20.

6. Patrick Lynch of Pennsylvania State University Law School thinks educators who call children "fat slob" are engaging in emotional child abuse. He wants to see legal remedies for such cases. See Don Oldenburg, "Child Abuse: The Emotional Side," *Washington Post*, September 22, 1987, p. D5.
7. Jan H. Blits, "What's Wrong with Children's Rights?" *This World* (Winter 1984): 6.
8. Shulamith Firestone, *The Dialectic of Sex* (New York: Morrow, 1970), p. 118.
9. Lyla H. O'Driscoll, "Toward a New Theory of the Family," in Joseph Peden and Fred Glahe, eds., *The American Family and the State* (San Francisco: Pacific Research Institute for Public Policy, 1986), p. 97.
10. John Holt, *Escape from Childhood* (New York: Dutton, 1974), pp. 158–59.
11. Ibid., p. 199.
12. Richard Farson, "Birthrights," in Beatrice Gross and Ronald Gross, eds., *The Children's Rights Movement* (Garden City, N.Y.: Anchor Press Doubleday, 1977), pp. 325–28.
13. Firestone, *The Dialectic of Sex*, pp. 114–15.
14. Klaus A. Ziegert, "Children's Rights and the Supportive Function of Law: The Case of Sweden," *Journal of Comparative Family Studies* (Summer 1987): 170.
15. Ibid., pp. 166–70. For information on the drug problem, see Lincoln Fry, "Drug Abuse and Crime in a Swedish Birth Cohort," *British Journal of Criminology* (January 1985): 46–59.
16. Sam Janus, *The Death of Innocence: How Our Children Are Endangered by the New Sexual Freedom* (New York: Morrow, 1981), p. 154; see chapter 5 for a discussion of incest.

PART IV

THE EMANCIPATION
OF THE ID

8

Origins of the Sexual Revolution

Picture this: It's the 1950s and two people are discussing what might be done in the years to come to reduce the already low rate of illegitimacy. They wonder aloud what might happen if (a) sex education were to be introduced into the school curriculum, (b) an inexpensive birth control pill were to be made available, and (c) abortion on demand were to be legalized in every state. Is there any doubt what they would have said?

So what happened? Why didn't things pan out the way they were supposed to? Why were the results counterintuitive? What did people do with the information, technology, and rights that they were given? How could it be that illegitimacy rates exploded while the opportunities to avoid pregnancy and childbirth multiplied? What went wrong?

Perhaps the answer to the above series of questions can best be illuminated by posing a slightly different scenario: It's the 1950s and two people are discussing what might be done in the years to come to *increase* the rate of illegitimacy. What would they have said? In all likelihood they would have focused on what could be done to lower the social penalties for illegitimacy. Why? Because as everyone concedes, the principal reason that illegitimacy rates were so low in the 1950s had everything to do with fear, guilt, shame, and stigma. Remove the controls and all hell would break lose. It did.

There is a lesson to be learned here. Giving people the means to avoid the consequences of temptation is not likely to yield less vice. What needs to be checked is temptation itself. And if temptation is ratified by society, then all the books, gadgets, and operations in the world will not be able to make up the difference. When freedom is defined as the abandonment of constraint, certain antisocial patterns follow. It matters not a whit whether new social utensils are at hand. What matters is moral resolve.

By now almost everyone agrees that a sexual revolution of sorts has taken place in the past few decades. At the extremes there are those who would deny it and hype it, but this is to be expected in a society that makes instant celebrities out of iconoclasts. It is a tribute to the trashing of moderation—in discourse as well as behavior—that those who most challenge common sense are treated as the high priests of wisdom. The new freedom has been kind to dissidents of every stripe, and this is why so many people have fun defying the obvious.

At one end of the spectrum there is Ben Wattenberg; at the other, Shere Hite. Where Wattenberg understates, Hite overstates. Wattenberg is a gadfly, a thoughtful observer who delights in challenging the prevailing winds of pessimism. He forthrightly objects to those who make a career out of bad news, and offers plenty of reasons that they are wrong. But in doing so he occasionally overextends himself, trying so hard to look at the positive that he glosses over real failures. This is particularly true when he discusses changes in sexual attitudes and behavior.

Wattenberg raises three objections to what passes as the popular conception regarding changing sexual mores. First, he argues that the sexual revolution has been less dramatic than reported. Second, he maintains that the consequences of the revolution have been minimal. Third, he contends that there is no need to worry because self-correcting mechanisms are already under way.[1]

There are a few problems with this formulation. To begin with, if Wattenberg's first two objections are correct, then the third needs explaining: self-correction means reparation, and reparation follows damage. Second, it is true that repair is under way, but it is going to be a long process, precisely because Wattenberg's first two contentions are false. Damage has been done, and it is families and communities—hence society— that have been impaired.

Wattenberg examines the data on sexual activity among youth and admits there have been some big changes. But he takes comfort in the fact that previous generations had similar misgivings, and therefore concludes that there is much hullabaloo about nothing. For instance, Wattenberg offers as testimony a quotation from a mother in 1929 who was complaining about the path-breaking phenomenon of girls calling boys for dates; this is supposed to quell our fears about contemporary examples of moral waywardness. But it is one thing to note episodic violations of folkways, quite another to record widespread violations of mores. In the 1920s, most precocious girls didn't wind up pregnant. Today many who aren't precocious do. That's the difference.

As to the consequences of the sexual revolution, one can begin with herpes and AIDS and work down to the psychological effects of divorce on children. It's not a pretty picture. Again, it does no good to pretend that the problem isn't so bad after all. Such wishful thinking only delays the day of reckoning.

Perhaps the biggest mistake is in thinking that there are "self-correcting" mechanisms out there just waiting to make amends. But there is no such thing as an invisible hand when it comes to morality. It is either nourished or it isn't. Repair to the social fabric is under way, but there is nothing mysterious about it. It's the product of human effort, of people organizing to do something about the problems that beset us. It's the result of hard, and still controversial, work.

Shere Hite muddies the debate even further. She wildly exaggerates the extent of the sexual revolution, and plays fast and loose with the data. Wattenberg, to his credit, is meticulous in his use of data; it's his conclusions that are questionable. Hite, however, violates the canons of social research just to make her point. She has been roundly criticized by social scientists for her work but continues to enjoy a respectable reputation among many journalists, and hence the readership of mass-market publications.

Hite has authored three huge "surveys" of the population on the subject of sexuality. None of her studies meets the minimal requirements for survey research, hence her samples are unrepresentative, misleading, and without scientific value. Placing ads for women to volunteer information about their sex lives in the pages of men's magazines (*Oui*) and local tabloids with limited appeal (*Village Voice*) is not exactly a textbook way of surveying the population. Yet she continues to affect the discussion because of the extreme "findings" of her work.

Her latest report, *Women and Love, a Cultural Revolution in Progress*,[2] purports to have uncovered data that indicate there is a major revolt going on in American households. She asserts that 70 percent of American women cheat on their husbands, and that 76 percent of the cheaters feel no guilt. How did she arrive at such a conclusion? By tallying the responses of the 4.5 percent of the women surveyed who bothered to answer 127 essay questions on the intimacies of their sex life and then took the time to mail the results to a total stranger. It's actually worse than that. Each woman was told she could skip any question she felt like skipping, and because Hite doesn't report how many people answered each question, we have no way of knowing whether it's 70 percent of a thousand women who cheat or 70 percent of ten.

Good data on sexual behavior are always hard to come by, but not impossible. And regardless of the degree of difficulty, the right thing to do in any research is to be honest about the limitations of the chosen methodology and stick closely to accepted investigatory procedures. Not to do so is unethical and possibly harmful to the well-being of others.

The nonbelievers and true believers aside, a sexual revolution of considerable, but not gargantuan, proportions did take place over the past quarter century or so. Why it occurred is the first line of inquiry. What the consequences were will be discussed in the next two chapters.

At least ten causes of the sexual revolution can be identified. In no particular order of significance, the effects of each of the following need to noted: World Wars I and II; new birth control practices; increasing levels of tolerance; decreasing levels of religiosity; changes in the schools; the role of the media; changing demographics; economic prosperity; welfare; and the rights revolution. Cumulatively, they brought about sizable changes in sexual attitudes and behavior.

There is a strong, and historically universal, relationship between war and changing sexual mores. British scholar John Costello has studied the phenomenon as thoroughly as anyone, and it is his conclusion that "the relaxation of moral restraints endemic in war influenced sexual relationships and the relations between the sexes throughout human history."[3] Indeed, war is the single most powerful variable explaining sexual emancipation, of both men and women, in history.

War fosters both interdependence and independence. As everyone acknowledges, war demands collective effort and thus has a solidifying effect on human relations. But it also generates independence: young single men are freed from the reach of their fathers, and married men and women are freed from the reach of each other. War affords men and women uncommon opportunities for sexual experimentation, the kind that all parties realize are transient and short-lived. It is fertile ground for widespread departures from the norm.

World War I was no different. It effectively terminated what was left of the Victorian era and ushered in what was to be called the "Roaring Twenties." It boosted considerably the suffragette movement and made the rights of women a more respectable and participatory enterprise than ever before. Skirts were shortened and inhibitions relaxed. It was no longer taboo for women to smoke in public or campaign for birth control. Newly trumpeted Freudian fears about stifling sexual desires took hold, and the automobile allowed a perfect place to vent such concerns; petting became the number-one demonstration of affection.[4]

World War II turned up the heat of the sexual revolution even higher. An entire generation of young men and women experienced the loneliness, separation, and uncertainty that accompanies war. In such times the unthinkable becomes thinkable and the unaccepted accepted. The overriding sense of urgency that war induces finds expression in the bedroom as well as the battlefield. Nothing is as it was, and there is no time like the present. The immediateness of war ignites and inflames; it pulls the plug on passion and empties energies hitherto held in reserve. It liberates.

The fear of venereal disease led the Allied armies to distribute condoms freely and widely, though the rates of syphilis and gonorrhea continued to climb throughout the war. Sexual adventures were also recorded at home, as young women took advantage of an unprecedented degree of sexual freedom. Shotgun marriages ballooned in the 1940s and the birthrate shot up as well. Perhaps the biggest effect, however, was the seeds that the war sowed in launching the women's movement of the 1960s. Once the "baby boomers" left home for college in the sixties, many of their mothers sought to recapture the independence that working outside the home gave them during the war.

The introduction of a birth control pill in 1960 radically reshaped sexual attitudes and behavior. But it did not happen overnight. Earlier in the century a sociologist by the name of William Ogburn had theorized that social change begins with developments in the material end of culture (for example, technological innovations) and then proceeds to affect the nonmaterial component (for example, norms and values). He maintained there was always a discernible lag effect between the two variables. Ogburn's theory of cultural lag finds support when considering the social effects of the pill: changes in sexual mores lagged behind the technological breakthrough of the new birth control device.

In the mid-1980s, Walter Goodman of the *New York Times* posed the right question on the subject of the pill and its progeny: "Does the availability of the pill make it easy for young couples to avoid emotional ties or does it permit them to make commitments, when they are ready, without being forced into them?" He then gave a sensible answer: "The current figures on divorce and on single-parent households cannot be testaments on commitment."[5] The pill proved to be especially attractive to upper-middle-class women, many of whom wanted to experience the rights of sexual freedom but were unprepared to shoulder the responsibilities of motherhood.

The legalization of abortion on demand in 1973 carried the process one step further. More than even the pill, abortion has come to signify the rights-without-responsibilities mind-set of our culture. The decision in *Roe v. Wade* sent a message loud and clear to both men and women: if you want to play, you need not pay. The support that men have shown for the Supreme Court decision has been misinterpreted by feminists who think that men have suddenly become their allies. On the contrary, men read *Roe* with their own self-interest in mind. Take away the possibility of having to make monthly child support payments, and what's to stop an otherwise reckless male from exploiting any women he can get his hands on?

The liberation of the id took a giant leap forward when tolerance became the defining virtue of the new freedom. Ever since the 1960s, there has been a steady, almost deafening, drumbeat of rhetoric proclaiming the horrors of past attitudes on sexuality and the wonders of full-blown liberation. Some, like Norman O. Brown,[6] have even suggested that sexual repression is dangerous. But very few of these sages have been prepared to compute the damage that has been done by abandoning constraint altogether.

Social scientists in general, and anthropologists in particular, approach the subject of sexuality with an extremely relativistic bent. The usual approach is to begin with a recitation on how different our moral standards are from many, indeed most, societies in history. Though the stated precept is that there is no "right" way to construct sexual mores, the real message that comes through is that our way of doing things is repressive, unnecessary, and unjust.

Here's how it works. We are introduced to a long list of primitive cultures, usually found on some remote island or village, where sex is free and open. A comparison with our own society follows, with the predictable conclusion that we are oppressed and they are free. Of course, many of these liberated peoples also practice cannibalism, subject women to clitorectomies, and decapitate their adversaries, but this seems not to count. What counts is sex and the lack of taboos.

The new-freedom approach to sexuality is nothing if not antireligious. It loathes the idea that religion teaches restraint, and seeks to deprecate its influence by mockery. For example, when the pitch for another round of tolerance is made, the discussion typically focuses on the nefarious influence that religion has exerted on human sexuality. The church, in particular, is scorned. After bashing the teachings of Saints Paul and Augustine, the Jesuits get it next, followed by a tirade against the Puritans. To anyone so naive as to believe this diatribe (the intended audience is most often college students), the logical inference to be drawn is that religion enslaves while the rejection of it enlightens. This, of course, is a "value-free" interpretation.

The new freedom regards anything that stands in the way of total sexual emancipation as the enemy of freedom. The prevailing assumption is that human beings are, at bottom, free and uninhibited spirits, lacking in notions of right and wrong. From this baseline it is argued that civilization has imposed artificial and wholly unnecessary restraints on us, making true freedom impossible. To experience the promise of liberty, we need to return to our original state of nature and start from square one. Only then we will be able to recapture the completeness of the human condition.

Such thinking is the stuff that fantasies are made of, not serious proposals for liberty. Human passions are capable of great good and great evil, as even a cursory reading of history will reveal. To get the best out of human beings, deliberate efforts must be made to channel the passions in a socially constructive way. Our appetites do not naturally incline to moral ends, and this is why the rational faculties that humans possess are indispensable to the task. Moral ground rules are established so that men may live in peace. The imposition of a moral code, temperately conceived and judiciously administered, is the first mark of a people dedicated to the interests of human liberty. Its absence is not freedom but slavery.

Be that as it may, the plea for moderation is drowned out by new-freedom demands for tolerance and uninhibited pleasure seeking. Hedonism is the only word that can describe the ambition of those who first launched the crusade for total sexual freedom. Kate Millett is on record as saying that the goal of the sexual revolution is to do away with all existing taboos so that a single permissive standard can be instituted.[7] Gore Vidal envisions a sexually free society to be a bisexual one, and looks forward to the day when "it is possible to have a mature sexual relationship with a woman on Monday, and a mature sexual relationship with a man on Tuesday, and perhaps on Wednesday have both together. . . ."[8] What the weekend will be like he does not say.

The evidence of the new tolerance is everywhere apparent. In Blumstein and Schwartz's study of male-female sexual relationships, the first words that earned the distinction of having quotation marks wrapped around them were *betrayal* and *loyalty*. A little later the reader advances to a section on cheating, infidelity, and adultery, only to learn that these old-fashioned and negatively sounding words have been replaced by the more contemporary term of "non-monogamy."[9] This is the doctrine of moral neutrality at its best: in one stroke, deviance has been eliminated from language, and, it is hoped, from the mind as well.

Tolerance for sexual behavior of every kind knows no finish line. It's a slope so slippery that, once stepped upon, there are no brakes: it's a sheet of ice. Everything goes, including pedophilia. When Dr. Ruth counsels that "there are no limits" to sexual enjoyment, the teenaged boy who is trying desperately to bring his girlfriend to orgasm can be forgiven if he resorts to unnatural methods. Correction: there is no such thing as unnatural in the lexicon of new freedom.

When *Ms.* magazine starts running articles on "Toys for Free Grown-ups: A Consumer Guide to Sex Gadgets, Potions, and Videos," there is good reason to believe that the new freedom has cornered the market. When feminists show as much concern for mastering the latest techniques of sexual excitement as they do for learning how to compete successfully in the world of work, then a change in priorities is evident in culture. And one can't help but note how many of these newly liberated persons find it absolutely necessary to be tied up and beaten in their sex lives. Is there freedom after bondage? No one says.

What do Americans want anyway? Do they like the new freedom or don't they? Yes and no. In one major survey, 42 percent of the public said that these days people have healthier and more relaxed ideas about sex. But 48 percent said that there is too much sexual freedom and loose living. It would have been interesting to know what segment of the population believes that loose living is a function of more relaxed ideas about sex. Similarly, pollsters like to dichotomize the population into two discrete groups when asking questions regarding changes in sexual attitudes and behavior: Have we become more tolerant, or are simply witnessing moral decay?[10] That the right answer might be both seems never to have crossed the examiner's mind.

Or consider this. The same pollster organization, in two different surveys, uncovered some very revealing findings. When asked whether they would welcome or reject "more emphasis on traditional family ties," fully 86 percent of those sampled said they would welcome such a shift.[11] But when asked whether they desire a "return to traditional standards regarding sexual relations," only 21 percent said yes.[12] It seems nearly everyone yearns for the ties that traditional family living provide, but few are willing to make the sacrifices that are necessary to achieve such a status. Or in today's vernacular, we want to experience the solidarity that the Waltons exhibit while living the life of "Miami Vice."

Interestingly, attitudes toward religion show the same ambivalence. We want the sense of belonging and incorporation that religion affords, but don't want to submit to its strictures. Religion constrains and that is why new-freedom enthusiasts find it so menacing. It is one of religion's prime social functions to subordinate the will of the individual to the interests of others. Such teachings are resisted, of course, in a society that thinks of the individual as the be-all and end-all of existence.

When the conventional religions lost their hold on many young people in the 1960s, they left fertile ground for a sexual revolution. Young people quite naturally incline to sexual adventure, so it was to be expected that when religion lost its grip, experimentation would follow. It did. One doesn't have to be a pure ascetic to be jolted by sharp changes in sexual attitudes and behavior. The new freedom left its mark on everyone, religious or not.

At about the same time that religion receded in influence, the schools lost out as well. It used to be that young people were disciplined in the home, church, and school. But beginning in the 1960s, all three institutions lost their nerve. When authority came under attack, those who exercised it took shelter. Parents traded correction for communication, clergymen practiced compassion instead of counseling, and teachers gave up altogether. The new freedom is nonjudgmental, and that's exactly what the young and the restless want to hear. Who can blame them? Certainly not the nonjudgmental: the very concept of blame is without meaning.

It is of symbolic importance that when prayer was thrown out of the schools, sex education was invited in. The secularization of the schools in the 1960s represents the triumph of the new freedom and the end, at least temporarily, to moral education. Human sexuality workshops replaced Bible study, and students learned more about condoms than chastity. This is not to suggest that the schools became hedonistic. They did not. But they did change, in a dramatic way, the language of morality. It was the atmosphere of the schools that changed most of all, and with it, the values and behavioral patterns of the students.

The overnight conversion to co-ed dorms on college campuses in the 1960s must be counted as among the new freedom's fastest victories. What was especially startling about this development was the extent to which private, religiously affiliated colleges and universities adopted the new rules. The near-absence of resistance to sex-integrated dorms, on the part of both parents and school administrators, is a tribute to progress—1960s style. What effect co-ed dorms had in inspiring promiscuity is not known, though more than a few college girls went home to mom and dad with half a family and no degree.

Media spokesmen are fond of saying that they merely reflect social changes, and are not responsible for causing any moral transformations. In truth, they do both. It is often difficult to determine which is the chicken and which is the egg, but it is not at all hard to discern which societal forces have at least some impact. That the media play a role in shaping public attitudes toward sexuality is something every producer will admit, albeit some prefer to do so in private. Titillation is their specialty, though each new round of sexual badgering makes it harder and harder just to tease. The more the audience gets, the more it wants. Drawing the line is no longer the censor's nightmare: deciding whether to draw it at all is.

Hollywood loves to debate the merits of labeling a movie R or X. Though an R will usually earn more bucks than an X, *Deep Throat* proved that chic-porn can be lucrative with the yuppie set. PG-13 was added to calm the fears of awakened parents, and plain old PG has come to mean that pubic hairs will not be shown. G movies come to town about as often as the circus, so mom and pop have to rent-a-Disney and hope that the lockbox stays locked. And as everyone quickly learns, all the controversy over ratings is largely a waste of time; there are no more Saturday afternoon movies, just Saturday movies.

Before the days of the new freedom, the most daring thing on Saturday night television were the June Taylor dancers. Now the family show has been upstaged by the movie, and practically every one of them begins the same way: "Parental discretion is advised." Parents can be forgiven if they've run out of advice to give, and need not feel defeated if being discreet no longer works. Sometimes banishment is to be preferred. It's the commercials that have become the boldest anyway, and they don't believe in viewer forewarnings. Calvin Klein likes it that way, and so, in fact, does the public: his photo of six half-nude bodies advertising his designer underwear was judged the most popular print advertisement in the United States in 1986 in a national survey by *Adweek* magazine.

A sexual revolution depends on young people, and that is exactly what America had in abundance in the 1960s. All those kids born after the war came of age in the sixties, swelling the ranks of teenagers to record levels. By late in the decade, the median age hit seventeen, bringing about the birth of a youth culture. If none of the other events had occurred, the changing demographic composition of society would have been enough to trigger some changes in sexual attitudes and behavior. As it turned out, the raw stuff of a sexual revolution was coupled with all the right cultural ingredients, making an attack on constraint all but inevitable. Hugh Hefner couldn't have written a better script.

The economic prosperity of the 1960s was another reason that moral conduct underwent considerable change. With low unemployment and low inflation, the stage was set for risk-taking behavior. It has historically been the case that when affluence strikes, the moral guard of society drops, sometimes to precarious levels. Though it is true that the fall of the Roman Empire was due in large part to barbarian invasion, it is also true that the moral resolve of the Roman elite had already been broken. The prosperity that preceded the fall was accompanied by a growing leisure class, and with it, a sharp increase in premarital sex, concubinage, cohabitation, adultery, divorce, abortion, and homosexuality. Appropriately, it was the Romans who invented the word *sex*.

Not everyone shares equally in prosperity, so it is to other economic considerations that we must turn to explain the collapse of moral standards among many of the poor in the 1960s. There is no reason to believe that poor people are less chaste than rich people, and that means that something other than pure material conditions must account for the moral transformation of poor neighborhoods. That something is welfare.

Before the 1960s, most able-bodied poor people preferred to work at low wages before ever taking a handout. But when the Great Society programs made welfare legitimate, everything changed. Although it exaggerates to say that welfare made having babies a financial asset, babies were certainly not the heavy liability they once were. And at least for some, that fact alone carried great moral significance. Add to this the general climate of times, and the inducements to promiscuity were well in place.

Finally, there is the matter of the rights revolution. A sexual revolution depends almost exclusively on the behavior of women, not men. Men have been, in any society, the ones most given to sexual adventure. Why this is so is debatable, but the fact is not. It is women who have typically demonstrated restraint, so that if and when they decline to do so, a sexual revolution is all but inevitable. And that is what happened in the 1960s: as the double standard collapsed under the weight of the rights revolution, women began to mimic the sexual adventurism of men.

As moral standards fell and liberation reigned, homosexuals watched approvingly and prepared to join the fight. Once they adopted the mantle of rights, the very idea of moral criteria came under attack. Ever since then, it is evident that rights have become more of a weapon to be used against society, and less a relief for the individual.

There are plenty of signs that the sexual revolution is in retreat. *Time* magazine put it rather bluntly when, midway through the 1980s, it announced "The Revolution Is Over." Caution and commitment, it said, were the new "watchwords" of the eighties.[13] As recent events have shown, there is much to be cautious about, and every reason in the world that commitment is important. But some learn more quickly than others, and the cleanup has only begun.

Notes

1. Ben Wattenberg, *The Good News Is the Bad News Is Wrong* (New York: Simon and Schuster, 1984), ch. 38.
2. Shere Hite, *Women and Love, a Cultural Revolution in Progress* (New York: Knopf, 1987).
3. John Costello, *Virtue under Fire* (Boston: Little, Brown, 1985), p. 2.
4. Ibid., ch. 1.
5. Walter Goodman, "There's Nothing Dated about the Bard's View of Chastity," *New York Times*, July 28, 1985, sec. II, p. 3.
6. See Norman O. Brown's best known works, *Life Against Death* (Middletown, Conn.: Wesleyan University Press, 1959), and *Love's Body* (New York: Random House, 1966).
7. Kate Millett, *Sexual Politics* (Garden City, N.Y.: Doubleday, 1970), p. 62.
8. Quoted by Dennis Altman, *Homosexual* (New York: Avon Books, 1971), p. 105.
9. Philip Blumstein and Pepper Schwartz, *American Couples* (New York: Morrow, 1983), pp. 194, 267.
10. Reported in Herbert McClosky and Alida Brill, *Dimensions of Tolerance* (New York: Russell Sage, 1983), p. 197.
11. The poll was taken by Yankelovich, Skelly and White and reported in Wattenberg, *The Good News Is the Bad News Is Wrong*, p. 283.
12. This was another Yankelovich, Skelly and White poll. See Daniel Yankelovich, *New Rules* (New York: Bantam Books, 1981), p. 98.
13. John Leo, "The Revolution Is Over," *Time*, April 9, 1984, p. 74.

9

The Legitimacy of Illegitimacy

If freedom is measured by the absence of constraints, then no segment of the population is more free than adolescents. They are the least burdened with responsibilities and the least encumbered by social strictures. Today more than ever before, young people enjoy fewer restrictions on their behavior and less abridgment of their rights, making them ideal candidates for measuring the impact of the new freedom. Unfortunately, a record number of young people miss out on the opportunity to experience their liberties: adolescent mortality rates are at an all-time high as the level of homicides, suicides, and accidents continues to mount. Add to this the unprecedented degree of psychological disorders that exists among teenagers, and the result is a declining proportion of young men and women who are capable of meaningfully exercising their liberties.

It is not surprising that sooner or later the new freedom would catch up with us. A reckless idea of freedom can have only reckless consequences, as both logic and experience amply demonstrate. Young people have always been inclined to partake of risky behavior, but only in recent years has the incidence of risk taking soared. Once the dominant culture advanced a "go-for-broke" mentality, many young people tried to do exactly that, hoping to roll back the tide of social constraints. It proved to be an uphill battle for most; some, it is now clear, went right over the edge.

Among the most wounded adolescents in the age of liberty without limits are teenaged mothers and their children. The fathers, which is to say the young boys, have almost uniformly dodged their duties, cashing in on the new-freedom's sanctioning of rights without responsibilities. It is sad to note that as the rights of women were being trumpeted by well-educated, affluent females, young boys were taking liberties with young girls, thus creating the feminization of poverty that feminists would come to deplore. Nowhere has there been more inequality between men and women than in the realm of teenage sexuality: he grabbed his rights and ran, leaving her with all the responsibilities. When a society's definition of freedom is totally open-ended, it is to be expected that some, perhaps many, will gravitate to a negative interpretation: freedom from.

Whatever doors the women's movement succeeded in opening is of little good to most teenage mothers; they lack the requisite skills to exploit their newly won opportunities. Only half of those who give birth before age eighteen complete high school, compared to 96 percent of those who postpone childbirth. Their earnings potential is seriously impaired, and the fact is that of those who drop out of school, most stay out for good. Female-headed families, as everyone knows by now, are much more likely to be poor: 40 percent of such families are in poverty, while only 7 percent of intact families are. The cost of all this to the taxpayer is significant: $16.6 billion was spent in 1985 on teenage childbearing, a figure that includes expenditures for administrative overhead, payments for Aid to Families with Dependent Children, Medicaid, and food stamps, but doesn't include the cost of housing, special education, foster care, day care, and the like.

The only ones who fare worse than teenage mothers are their children. There is a link between the age of the mother and the likelihood of giving birth to a low-weight baby, a factor that is itself related to numerous physical and mental handicaps. It is known that children of teenage mothers are more likely to die in infancy, have poorer health, be subjected to child abuse and neglect, do poorly in school, and have higher rates of delinquency than children reared in two-parent families. Moreover, babies born to single mothers are four times more likely to grow up poor than children of two-parent households. In short, if one were to concoct a recipe for social disaster, there would be no better model to build on than the present phenomenon of teenage motherhood.[1]

Exact figures on premarital sex are unobtainable, due, in part, to the prevailing winds of culture: in times of sexual reticence, the reported number is in all likelihood lower than what really exists, while in times of sexual permissiveness, a certain allowance must be made for hyping the actual level, the assumption being that social pressure is felt as much in times of sexual inhibition as well as exhibition. Be that as it may, the reported figures indicate a sizable leap in premarital sexual intercourse in the twentieth century. For example, Kinsey found that of women born between 1900 and 1920, 36 percent had premarital sex by their twenty-fifth birthday. By the early 1960s, it was estimated that approximately one-half of American women engaged in premarital sex. By 1975, the figure climbed to its highest level: 80 percent. It has since abated somewhat, as fear of contracting herpes, AIDS, and other communicable diseases has taken hold.

The biggest increase in premarital sex undoubtedly took place in the 1970s, just as the sexual revolution went into high gear. Among unmarried teenage women, the increase is believed to be on the order of two-thirds. By the late 1980s, the most widely quoted figure was that by age nineteen, three-quarters of all the boys, and almost two-thirds of all the girls, had experienced premarital intercourse. In terms of teenage pregnancies, it is known that the rate doubled in the 1970s, and reached a level of more than three thousand a day by 1988. There are now more than one million teenage pregnancies each year, resulting in a half million abortions; the majority of those children who aren't aborted are born illegitimately.

Birth rates do not necessarily follow pregnancy rates. In fact, the teenage birth rate in 1987 was lower than in 1957, this despite the huge increase in the pregnancy rate. In the 1950s, it was not uncommon for teens to marry and have children. In the 1980s, teens engaged in more sex but were less inclined to marry, due largely to the legality and easy availability of abortion, and the declining stigma attached to unwed motherhood. This transformation was reflected in the 1970s, when pregnancy rates soared while both births and birth rates plummeted. There was a 25 percent decrease in the birth rate between 1970 and 1984, due to a doubling of the abortion rate during that period.

It is troubling, to put it mildly, to note that between 1960 and 1980, that is, in the very period when absolute freedom became a reality, the illegitimacy rate among teens jumped by more than 200 percent. In 1985 almost 60 percent of the 478,000 teenagers who gave birth were unmarried, a sharp increase from 1970, when the proportion was less than a third. We are now faced with the reality of declining fertility rates among teenagers but increasing rates of unwed motherhood, which is to say that although teenage girls are bearing fewer children, the proportion of fatherless children is rising.

By the mid-1980s, childbearing by all unmarried mothers accounted for more than one in every five babies born, reaching the highest level since the federal government started collecting data on the subject in 1940. In New York City alone, more than one in three babies born is now born out of wedlock, a ratio that is triple what it was twenty years ago. Among blacks, nationwide, the figures are worse still: three in every five black babies born is illegitimate, which is more than four times the white ratio. And 90 percent of black teenage mothers give birth out of wedlock.

Interest in teenage pregnancy became a matter of national debate with the 1976 publication of a Planned Parenthood report on the subject. The report, done by Planned Parenthood's research arm, the Alan Guttmacher Institute, declared that nothing less than a "teenage pregnancy epidemic" was facing the United States. It called for an immense increase in public financing to combat the problem. Its plea did not go unanswered; a record amount of public funds, as well as new family planning legislation, was quickly made available.

Planned Parenthood got what it wanted: in 1978 federal legislation mandated that contraceptive services be made available to adolescents, without parental notification. But the problem only got worse. In 1981 the Guttmacher Institute was back pleading for more money, this time in response to its latest findings. The most widely touted figure was the projection that four in every ten girls aged fourteen would become pregnant at least once during their teenage years. It also said that the average age of first sexual experience was sixteen. As important as any finding, it was revealed that previous differences of the level of sexual activity on the basis of race, class, and religion were disappearing.

Planned Parenthood got what it wanted: in 1982 it was reported that more than three-quarters of sexually active teenage girls had received counseling services about contraception during the previous three years. But the problem only got worse. In 1985 the Guttmacher Institute was back pleading for more money, this time in response to its latest findings. It now appeared that the United States had the highest teenage pregnancy rate in the industrialized world, as data from several countries were collected and analyzed. Not unexpectedly, the report concluded with a plea for yet more of the very same programs that had proven to be ineffective all along. Planned Parenthood, of course, is one of the major beneficiaries of such programs.

The 1985 report proved to be the most influential of all the studies, including the two that were released in 1988 (they added little to the 1985 report). There were two parts to the study: one part compared teen birthrates in thirty-seven developed countries; the other was a case study of six countries, including the United States. Birthrates were chosen for comparison in the first part of the study because data on abortion were generally not available, and thus estimates of pregnancy rates could not be made. The case study analysis looked at teen pregnancy rates, defined as births plus abortions. The purpose of the research, as the report made clear, was to gain information about reproductive behavior that might be used to affect public policy.

As is often the case in social science research, there is more than one interpretation of the data that can be made. Predictably, the Planned Parenthood researchers found that the data supported the mission of the organization: the best way to proceed in curbing teen pregnancies is through the distribution of contraceptives and the expansion of family planning clinics in the schools and communities. "In sum," the study concluded, "increasing the legitimacy and availability of contraception and sex education (in its broadest sense) is likely to result in declining teenage pregnancy rates."[2] But as we shall see, this conclusion is not as obvious as the study asserts. Furthermore, as Fordham sociologist James R. Kelly has observed, there are so many gaps in the data as to preclude the existence of any confident conclusions.[3]

In the thirty-seven-country study, it was found that there was a positive relationship between levels of maternity leaves and benefits and the teenage birthrate. The experience of the United States, in this regard, was anomalous: although there is no national policy in this area, the maternity policies that are generally available to working women are far less generous than exist in most other developed countries, yet the fertility rate is higher in the United States than in most other developed nations. What the data seem to be saying is that, on the whole, the more liberal the maternity policy, the higher the birthrate, suggesting that if the United States were to follow the lead of the other developed nations, as is often recommended, we would in all likelihood increase the gap in fertility rates beyond the present level.

The study found that where the minimum age for marriage was high, the birthrate for older teenagers was low. Again, the U.S. experience was atypical, suggesting that what is true for others is not necessarily true for us. Although there is no national minimum age for marriage in the United States, the age set by most states is higher than what is generally found elsewhere, yet the teenage birthrate is considerably higher here. There is no reason to believe that raising or lowering the minimum age for marriage is likely to have much effect on birthrates in this country.

One finding that the researchers found convincing was the relationship between distribution of income and birthrates: the more equitable the distribution, the lower the birthrate. The United States was judged to be a country that has greater inequalities of income than most other developed countries, thus explaining, to some degree anyway, why we have such a higher birthrate. But there are some problems with this line of thinking that the study failed to address.

First, the correlation between the proportion of total household income distributed to the top 10 percent of the population and the birthrate for women under the age of eighteen was .06, which is to say that it is practically nonexistent. The correlation for women aged eighteen and nineteen was .00, which is to say there is no association whatsoever. There is a stronger but not very convincing correlation when the proportion of total household income distributed to the bottom 20 percent is considered: it's − .41 for women under eighteen and − .14 for women aged eighteen and nineteen.[4] These four correlations are not on the order that most social scientists get excited about.

According to the study, the United States and Canada both were scored as being among those countries that have the least equitable distribution of income. But if this is true, then it needs to be explained why the Americans have a teenage birthrate almost double the Canadian. Once again, generalizations from the data prove to be difficult. A third criticism that can be made is the lack of uniformity in the way income distribution statistics are collected. For example, there are other studies that show that the United States has a relatively equal distribution of income, much more equal in fact than most other countries.[5]

Finally, there is the matter of not counting noncash transfer benefits when tallying income distribution figures, and leaving out of all consideration the proportion of taxes paid by the top 10 percent and the lowest 10 percent of income earners. Not to count such items as food stamps, Medicaid, day care provisions, housing subsidies, free lunch programs, and so on is to offer a skewed interpretation of the way income is actually distributed. And not to count the fact that the richest segment of U.S. society pays a highly disproportionate share of total taxes further distorts reality.

One of the most contentious findings was the apparent link between openness about sex and fertility. It was maintained that the countries that are the most liberal in sexual matters generally have the lowest birthrates. The United States was scored as being sexually restrictive and could therefore benefit by becoming more liberal. Openness about sex was defined on the basis of four characteristics: media presentation of female nudity, the extent of nudity on public beaches, sales of sexually explicit literature, and media advertising of condoms.

As to the first item, female nudity in the media, it is difficult to see how the American media could be considered as anything but "open." There is more nudity, including frontal nudity, of women, and for that matter of men, on television and in the movies than ever before. Cable television and home videos have made it possible to watch as much nudity as anyone would want. Moreover, the movies produced by Hollywood have become so explicit that what previously merited an R or X rating, now receives a PG-13. And interestingly, all the European countries have some kind of government censorship system that screens for excessively obscene movies.[6] We have none.

It is true that nude beaches are more common in Europe than in the United States, but they are not more common in Canada than in the United States, yet Canada doesn't have the problem that we have with regard to teenage births. And besides, there is no doubt more nudity on the beaches of sunny California than anyplace else in the country, yet it is well known that California has a bigger problem with teenage pregnancy than all but one of the fifty states.[7]

The sale of sexually explicit literature is more common in big cities than in the countryside, yet teen pregnancy is more an urban problem than a rural one. In fact, it is in places like New York's Times Square, where sexually explicit literature thrives, that all sorts of antisocial problems abound. If anything, there seems to be a link between the extent to which sexually explicit literature has become a commonplace throughout the United States and an increase in teenage pregnancy rates. And as for the advertisement of condoms on television, it has since become network policy to offer such ads.

It should be noted as well, that at the time of the Guttmacher report, problem-free Canada had the same policy of not showing such advertisements.

In part two of the report, the United States was contrasted with the following countries in a case study analysis: Canada, England and Wales, France, the Netherlands, and Sweden. These countries were chosen partially because data were available on abortion rates, which when added to birthrates yields an approximation of pregnancy rates, and because all five countries have lower estimated pregnancy rates than the United States. It needs to be mentioned that even when the substantially higher pregnancy rates among blacks are controlled for, the rate among white teenagers is still higher than the other five countries in the study.

One problem that the researchers immediately ran into was the lack of data on pregnancy intentions: the United States was the only country to keep such data. It was known, however, that the proportion of American teenagers who get married is at least twice as high as in the other countries. And of all those who do get married, American teenagers are much more likely to bear children. So right away we would expect pregnancy rates to be higher in this country than the other ones, having nothing to do with the kinds of problems that most Americans spend time worrying about. It should be remembered, however, that Planned Parenthood is dedicated to population control, so whether teenagers, or for that matter nonteenagers, are having more children, it is an organizational imperative to try to reduce pregnancy and fertility rates.

Even given some reservations about the meaning of the data, it is still the case that the teenage abortion rate is higher in the United States than in the other countries, making it likely that the rate of unintended pregnancies is greater. After comparing and contrasting the United States with the other countries on a number of issues, the Guttmacher study came to the conclusion that the relatively high American teenage pregnancy rates were primarily due to the existence of conservative attitudes on the subject of sexuality. If Americans would only adopt a more sophisticated attitude toward sex, the report suggested, their teenage pregnancy problem would soon abate.

In looking at some of the differences between the United States and the other five countries, it was noted that attitudes toward the pill varied greatly. In the other countries, the pill was widely regarded by the medical profession to be a safe and reliable form of birth control. Not so in the United States. For years the medical community has made its reservations known about the possible long-term negative consequences of the pill, and there is reason to believe that this reservation has been readily translated into a greater reluctance on the part of American women to use it. In addition, the requirement of a pelvic examination before the pill can be prescribed, an uncommon practice elsewhere, is believed to act as a further deterrent to its use.

The Guttmacher study makes plain its adamant support for making contraceptives easily available to teenagers. Yet on this score, there is little that the United States can do that it is not already doing. In comparison to the thirty-seven countries that made up the first part of the study, the report noted that "the United States does not appear to be more restrictive than low-fertility countries in the provision of contraceptive services to teenagers."[8] Similarly, the report calls for the free distribution of contraceptives, yet admits that "indigent teenagers from eligible families are able to get free care [contraceptive services] through Medicaid, and others do not have to pay anything because of individual clinic policy; otherwise, clinic fees are likely to be modest."[9] In essence, pleas for making contraceptives more easily available are without much significance: they are already available without cost or hassle, and this is especially true for the teenagers who have the highest pregnancy rates.

The report recommends that "postcoital methods," such as abortion, be granted greater approval. The researchers looked favorably on the experience of Sweden, which has for some time provided abortions free of charge. Yet the researchers' own data belie such confidence. The evidence collected on many countries indicates that publicly funded abortions are associated with high teenage birthrates,[10] thus confounding the suggestion that one way to get a grip on the problem is to provide for free abortions. Nowhere in the report is there an attempt to reconcile this finding with the tacit approval that is given to government-paid abortions.

As in the first part of the study, the case-study section of the report stresses the need to be more open about sex. The researchers found it significant that Europeans generally had a more relaxed attitude toward sex than Americans. The more energetic role that religion plays in the United States was seen as having a negative effect in developing a more tolerant attitude toward premarital sex. Though the connection wasn't stated with any degree of precision, the researchers apparently thought that a more casual attitude toward teenage sex resulted in lower rates of pregnancies. It is not clear why this should be so. Indeed, it is not clear why the opposite isn't true.

Two ways of demonstrating a more tolerant attitude toward sex, and two principal ways that the report endorses as having a desirable impact on teenage pregnancies, are extensive use of sex education and the establishment of school-based family-planning clinics. These recommendations form the core of the study's conclusions. More information and accessibility, the Guttmacher Institute believes, will do more to curb teenage pregnancies than any other initiative.

It is striking to note the correlation between the expansion of sex education and unwanted teenage pregnancies: the more we have of the former, the more we have of the latter. No one doubts that the correlation is true, the only question being whether there is a cause-and-effect relationship. It is impossible to know for sure, but what is not uncertain is the fallaciousness of the proposition that more sex education yields fewer unwanted teenage pregnancies. Yet this is precisely what Planned Parenthood recommends, despite the data uncovered by its own researchers.

In 1985 fully seven in ten of all high school seniors had taken sex education courses, the highest level ever recorded. The year 1985 was also the year when the Guttmacher Institute was calling attention to the record level of teenage pregnancies in the United States, urging more sex education as a remedy. It is safe to say that merely providing more information about sex is not having the expected result. Not only is it true that more high school students are enrolled in sex education courses than ever before, but they are receiving their first lessons in the subject at an earlier age than at any time in the past. Still, the evidence is clear that sex education does not alter the sexual activity of adolescents.[11]

All this has forced even some Planned Parenthood researchers to question the efficacy of sex education. For instance, Asta M. Kenney, an associate for policy development with the Guttmacher Institute, has written that "the evidence that sex education leads to a reduction in teen pregnancies is not compelling. . . ."[12] What is compelling is that this should be admitted by a Planned Parenthood staffer. But the fact remains that the organization has yet to abandon sex education as its chosen strategy for combating teenage pregnancies. In fact, its support for the educative approach, as shown in its endorsement of school-based clinics, is stronger now than ever.

The use of school-based health clinics to combat teenage pregnancy has proven to be the most divisive idea to surface in some time. The central purpose behind this initiative is to make available to adolescents the entire range of pregnancy-related services, housed in or near middle schools and junior and senior high schools. Most clinics prescribe contraceptives; others distribute them; some actually perform abortions.[13] Proponents say that progress can be made against teenage pregnancies only by inducing adolescents to learn more about the proficient use of contraceptives. There is no better way to do this, they argue, than by bringing the services directly to them in the schools.

Advocates of school-based clinics have run into a number of problems, not the least of which has been the charge of racism. Because the teenage pregnancy problem is much worse in the black than in the white community, most proposals have initially targeted schools that are mostly black. In New York City black leaders and parents maintained that the selection of schools indicated racist motivations on the part of public officials. In Chicago parents of students at the all-black DuSable High School filed a lawsuit against the Board of Education and others, arguing that the clinic was designed to reduce the black population. Other charges that have been levied in these instances include violation of students' rights to privacy, religion, and parental and pastoral guidance.

Much of the enthusiasm for school-based clinics stems from the purported success of two such operations, one in St. Paul and one in Baltimore. In the early 1970s St. Paul was one of the first cities to establish school-based clinics in some of its high schools. By the late 1970s the statistics collected by the clinics reported that a drop in the number of teen births had coincided with an increase in female participation in the clinic program. It was instantly branded a success and held up as a model for the rest of the country. But serious questions were quickly raised, casting doubt on the alleged success.

To begin with, there was no control group, that is, no attempt was made to evaluate whether schools that were similar in demographic portrait but didn't have clinics had seen a similar drop in fertility. Second, there was a substantial drop in the population of the high schools over the period when the alleged decline in the number of births took place, making it possible that the overall decline in births was attributable to the decline in the female population. Third, the data indicate a decline in the number of births but provide no insight into the pregnancy and abortion rates, thereby allowing for the possibility that the decline in births was a function of increased abortions. These and other criticisms of the methodology have been made by Michael Schwartz and Barrett Mosbacker.[14]

The Baltimore study, although better in some respects, was also plagued with difficulties. A team of researchers from Johns Hopkins University presented data that indicated that school-based clinics reduced both the pregnancy and birth rates of the students. The decision to provide data on pregnancies, and not just births, was an improvement over the St. Paul study. The methodology also included a control group, and thereby mitigated even more problems. But as Stan E. Weed pointed out in the pages of the *Wall Street Journal*, the study left many questions unanswered.

Over 30 percent of the female sample dropped out between the beginning and conclusion of the measurement period. The size of the sample was small (ninety-six girls) and the data combined clinic with nonclinic students, making it hard to judge the program's effects. Documentation of pregnancy, abortion, and sexual activity was sparse, not lending itself to the kind of careful analysis that is required for tests of reliability.[15] Still other questions have been raised by Tobin Demsko in his analysis of the Baltimore study.[16] It also needs to be mentioned that this study had as a component the placement of counselors in the schools, whose job it was to teach the virtue of abstinence and the merits of responsible sex. How much effect this had in reducing pregnancy rates is not known.

Far and away the most comprehensive studies on the effect that family planning programs have had on teenage pregnancies and births have been conducted by Stan E. Weed and Joseph A. Olsen for the Institute for Research and Education. Weed and Olsen used data from every major demographic source, including the Guttmacher Institute, the U.S. Census Bureau, the National Center for Health Statistics, and the U.S. Centers for Disease Control. They also availed themselves of data collected by all fifty states, and the District of Columbia. Unlike many other researchers, Weed and Olsen focused on teenage pregnancy rates, not just birthrates.

Through the use of regression analysis, Weed and Olsen confirmed the assertions of population control groups like Planned Parenthood that increased accessibility to family planning programs is related to a decrease in teenage birthrates. "However," they noted, "instead of the expected reduction in overall teenage pregnancy rates, greater teenage involvement in family-planning programs appears to be associated with higher, rather than lower, teenage pregnancy rates."[17] What they found, then, was quite different from what the family planning community had expected: clinics are associated with decreased childbirths but increased pregnancies and abortions.

The report was immediately greeted with a storm of protest, suggesting the politically volatile nature of the study. Special interest groups have never taken well to criticism, and this is especially true of organizations, like Planned Parenthood, that are wedded to government expenditures for sustenance. Reporters made inquiries into the motives, ideology, and religion of Weed and Olsen, hoping to smear the report through the use of *ad hominem* attacks. Nonetheless, because some of the questions raised were legitimate, the two researchers sought to incorporate the constructive criticisms into their research design and launch a second study.

The second study was even more refined than the first, using different types of research data and analytical strategies. The four major conclusions confirmed the findings of the first study: "First, family-planning program involvement is associated with lower teenage birthrates. Second, family-planning program involvement is associated with higher, not lower abortion rates. Third, greater family-planning program involvement does not result in a reduction in teenage pregnancy rates. Fourth, the reduction in teenage fertility that has been attributed to family-planning program involvement is in turn due to its impact on the continuation, and not on the occurrence of pregnancy among teenagers."[18]

The work done by Jacqueline Kasun makes the position of Planned Parenthood even more tenuous. Her analysis of the data, collected in part from the Guttmacher Institute, indicates that the logic of Planned Parenthood has backfired: "States that provide easy access to publicly funded birth control tend to have higher rates [of teenage pregnancies, out-of-wedlock births and abortions]." She also points out that California, which allows free access to contraceptives and abortions without parental consent, and spends more money than any other state on birth control, has the highest rate of white teenage abortion and the second highest pregnancy rate.[19] So much for the accessibility argument.

Though some of the most critical data on school-based clinics did not appear until after the 1985 Guttmacher report, there is no reason to believe it would have stemmed the enthusiasm of the Planned Parenthood researchers had it been made available earlier; the organization has since stood fast in its convictions. And that is because Planned Parenthood is not particularly concerned with how the teenage birthrate is cut: if the price we pay is an increase in pregnancies and abortions, so be it. Moral considerations are of secondary significance to organizations that are exclusively results-oriented.

Planned Parenthood's unwillingness to weigh the moral issues involved in its crusade against teenage births accounts for its glowing references to Sweden as a model for U.S. programs. Over and over again the point is made that Sweden is more advanced, progressive, tolerant, enlightened—whatever—than parochial, religiously infused America. There is no doubt about the low rate of teenage pregnancies in Sweden, but there is considerable debate about whether the price the Swedes (especially the children) pay for such "progress" is worth it. Yet those who cling tightly to notions of distributive justice have little to say about the inequitable way in which the burden of progress is distributed; the most defenseless segment of the population carries the brunt of the burden.

The Guttmacher report on the six countries that make up the case-analysis section of the study shows Sweden to be the only country where a majority of teenage pregnancies end in abortion. It is also by far the lowest in percentage of pregnancies that result in marital births.[20] To get a sense of what has been going on in Sweden, consider this: in the period following World War II, there were, on the average, 125,000 live births a year; in 1985 there were 98,480. The liberalized abortion laws of the 1970s allowed for 31,000 abortions in 1985. As for out-of-wedlock births, Sweden leads the world with a staggering 50 percent illegitimacy rate. Things are so bad that the Swedish Institute has openly admitted that "cohabitation outside marriage is common and more unstable than marriage."[21] Hence, the growing number of bastards.

It should be clear by now that the prescription advocated by Planned Parenthood, and organizations like the National Research Council, does not work. More sex education and more readily available contraceptives are not the answer to unwanted teenage pregnancies. Indeed, there is good reason to believe that by fostering these ideas we have unwittingly created a climate of acceptability, a milieu in which adolescents come to the conclusion that it's okay to engage in sex, just as long as there are no long-term negative consequences. Hence the increase in promiscuity and abortion, two problems that Planned Parenthood chooses not to address. And by holding up Sweden as a model, despite the fact that it has the highest illegitimacy rate in the world, Planned Parenthood makes plain that its *only* interest is that of population control.

The psychological and social cost that is incurred by high rates of promiscuity, abortion, and illegitimacy is incalculable. Together, these three problems make hollow any alleged victory there might be in declining birthrates among teenagers. There is nothing to celebrate when more and more young people are stimulated to become sexually active at an increasingly earlier age, unprepared as they are for the consequences of their behavior. Yet this is precisely what has happened.

In a report on teenage pregnancy issued by the House Select Committee on Children, Youth and Families, it was noted that despite the expansion of sex education programs and accessibility of contraceptives, "there has been no change in the percentage of sexually active teens who become pregnant, but there has been a huge increase in the percentage of teens who are sexually active. And this increase in sexual activity has led to a proportionate increase in pregnancies to unmarried teens."[22] Another way of putting it is this: the more the new freedom succeeds in lifting the social lid on the libido, the more sexual experimentation there is among those with the strongest natural sex drive—youth —and the more they experiment, the greater the increase there is in human suffering for themselves, the children they conceive, and the society they live in.

There is a direct correlation between increasing tolerance for promiscuity and the consequences of sexual experimentation. There is more promiscuity, teenage pregnancy, abortion, and illegitimacy than ever before because there is more tolerance for immorality than ever before. The very fact that the word *immorality* has itself become practically obsolete, especially among the cultural elite, is testimony to the collapse of standards. When it is used, it is typically surrounded by quotation marks so as not to imply any personal disapproval. And when scholars set out to measure increases or decreases in the public's level of tolerance toward such things as extramarital sex, they invariably score as intolerant those who regard the practice as "morally wrong."[23]

Approximately four in ten Americans regard premarital sex as morally wrong, a figure that is subliminally understood by adolescent boys and girls. Illegitimacy has similarly been legitimatized, even to the point of having been lost to the lexicon of human sexuality. (The Swedish government offically stopped usage of the word decades ago.) The declining stigma attached to illegitimacy has fallen so far that less than 5 percent of today's unwed mothers give their babies up for adoption; the figure in the early 1960s, just before the new freedom began to flourish, was 35 percent.

Perhaps the most unfortunate aspect of all this is the fact that today, more than ever before, there are millions of young couples who (a) can't have children, (b) are in every way adequately prepared to adopt children but (c) can't do so because a record number of unwed mothers are keeping their children, even though most are unable to provide for them adequately. Again, this is a no-win proposition all the way around. The biggest price, of course, is exacted from those least able to bear it: the children.

And what does Planned Parenthood have to say about the increasing tolerance and decreasing stigma attached to sexual adventurism? Evidently we haven't gone far enough to suit Faye Wattleton, president of the New York-based organization: "We are still very much governed by our puritanical heritage."[24] Ms. Wattleton is apparently oblivious to the fact that when we were most puritan, we had the fewest problems. Of all the ideas presented by Planned Parenthood, none is more lacking in foundation than the notion that openness about sex is tied to fewer teenage problems.

Alfred Moran, speaking as an official of the organization, seems to understand this but, like Wattleton, still recoils at the suggestion that we ought to move in the other direction. He admits that television shows, movies, magazines, and rock lyrics are laced with sexual innuendo, and even goes so far as to say that the problem of teenage pregnancy is "an inevitable byproduct when our sexuality is exploited by the sales pitch."[25] And what does he recommend we do about it? Advertise condoms on television.

Moran knows what the problem is—a culture rife with sexual provocation—yet adamantly refuses to hold the custodians of culture responsible for their irresponsibility. He will not seek to resolve the problem of teenage pregnancy by attacking the problem at its source because, in his words, "No one wants to return to the hypocritical pseudo-morality of the Victorian age. . . ."[26] The only other choice, according to Moran, is to stick with what we have and advertise condoms on television. To get a sense of what Moran is saying, consider this: If the same logic were applied to crime control, we would abandon all efforts at addressing the causes of crime and concentrate exclusively on such prophylactic measures as advertising bulletproof vests on television.

Moran is unwilling to point a finger at the media because he himself is hostage to new-freedom thinking. Being open-minded is interpreted as being morally neutral, especially in matters of sexuality; therefore, the best that new-freedom devotees can do is recommend control measures when things get out of hand. They would prefer to see pornography on Saturday morning television before ever bringing pressure to bear on the producers. They believe that nothing is worse than being tagged "Victorian," even if those who do the tagging are child pornographers. They think that all calls for moderation and constraint are nothing more than appeals to censorship. In short, their ability to make critical distinctions has been impaired.

The media are not alone in working against a semblance of constraint in our culture. Civil libertarians are responsible as well. If someone introduces a bill requiring parental consent before teenagers can avail themselves of contraceptives at a federally funded clinic, the "reproductive-freedom" people at the local ACLU immediately try to stigmatize such efforts by labeling them "squeal rules." The ACLU sees all such attempts at constraint as violative of the "constitutional rights" of adolescents, though no such rights are found anywhere in the Constitution. For the ACLU, those who want to restore a measure of accountablility are promoting "chastity acts," legislation that enfeebles the liberty of youngsters to make up their own rules of sexual behavior.

If progress is going to be made against the problem of teenage pregnancy, more time will need to be spent listening to what teenagers have to say about the problem. All the graphs, correlations, and equations in the world can never be an adequate substitute for listening, an art unfortunately not cultivated in graduate programs. Do teenagers choose to get pregnant? Is ignorance the problem? The best answers to these questions come from the responses culled by journalists.

At age thirteen, New Yorker Roseann Collado became pregnant and, one year later, did so again. That is not an uncommon experience: in two years, most teen mothers become pregnant again, making incoherent arguments about ignorance. Roseann lives in a neighborhood where teens who don't have kids are the outcasts: "Basically the whole block is all young girls with kids," said the north Bronx native. "They're all young, 14 or 15. The oldest one is my best friend, she's 17 with an 1-year-old. She did it to get out of the house. The youngest girls sleep with anybody they can get. To me, they want to be like everybody else."[27]

Most scholars have a hard time understanding commentary such as this. Given their tendency to view the world through the lens of rationalism, they find it implausible that any unwed teenage girl would choose to get pregnant so as to achieve independence and status. But many do. Listen to what *New York Times* reporter Esther B. Fein concluded in her study of life in the projects, low-income apartment complexes where teenage pregnancy is commonplace: "Sex, many young people said, is one area in their lives where they can take control, and it does not cost them anything. Despite the threat of pregnancy and the prospect of child rearing at so young an age, teen-agers in the project said they usually did not practice birth control. They are not ignorant of birth control methods, they said, they just do not want to use them."[28]

Three in four unmarried teen mothers say their mothers were unmarried teenagers. Eighty-two percent of girls who give birth at age fifteen or younger were themselves born to teenage mothers. These statistics indicate that no amount of sex education is going to do the job. The problem is cultural. Our culture induces the very kind of present-orientation that disables teenagers from thinking about the consequences of their behavior. The problem is especially acute among those in the lower class. A socially destructive "get-it-while-you-can" attitude is pervasive, the roots of which are found in a concept of liberty that defines freedom as the abandonment of constraint.

Another popularly cited reason for getting pregnant is love. Many teenage girls sincerely believe that by giving themselves to a young man (the term *boy* would be more accurate), they will secure his love. This is what one girl told Sharon Thompson, author of an insightful study of teenage pregnancy, reported in the pages of the *Village Voice*: "*Come to think of it, I got pregnant as an escape from my family, and plus I wanted somebody, you know, to love and somebody to love me back, and I thought this guy was the right man for me, so I wanted his child, and— mainly those reasons. Those three reasons. So I got pregnant on purpose.*"[29]

When Thompson asked the girls in her survey why they didn't use contraceptives, most simply said, "It never crossed my mind." How can this be? They know about contraceptives, can get them for free, are not ashamed to use them, are in no danger of being stigmatized, yet choose not to use them. "Girls frequently explain they didn't use birth control," reports Thompson, "because intercourse took place 'spontaneously.' "[30] Exactly. Most teenage girls become pregnant not so much on purpose (though some do), but because they (and the boys as well) lack the discipline to say no. It's not as though these girls consciously set out to get pregnant, they simply go about life on an ad hoc basis, rarely planning ahead for anything, including the prospects of pregnancy. If it happens, it happens.

Unwed fathers are, of course, just as delinquent as unwed mothers. In almost every case, they accept little or no responsibility for their behavior. They know about condoms, but seldom use them. There are four principal reasons that teenage boys don't use condoms. First, the use of a condom is predicated on the idea that one has enough foresight to possess the device before a sexual encounter occurs. Right away that excludes most adolescent boys, and nearly all of those in the lower class. Second, being in possession of a condom isn't good enough: one has to have the discipline to interrupt the sex act to put the condom in place. Since it is lack of self-discipline that has led these boys to engage in irresponsible sex in the first place, it is unrealistic to expect that at this juncture they will turn over a new leaf.

Third, wearing a condom is deliberately rejected by many boys. Why? It isn't macho. Unwed father George Rivera spoke for many when he told a *New*

York Times reporter, "God didn't put rubber things on me. Why should I?" To Rivera, a condom "Looks like a balloon. To this day, I would feel uncomfortable putting one of those on."[31] Rivera's sentiments are not unusual. Hard as it might be to accept, in some neighborhoods there is a cultural prohibition against the use of condoms that no amount of sex education can affect. In short, the Planned Parenthood approach is of limited utility.

A fourth reason that boys don't wear condoms is that few see any reason for doing so: our society places virtually no penalty, socially or legally, on young boys for being promiscuous with their sex life. Think of it. If his girlfriend gets pregnant, it's her problem. If she wants the kid, she can have it. Who will support the baby? Her family. If that doesn't work out, there's always welfare, with the prospect of a new apartment to boot. His paycheck (assuming he collects one) won't be trimmed for child support, and in any case the law will allow him to go scot-free. She can finish high school in many parts of the country without paying for day care, and may even be allowed to drop the kid off at a school-based facility. Failing all that, there's abortion; for about the price of a black-and-white television set, most girls can purchase the services of an abortionist. On their lunch hour. Is there any socially imposed reason for the young man to act responsibly?

It would be a mistake to think that middle-class kids are immune to the effects of the new freedom. They are not. Here's what one sexually active teenager told her English teacher at a middle-class high school in Alexandria, Virginia: "There's a feeling that it's okay for us to have sex because we're educated and know what's going on. We're not going to get pregnant and burden society with unwanted children. We're going to college and have a future. If we do slip up, we'll get an abortion."[32] Notice the attitude. It's okay to fool around because chances are no one (save the unborn child) will have to pay a price for the irresponsible action. Exercising rights without incurring responsibilities is, of course, one of two major components of the new freedom.

The other major component of the new freedom is moral neutrality. It, too, finds expression in accounting for teenage pregnancy, as another girl from the same school told her former teacher: "In eighth grade, if a couple was sleeping together, it was big news. But it's no big deal in high school. If a couple is dating for a few months, everyone just assumes they're having sex. *There's no stigma at all to it. Girls no longer try to hide it.*" (Emphasis added.)

This next comment should jolt parents who accept the new freedom: "It's hilarious to watch my mother try to find out about my sex life. I've grown up with all these messages about being open—the 'You can tell me anything, dear—I'm from the '60s' kind of stuff. She's had the 'Joy of Sex' on the living-room bookshelf since I've been in sixth grade. But now that I'm 17 and have a boyfriend she's getting desperate to know what's going on.'' As for divorced parents who are having affairs, the role model that is being presented is even more perverse: ''When your mother has a Friday night date and he's in the kitchen eating breakfast Saturday morning, how can she preach about premarital sex.''[33] Answer: she can't.

So what works? Clinics? No, and for some of the reasons already stated. Clinics treat the symptom and not the cause. It is ironic that some of the same people who have for years told us that we need to get to the root cause of the problem (of discrimination, crime, and so on) now abandon all such efforts when faced with the problem of teenage pregnancy. There is a reason for this exceptionalism: to treat the cause, namely, promiscuity, would require a more censorial approach, and the problem with that is it violates the ethos of the new freedom.

Putting a clinic in the basement of a high school is worse than a Band-Aid tactic: Band-Aids help a little; school-based clinics make the problem worse. It is no surprise that teenage pregnancies, and abortions, increase as clinics are set up in local schools. It is a mistake to expect a student to learn about the desirability of abstinence in a sex education class (assuming that is what he's taught), and then follow through on that advice when the school clinic is giving advice on what to do when abstinence fails. Putting a clinic in a school basement is on the order of putting a bakery in the lounge of a diet clinic: mixed messages are sent, and everyone knows which one will be controlling.

Those who promote school-based clinics usually entertain a morally neutral stance on matters of sexuality. It's up to the individual, they contend, to make up his own standards. Or lack thereof. It is this attitude that contributes to the problem and stands in the way of progress: we can't get to the cure (imposition of constraints) because we won't address the cause (the new freedom's abandonment of constraints).

Another way to conceptualize the issue is this: Imagine that a pill has been developed that allows people to eat as much as they want without ever gaining weight. The consequences of overeating have now been solved. Is there cause for celebration? It depends. For those whose only concern is looking bad, much has been achieved. But that doesn't exhaust the concerns. Doesn't gluttony count for something? Taking it a step further, isn't there every reason to believe that such a pill would actually induce more people to become gluttonous? Isn't this exactly what is at stake when condoms are distributed to students, that is, we stimulate promiscuity by removing its consequences, thereby solving the effects of immorality while simultaneously fostering immoral values?

People who are promiscuous with their eating habits, or with their sex life, are exhibiting values that have long-term effects. Those who are not accustomed to practicing self-discipline in their sex life, for example, are not likely to be successful in invoking self-restraint in other instances. Those who have been neglectful of developing virtue cannot simply decide to become virtuous when it suits them: virtue is a continuous property, one that cannot be turned on and off like a spigot. It's like anything else: practice makes perfect or, conversely, the lack of practice yields imperfection. We are, to a large degree, what we nourish ourselves to be. And that is why programs that give tacit approval to promiscuity cannot help but feed a promiscuous life-style.

One way to get at the problem of teenage pregnancy would be to curtail the right of minors to get abortions and to hold the parents of minors financially responsible if their children have babies. Wisconsin is doing the latter, but not the former (in fact, it expressly allows for abortion without parental consent). In 1985 the state legislature of Wisconsin unanimously passed a law that provided abortions without the necessity of parental consent and the so-called grandparents liability law. By holding parents financially responsible for the behavior of their children, the law succeeds in imposing the kinds of constraints that help deter irresponsibility. Not surprisingly, Planned Parenthood objected to this approach but raised no objection to the idea of abortion without parental consent.

Perhaps the best effort at tackling the issue of teenage pregnancy has come from the Reagan administration. In 1981 Senator Jeremiah Denton introduced legislation to provide an alternative to the condom-distribution, school-clinic, abortion approach of Planned Parenthood. The legislation made federal monies available to local organizations, including religious organizations, that sought to promote abstinence (an ACLU attempt to strike down the law lost in the Supreme Court). Funds were not to be dispensed to organizations that promoted abortion.

Unlike other legislation in this area, Denton's bill was based on the belief that prevention of adolescent pregnancy depends on strong family values. That is why the legislation, known as the Adolescent Family Life Act (AFLA), sought to promote self-discipline and other prudent approaches to the problem: these measures give due recognition to the primacy of the family in value formation. Other aspects of the AFLA include pregnancy testing and maternity counseling, adoption counseling and referral services, prenatal and postnatal care, nutrition information, referral for screening and treatment of venereal disease, and referral to appropriate pediatric care and mental health services. The target population, as the act stipulates, is the poor.

If the campaign against teenage pregnancy is going to succeed, legislation modeled on the AFLA will have to become the rule, and not the exception to it. It cannot be stressed too much that it was the sexual revolution, with its new-freedom lack of values, that gave birth to the problem in the first place. Noted sociologist Kingsley Davis said it all when he summarized the failure of contraceptives to reduce teen pregnancy: *"The current belief that illegitimacy will be reduced if teenage girls are given an effective contraceptive is an extension of the same reasoning that created the problem in the first place. It reflects an unwillingness to face problems of social control and social discipline while trusting some technological device to extricate society from its difficulties. The irony is that the illegitimacy rise occurred precisely while contraceptive use was becoming more, rather than less, widespread and respectable.*[34]

As Davis says, the lack of adequate social control and discipline is at the heart of the problem. If we had set out to promote a more hospitable environment wherein adolescent recklessness would thrive, we couldn't have done any better than to follow the thinking of the new freedom. When society drops its guard, everyone takes note, and none more attentively than young people. Conversely, when society lifts its guard, none feels its sway more forcefully than youth. Unfortunately, that has yet to happen.

Notes

1. For an excellent discussion of this issue, see Irwin and Sara McLanahan, *Single Mothers and Their Children: A New American Dilemma* (Washington, D.C.: Urban Institute Press, 1986).
2. Elise Jones et al., "Teenage Pregnancy in Developed Countries," *Family Planning Perspectives* (March/April 1985): 61.
3. For a trenchant analysis of the Guttmacher study, see James R. Kelly, "Numbers versus Principles: Moral Realism and Teenage Pregnancies," *America*, February 14, 1987, pp. 130–36.
4. Jones et al., "Teenage Pregnancies in Developed Countries," p. 62.
5. See *The New Book of World Rankings* (New York: Facts on File 1984). Of sixty-nine countries surveyed on a scale of income distribution measuring the percentage of national income received by the richest 10 percent, only fourteen had a more equitable distribution than the United States, placing the United States in the lower middle range (see table 67, p. 101). There are other ways of measuring income distribution as well, such as the use of Gini Ratios, which show the United States to be among the most equitable countries in the world.
6. See the findings of the study submitted to the British Parliament, *Report on the Committee on Obscenity and Film Censorship* (London: Her Majesty's Stationery Office, 1979), p. 142.
7. See the extrapolations of the data, provided in part by the Guttmacher Institute, made by Jacqueline Kasun, "The State and Adolescent Behavior," in Joseph Peden and Fred Glahe, eds., *The American Family and the State* (San Francisco: Pacific Research Institute, 1986), pp. 338–39.
8. Jones et al., "Teenage Pregnancy in Developed Countries," p. 54.
9. Ibid., p. 58.
10. Ibid., p. 62.
11. See the review of the literature by James W. Stout and Frederick P. Rivara, "Schools and Sex Education: Does It Work?" *Journal of Pediatrics* (March 1989): 375–79.

12. Asta M. Kenney, "Teen Pregnancy: An Issue for Schools," *Phi Delta Kappan* (June 1987): 732.
13. Tobin W. Demsko, "School-Based Health Clinics: An Analysis of the Johns Hopkins Study," *Research Developments* (Washington, D.C.: Family Research Council, 1987).
14. Michael Schwartz, "Lies, Damned Lies, and Statistics," *American Education Report* (March 1986). See also Barrett Mosbacker, "Teen Pregnancy and School-Based Health Clinics" (Washington, D.C.: Family Research Council, 1987).
15. Stan E. Weed, "Curbing Births, Not Pregnancies," *Wall Street Journal*, October 14, 1986, p. 36.
16. Demsko, "School-Based Health Clinics."
17. Stan E. Weed and Joseph A. Olsen, "Effects of Family-Planning Programs for Teenagers on Adolescent Birth and Pregnancy Rates," *Family Perspective* (Fall 1986): 167.
18. Stan E. Weed and Joseph A. Olsen, "Effects of Family-Planning Programs on Teenage Pregnancy—Replication and Extension," *Family Perspectives Journal* (Fall 1986): 190. Copies of both studies by Weed and Olsen are available from the Family Research Council, Washington, D.C.
19. Kasun, "The State and Adolescent Sexual Behavior," pp. 338–39.
20. Jones et al., "Teenage Pregnancies in Developed Countries," figure 4, p. 56.
21. Paul Lindblom, "The Swedish Family: Problems, Programs and Prospects," *Current Sweden* (August 1986): 5.
22. The quotation is from the December 1985 report, cited by Mosbacker, "Teen Pregnancy and School-Based Health Clinics."
23. See especially the influential research by Herbert McClosky and Alida Brill, *Dimensions of Tolerance: What Americans Believe about Civil Liberties* (New York: Russell Sage, 1983); chapter 5 offers the best example of this attitude.
24. Quoted in "Children Having Children," *Time*, December 9, 1985, p. 82.
25. Alfred F. Moran, "Video Contraception," *New York Times*, September 8, 1982, p. 29.
26. Ibid.
27. Quoted by Jane Perlez, "Children with Children: Coping with a Crisis," *New York Times*, December 1, 1986, p. B6.
28. Esther B. Fein, "At a City Project, Price of Survival Is Vigilance," *New York Times*, July 10, 1986, p. B5.
29. Sharon Thompson, "Pregnant on Purpose: Choosing Teen Motherhood," *Village Voice*, December 23, 1986, p. 36.
30. Ibid., p. 32.
31. Quoted by Samuel G. Freedman, "Young and Unwed: New Focus on the Fathers," *New York Times*, December 2, 1986, p. B5.
32. Quoted by Patrick Welsh, "Sex and Today's Teen-Ager," *Washington Post*, November 29, 1987, p. L1.
33. Ibid., p. L2.
34. Quoted by Mosbacker, "Teen Pregnancy and School-Based Health Clinics," p. 2.

10

The Meaning of Gay Rights

When the 1970s began, the sexual revolution was already in high gear, demolishing traditional conceptions of morality at a record pace. Dennis Altman, a spokesman for the homosexual community, was declaring that "we need to move towards a full acceptance of the erotic qualities of humankind and of the many different kinds and levels of sexual encounters that are possible." Many did just that, following Altman's advice that "casual sex can be a good way of getting to know people."[1] Unexpectedly, by the end of the 1980s, many of those who practiced what Altman preached were dead.

The gay rights movement, which began in earnest in New York and California in 1969, has long championed the idea that homosexuals have much in common with blacks and women: they are a stigmatized minority seeking full incorporation into American society. But the comparison has always been flawed, principally because to be gay is to be part of a sexual life-style, an identity wholly different from race and gender.

There is no such thing as a black life-style, nor is there an identifiable life-style associated with women. As is true of white men, there are class differences (as well as religious cleavages) within the black and female population, but there is no such thing as a black or female style of life. Moreover, the full incorporation of blacks and women into society has never beeen predicated on a fundamental challenge to the sexual mores of the dominant culture. Whatever has been said of blacks and women, no one has ever seriously maintained that their very status was that of a social deviant; homosexuals can make no such claim.

The major difference is this: Homosexuals *must* challenge accepted standards of morality if they are to win. The same is not true of blacks and women. Whereas blacks and women have had but one goal—total inclusion— gays have had two: total sexual liberation and total inclusion in society. But the problem is that by pushing for the former, they cannot achieve the latter. There's the rub. It's a dilemma that no other minority has had to face.

The dilemma would be mitigated, if not resolved, if homosexuals simply settled on winning tolerance for their life-style. But that is not what the rights activists want: Nothing less than complete social acceptance and approval will do. Homosexual activists are on record as demanding full societal affirmation of their life-style, and to that end they are prepared to seek legislation that fundamentally overturns any law that is supportive of conventional mores. To be explicit, the leadership in the homosexual community wants the new-freedom definition of liberty to prevail. If it does, they win. If not, they lose.

The idea that everything that constrains the individual is the enemy of freedom is nowhere more apparent than in the gay liberation movement. It is what defines the movement. Absent the ideology of the new freedom, the gay rights movement is unintelligible. The idea of rights and more rights, of a totally neutral moral code, this is the what fires the movement and gives meaning to its agenda. But as many found out, a steady diet of the new freedom kills. It's called AIDS.

If following the logic of the new freedom leads to liberticide in society, its legacy for homosexuals is suicide. AIDS is one the most tragic diseases ever uncovered, and one of the most unnecessary to have arisen in the first place. It arose because the lure of the new freedom proved to be too difficult to resist and too implacable in its consequences. When an entire segment of the population defines its freedom as unlimited bodily expression, certain reactions quite naturally follow. Nature has a way of saying enough is enough, even if society is unprepared to do so.

Heterosexuals who have practiced new-freedom sex have succumbed to a similar fate. It is believed that fifty million Americans—one in four—is infected by the genital herpes virus, herpes simplex type 2, with as many as a half million new cases developing each year. As is so with AIDS, most of those who have acquired the disease have done so through self-infliction, that is, genital herpes is largely a behaviorally based disease, one that implants itself in those who are promiscuous. Tragically, there are exceptions. Innocent children often pay the price of their parents' promiscuity: as many as one thousand babies are afflicted with herpes each year; half of them die or suffer brain damage, with the rest suffering lesser disorders.

What makes AIDS so devastating, so much worse than herpes, is that it utterly disables the immune system, thus making the body vulnerable to all sorts of diseases. Because there is at least a five-year lag between infection with the virus and diagnosis, it is difficult to estimate the ultimate damage that will be done. Although most of those who are infected with the virus do not develop full-blown AIDS, many of those with the virus do not get off scot-free, suffering as they do from dementia and other disorders; some die as a result of exposure to other diseases. AIDS takes its toll in many ways, psychologically, physically, and socially.

It is mostly homosexuals and intravenous drug users who get AIDS, making up better than 90 percent of those afflicted with the deadly disease. In the mid-1980s, there were some who sounded the alarm that the disease was making its way into the heterosexual population with great speed, but these voices have been shown to be unreliable. No one more wildly exaggerated the spread of AIDS than Masters and Johnson, the famous sexologists.

In a methodologically flawed study, Masters and Johnson made the remarkable assertion that AIDS was running rampant in the heterosexual population,[2] an assessment totally at odds with respected opinion on the subject. Masters and Johnson ignored the conclusions of people like Harold Jaffe, chief AIDS epidemiologist at the federal Centers for Disease Control, who a year earlier had said: ''We really have not seen much evidence for the spread of the virus [outside] risk groups. For most people, the risk of AIDS is essentially zero. . . .''[3]

Journalist Michael Fumento, who did an in-depth study of how AIDS is transmitted, came to the same conclusion that Dr. Jaffe did: those in the nonrisk group have little to worry about. But why is this so? It is because AIDS is ''extraordinarily difficult to transmit or contract, even by the standards of other sexually transmitted diseases (STDs).'' The reason homosexuals suffer from AIDS is due to the type of sex they engage in, namely, anal sex. As Fumento instructs, the rectum was not designed for penetration, so that unlike the vagina, it is ill-prepared for the insertion of a penis. The vagina can withstand the volatility of intercourse and childbirth; the rectum tears easily when forcible entry is made. Thus semen finds its way into the blood vessels of the rectum, making the transmission of AIDS possible.[4]

The man who experts think was most reponsible for spreading AIDS, Gaetan Dugas, was a prototype of new-freedom excess in the homosexual community. It is safe to say that a more irresponsible person would be hard to find among any segment of the population. Dugas, a French-Canadian steward who died at age thirty-one of AIDS, regularly abused both himself and thousands of others, treating his body in a way that insured self-destruction. Had AIDS never existed, Dugas, and those like him, would have died prematurely anyway. In fact, AIDS is only one of many venereal diseases to have hit the homosexual population.

Randy Shilts, the San Francisco reporter who covered the AIDS story from the beginning, had this to say of Dugas, a.k.a. Patient Zero: ''Sex just wasn't sex to Gaetan; sex was who Gaetan was—it was the basis of his identity.'' Ditto for tens of thousands of others, and for the thousands of sex partners they've experienced. Dugas not only gave new meaning to the word *promiscuous* but deliberately inflicted his lethal sex practices on others. After engaging in sodomy with one of the bathhouse clientele, Dugas would proudly announce, ''I've got gay cancer. I'm going to die and so are you.''

When told by doctors he must cease and desist, Patient Zero replied in textbook new-freedom form: "It's none of your goddamn business. It's my right to do what I want to with my own body."[5]

Gaetan Dugas may be the single most important person responsible for the spread of AIDS (it is said that 40 of the first 248 men to contract AIDS either had sex with him or with men sexually linked to him), but it would be ridiculous to conclude that had Dugas never been born, neither would AIDS have been born. AIDS is the pathological product of the new freedom, and Dugas was only one of millions who spun out of control, unable to resist the promise of unbounded liberty. AIDS is a manifestation of a culture that endorses a no-holds-barred attitude toward life, including sexuality.

Dugas had plenty of company, men who conspired to assault their bodies with more punishment than most care to imagine. And it was not just sex that they frantically engaged in, it was drugs. For about twenty years, from the midsixties to the mideighties, Quaaludes and cocaine, as well as other more exotic narcotics, became a staple of the sexually active homosexual population. The appetite for sex and drugs was positively insatiable in some communities, turning whole neighborhoods into a subculture of reckless abandon, and bringing to the attention of the medical community diseases it never contemplated would occur in human beings.

Some homosexuals interpreted the new freedom not simply in terms of sexual freedom but in terms of wholesale bodily liberation from anything and everything imaginable. Hence the innovation of "water sports," a term used to describe the practice of urinating on one's lover. Another cited behavior is the habit of eating the feces of one's mate, a practice quite unknown to other minority groups. Reports of bestiality have also surfaced, calling into serious question the idea that what is being discussed here is nothing more than an "alternative life-style."[6]

"Fisting" is another popular indulgence in the homosexual community, an exercise whereby one man puts his hand, or his arm if he can squeeze it, into the rectum of his lover; Crisco is used as a lubricant. There are even "fisting" bars in New York City, places where Kaposi's sarcoma, a rare cancer, is transmitted. One of them, the Mine Shaft, was known for open displays of fellatio and anal intercourse, as well as such sadomachistic techniques as whippings and torture. The Mine Shaft was a tax-exempt institution, one that never had its status checked by New York State after it secured its status in 1976. The homosexual brothel not only did not pay any state or sales tax but it never had a liquor license, and was never closed down even for this violation, though it was raided half a dozen times. In November 1985 the Mine Shaft was finally closed down, over protests from the ACLU.

It is a tribute to the new freedom that the cities that are universally acknowledged to be the most tolerant of homosexuality are the ones most plagued by the AIDS epidemic. AIDS is not the concern of Peoria, but it is the bane of New York, San Francisco, Los Angeles, Washington, D.C., Houston, and Miami. It is in those cities where tolerance for homosexual liberation became tolerance for sodomy, as practiced in the numerous bathhouses, bars, peep shows, public restrooms, theaters, pornographic bookstores, sexual prisons, sadomasochistic clubs, and torture chambers. It is in those cities where Gay Liberation Weeks and Gay Parades were loudly proclaimed. And it is in those cities where AIDS was announced as the leading cause of death among young men.

The argument being made here—that AIDS is a direct result of the homosexual community's embrace of the new freedom, and not a function of homosexuality per se—is given credence by the fact that studies conducted of the homosexual population before the 1960s showed little in the way of promiscuity. For example, the famous Kinsey studies on human sexuality reported that homosexuals actually had fewer sexual contacts than heterosexuals. Even as late as 1960, researchers were finding that homosexuals were relatively sexually inactive. But once the new freedom took root in the culture at large, and with great intensity in the homosexual population in particular, the stereotype changed from one of asceticism to promiscuity.[7]

By the late 1970s, social scientists Alan P. Bell and Martin S. Weinberg were able to conclude that promiscuity was the norm for a sizable segment of the homosexual population. Their study showed that almost half the white homosexuals, and about one-third of the blacks, had had at least five hundred different sexual partners; almost three in ten white males had over a thousand partners, while the figure for blacks was two in ten.[8]

Sociologists Philip Blumstein and Pepper Schwartz have given us the most comprehensive examination of human sexuality to date. Leaving no idiosyncrasy uncovered, Blumstein and Schwartz exhaustively cataloged the sexual proclivities of male and female, heterosexual and homosexual. They make it crystal clear that homosexual men are far more promiscuous than heterosexual men or women, or lesbians. Fully 82 percent have cheated on their lovers, making monogamy "a rare phenomenon" of homosexual relationships. Moreover, whereas married couples who cheat on each other try to keep their infidelity a secret, there is no such prohibition among homosexual men, 88 percent of whom are aware of their lover's unfaithfulness.[9]

Gay men cheat on their partners with great regularity, and most waste no time doing so, waiting less than two years in a relationship before finding someone else. As the relationship continues, say Blumstein and Schwartz, "virtually all gay men have other sexual partners." The rapidity with which partners are exchanged is a function of the "trick mentality," that is, the impersonal nature of homosexual encounters. For example, an astonishing 90 percent of the homosexual men in the Blumstein and Schwartz study admitted to having sex on the same day that they met another homosexual. Such a phenomenon, as the sociologists point out, is uncommon among heterosexuals and lesbians.[10]

But promiscuity alone does not explain why homosexuals get AIDS. It is a particular kind of sex, namely, receptive anal intercourse, that is tied to AIDS. And it is a specific type of homosexual experience, something called "rimming," that accelerates the chances of winding up with AIDS. "Rimming" is the term used to describe oral-anal sex, that is, the practice whereby a man's mouth comes into contact with another man's anus. Randy Shilts comments on why this "down-and-dirty" custom (as he calls it), is unhealthy: "The problems grew with the new popularity of anal sex, in the late 1960s and early 1970s, because it was nearly impossible to avoid fecal matter during that act. As sexual tastes grew more exotic and rimming became fashionable, the problem exploded. There wasn't a much more efficient way to get a dose of parasite spoor than by such direct ingestion."[11]

"Rimming" was not simply a fun thing to do, it was promoted by some influential homosexual writers as the "prime taste treat in sex," while others saw it as nothing less than "a revolutionary act." Even after AIDS was discovered, and after about one thousand men had died, San Francisco writer Konstantin Berlandt boldly confessed, "I love to rim. To some people, a tongue up the asshole can be relaxing, mesmerizing, even spiritually uplifting." Berlandt also argued that it was the exclusive responsibility of society to find a cure for AIDS, maintaining that he saw no reason that homosexuals should alter their life-style. Many of his readers agreed with this assessment.[12]

What gave rise to "rimming" and other perversions was the new-freedom climate of tolerance that places like San Francisco made famous. *New York Times* reporter Robert Lindsey affords a graphic picture of life in the Bay City's Castro district: "The late 1970's and early 1980's were a period of anything-goes sexual liberation for San Francisco's gay community. On some nights, thousands of men, many seminude or wearing costumes, women's clothing or heavily studded leather outerwear, overflowed onto the community's sidewalks, some taunting heterosexual couples who had ventured into their neighborhood as 'breeders.' " Where did they go? To the bathhouses. "It was not uncommon," writes Lindsey, "for some men to have sexual contacts with 20 or 30 partners in a single evening at bath houses that featured 'orgy rooms' and other facilities designed to encourage multiple sexual contacts."[13]

There is no way to discuss gay liberation, and the transmission of AIDS, without mentioning the role of the bathhouse. No other institution symbolizes the gay community more than the bathhouse, and no other institution is as revered. And that is why gay leaders everywhere resisted their closing, even after it was apparent that keeping them open meant certain death to those who frequented them. Randy Shilts does not exaggerate when he states that bathhouses "were biological cesspools for infection." The result: "Bathhouses guaranteed the rapid spread of AIDS among gay men." Then why weren't they closed? "Common sense," says Shilts, "dictated that bathhouses be closed down. Common sense, however, rarely carried much weight in regard to AIDS policy."[14]

Why didn't common sense prevail? Because of politics, that's why. To be specific, the new-freedom emphasis on individual rights, together with a doctrinal insistence on moral neutrality, literally disabled the thinking of those who should have known better, namely, the medical establishment. If it was inexcusable for gay leaders and civil libertarians to speak *only* to the issue of gay rights—while people were dying left and right—then it was a million times more irresponsible for health officials to adopt the same line. Over and over again, big-name doctors from big-name institutes and big-name health officials from big-league cities abdicated their responsibility by showing infinitely more interest in the civil liberties of homosexuals than in the public good they were pledged to uphold.

Even Shilts, who would like to put much of the blame for the AIDS epidemic on Ronald Reagan (he didn't respond quickly enough), admits that the "bathhouses had been allowed to stay open solely for political reasons."[15] Yes, and for reasons having absolutely nothing to do with Ronald Reagan. It was, as Shilts details, the leadership in the homosexual community that succeeded in intimidating state officials and health professionals from doing their jobs. And it was those politicians who were supposedly sympathetic to homosexuals, like Mario Cuomo and Michael Dukakis, who for years did nothing to close the bathhouses while giving not a dime for AIDS research.[16]

The fight to keep the bathhouses open was carried on in New York long after they were closed in San Francisco. One year after the director of public health in San Francisco, Dr. Mervyn Silverman, ordered the bathhouses closed in late 1984 (he worked hard to keep them open for years), homosexuals were still patronizing bathhouses in New York. Only now they were taking precautions, often encouraged by the worried owners. For example, signs were posted on the walls of the Hell Fire Club in Manhattan's lower west side describing the house rules, stating in no uncertain terms that "no bullwhips, electric prods or animals" could be used for sexual gratification. This was considered a compromise.[17]

The bathhouse owners did more to exploit homosexuals than any other group. Concerned only with profit, they dreamed up the wildest rationalizations for keeping their brothels open. Bruce Mailman, owner of the four-story St. Marks Bath in the East Village, stated those who (like Mayor Koch) called bathhouse owners "vile" and "merchants of death," were demonstrating "a regrettable lack of sensitivity to our constitutional rights," rights that included "the right of individuals to associate freely, to practice private sex and to operate a lawful business."[18]

But didn't the argument that homosexuals can't function without their bathhouses suggest that they were every bit as compulsive as their critics contended? Yes, and Mailman offered proof: "Closing bathhouses and other establishments catering to homosexuals will, as a practical matter, leave homosexual men with virtually *no havens for assembly*" (emphasis added).[19] The editors of the *New York Times*, it should be noted, accepted the same line: "The bathhouses seem to respond to an important need for some homosexuals. Though closing them might win some votes, that need will remain."[20] The *Times* then went on to recommend that the bathhouses remain open, without ever stating exactly what homosexual need was being served in these places and why this need was apparently unique to them.

Not all homosexual leaders tried to deny the obvious. "The movement of the 60's and the 70's legitimized promiscuity," commented Larry Kramer, a founder of the Gay Men's Health Crisis in New York City.[21] How right he is. The movement came straight out of the pages of the new freedom. For those caught up in it, the momentum often proved unstoppable, and that is why so many homosexuals continued to patronize the bathhouses even after a media blitz warned against doing so. For example, in 1983, 62 percent of San Francisco homosexuals surveyed said they continued to engage in high-risk sex at the same, or even higher rates, than before learning about AIDS.[22] The following year the figure had dropped to about a third.[23] However, in a study of students at the University of Maryland in 1987, it was found that 83 percent of the homosexual males had done nothing to change their sexual habits.[24]

The finding that homosexuals on campus refused to change their behavior is supported by other research in this area. There are two categories of homosexuals who have shown the least willingness to alter their sex life: the most-well-educated and the bathhouse patrons.[25] To the most-well-educated, the AIDS epidemic was something that struck the misfortunate but had little chance of infecting people like themselves, convinced as they were of their own invincibility. As for the bathhouse patrons, it comes as little surprise to learn that the most compulsive segment of the homosexual community would also be the least capable of reform. Both of these groups share a hostility to any advice that counsels restraint, thinking that the real intent of those who offer such guidance is to punish them.

It is very difficult to reach people when they ascribe malicious motives to anyone who questions the wisdom of their prevailing life-style. Not everyone who counsels restraint is a "sexual fascist" or some kind of homophobic demagogue seeking to capitalize on the public's fear of AIDS. Many homosexuals, including a growing number of their spokesmen, have adopted a more cautious approach. Indeed, judging from the death rate among homosexuals, and the incalculable suffering that AIDS causes, it is a mystery why those who favor no changes in behavior are considered friendly to homosexuals while those who ask for moderation are cast as the enemy. After all, it is the advice of the so-called "friends" that has made many a mortician rich.

In addition to casting aspersions on those who recommend a more temperate approach, serious debate on the issue of AIDS has been stifled further by sanitizing the discussion, resulting in what Shilts aptly calls "AIDSpeak."[26] For example, semen is called "bodily fluids," AIDS victims are referred to as "people with AIDS," promiscuous is dubbed "sexually active," venereal disease is known as "sexually transmitted disease," promiscuous men are labeled "nonmonogamous," and so on. No one beats Harvard professor Stephen Jay Gould (he thinks AIDS is a "natural phenomenon"), who refers to those AIDS patients who knowingly shoot narcotics into their veins with dirty needles as "minorities of life style."[27] There is so much emphasis on crafting "nonjudgmental" language that the enormity of the disease is lost.

Another way in which honest debate on this topic is muddied is by characterizing the issue as a "victimless crime." When innocent third parties, many of them children, die as a direct result of someone else's behavior, it makes no sense to pretend that victims are nonexistent. Those who give blood after being apprised that they are carrying the AIDS virus are no different from those who might seek to poison the water supply by dumping a toxic substance into a reservoir. Joseph Markowski of Los Angeles demonstrated his new-freedom consciousness when asked in 1987 why he sold his AIDS-contaminated blood: "I know AIDS can kill, but I was so hard up for money I didn't give a damn about other people."[28]

What is even more outrageous is the extent to which those who have intentionally victimized others are protected by the law from prosecution. Several cases have emerged. In 1986 two San Diego policemen were denied the right to find out the results of a blood test administered to the man who bit them while being arrested at a Gay Pride Parade. Though the homosexual boasted to the police that he had AIDS, a federal district court concluded that the bitten police officers had no right to find out the results of the blood test. A New York woman who gave CPR to an intravenous drug user with bleeding gums was similarly denied the right to find out whether the man tested positive for AIDS. The right to privacy has even been extended to a practicing surgeon with AIDS: none of his patients know that he is an AIDS victim, even though all could be infected by his blood during an operation.

All this is being done in the name of confidentiality. Unlike other communicable diseases, this one merits no testing, tracing, or notification. Some like it that way, even if it means innocent people die. Janlori Goldman of the ACLU's Project on Privacy and Technology is explicit in her preference: "The benefits of confidentiality outweigh the possibility that somebody may be injured."[29] ("Injured" is AIDSpeak for die.) The politics of AIDS is so strong that in New York City, where one in every three AIDS victims lives, the state Public Health Council and the New York City Health Board have refused to designate AIDS as a communicable disease. As Bruce Lambert of the *New York Times* said, "This was no oversight. Because of the intense emotions evoked by the disease, a deliberate decision was made to avoid traditional medical tactics against communicable diseases, such as tracing and quarantine."[30]

In the end, it is the new-freedom's emphasis on moral neutrality that is largely responsible for the problem. Dr. Robert Mendelsohn, author and physician, has been one of the few courageous voices in the medical community to make this point. According to Mendelsohn, both AIDS and herpes are partly iatrogenic, that is, they are doctor-produced diseases. How so? Both have thrived because of the nonjudgmental stance that doctors have taken toward these diseases; even the medical profession refers to promiscuous men as "sexually active" individuals. As Mendelsohn explains it, it was during the 1960s when doctors took the attitude that a person was entitled to any lifestyle he chose, it being the sole duty of the physician to treat and cure the disease.[31]

Consider what is at stake: there are people who are currently dying of parasites previously found in the bowels of sheep but never in humans, spreading their disease to unsuspecting men and women, while doctors ponder the civil liberties questions involved in duty-to-warn regulations. There is something terribly wrong when New York City's Health Commissioner, Dr. Stephen C. Joseph, can say in good conscience that the Department of Health "is not the guardian of public morality. We are the guardian of public health."[32] Really? And what does Joseph tell people who are overweight, or drug addicts, or alcoholics, or chain smokers? Does he not tell them to stop, to put an end to their irresponsible behavior? Isn't that part of *his* responsibilities? Does that make him a commissar of public morality?

It is a sign of the times that chain smokers who acquire cancer by damaging their lungs are stigmatized infinitely more than homosexuals who acquire AIDS by damaging their rectums. Smokers pay higher insurance premiums than nonsmokers, but those who have the AIDS virus pay the same rate as everyone else. Wassermann tests were a commonplace when an increase in syphilis was detected, but there are no routine tests for AIDS. In 1987 the citizens of Del Mar, California, entertained an initiative to ban smoking in public, except in specially built pens, but no such proposal to segregate AIDS patients—crazy as the idea is—has ever been, or could ever be, considered. A double standard is evident almost everywhere.

The existence of a double standard is testimony to the political muscle that homosexuals command. It is safe to say that homosexuals are among the most powerful groups to emerge in recent times. In the strict sense of the word, they can hardly be called a minority group. The term *minority group* is used by sociologists to describe a people who lack power vis-à-vis the dominant group. It is true that homosexuals are not the dominant group, but they are not a group that suffers for lack of power either. The evidence is pretty straight-forward.

In 1973, just four years after the gay rights movement began, homosexuals scored their first major victory: organized homosexuals succeeded in getting the American Psychiatric Association to stop labeling homosexuality a mental illness. The decision was the product of a campaign of intimidation, one that had absolutely nothing to do with some new scientific insight or research finding. Beginning in 1970, homosexual activists showed up each year at the annual meeting of the association, putting pressure on the psychiatrists to make the desired change. Through a combination of violence and insult, they made their point stick.[33] The decision to capitulate in the face of political pressure was the first of many to be made by people thought to be responsible.

In 1974, a Gay Caucus was established within the American Sociological Association, signifying the strength and legitimacy that homosexuals were achieving in academia. College presidents and deans would be lobbied next, and by the 1980s the presence of homosexual student groups was acknowl-edged on many campuses, especially at Ivy League institutions. Schools that rejected the demands of homosexuals were far and few between, and when they tried, they lost. In 1988 Georgetown University, a Catholic institution, lost in the Supreme Court in its bid to stay a D.C. appeals court ruling, and was ordered to extend to homosexual student groups the same privileges and recognition accorded other campus organizations, even though doing so breached the doctrinal prerogatives of the Church.

The homosexual rights movement has targeted the Catholic and Protestant churches for recognition as well. The mainline Protestant denominations, especially the Episcopalians and Presbyterians, have been under steady pres-sure to accept openly homosexuals as ministers. Strong support has been found in some quarters as people like New York Episcopalian Bishop Paul Moore have registered their approval of various homosexual rights goals. Moore, for example, thought it "immoral" that his Catholic colleagues at the New York Archdiocese found problems with proposed gay rights legislation in the city.

Some Catholic theologians, like Dr. Daniel Maguire of Marquette Univer-sity, have publicly proclaimed their endorsement of homosexual marriage. Then there is the Catholic homosexual group, Dignity, which believes so strongly in rights for all homosexuals that it has voted to admit the North American Man/Boy Love Association (NAMBLA) into membership in New York City's Community Council of Lesbian/Gay Organizations. NAMBLA is an organization dedicated to the proposition that homosexuals have a right to commit sodomy with minors.

Politicians at the federal, state, and local levels have been quite solicitous of homosexuals, especially those in the Democratic party. Presidential candidates Jesse Jackson and Paul Simon went out of their way during the 1988 campaign to pledge their unabiding support for the cause of homosexual rights. Indeed, the Democratic party adopted a resolution at the 1984 convention in San Francisco that required every state party to develop an affirmative-action type of "outreach" program to recruit homosexuals as delegates to the 1988 convention. As early as 1980 the Gay Caucus was already larger than the delegations of almost half the states.

In New York City, Mayor Edward Koch marches in the annual Gay/Lesbian Pride Parade, along with the commissioner of health, chairman of the Commission on Human Rights, and president of the Health and Hospitals Corporation, the three city agencies most involved in combating the AIDS epidemic. The officials continue to show support for homosexual rights, even though there is an outburst of anti-Catholicism that occurs each year at the parade; obscene remarks and gestures are made by the demonstrators when the march extends past St. Patrick's Cathedral.[34] Some dignitaries, like Koch, prefer to join the parade after it passes the church.

Homosexual rights legislation has succeeded in a number of cities in the 1980s. In New York, for instance, such legislation failed repeatedly for over two consecutive decades, before finally winning out in 1986; the bill passed after the discovery of AIDS and after the death of actor Rock Hudson. This is not an isolated case. Those who have followed the homosexual rights movement have been struck by the extent to which support for gay rights has generally accompanied the spread of AIDS. It is worth noting, too, that calls for barring youngsters with AIDS from school followed similar pleas for denying entry to youngsters afflicted with herpes, thus calling into question the charge of homophobia.

Perhaps the most sympathetic voices have come from the media. Television, in particular, has moved to counter any negative stereotype that homosexuals might have. Shows like the NBC movie "An Early Frost," and PBS specials like "The Times of Harvey Milk" and "Silent Pioneers," have cast homosexuals in a very positive manner. Evidence that the networks might be concealing the role that homosexuals have played in the transmission of AIDS was uncovered by the Center for Media and Public Affairs. By studying the tapes of more than a hundred nightly news broadcasts, taken over a period of better than four months in 1987, the researchers found that only 9 percent of AIDS victims were identified as homosexuals, though they account for 73 percent of all cases; no intravenous drug users were featured, though they constitute 20 percent of the AIDS victims.[35]

Another measure of success that homosexuals have registered is income earnings. For some time now, rights activists have maintained that homosexuals earn more than the median income, putting to rest, they say, speculation as to how much homosexuals contribute to society. The data support such claims. It is known, for example, that a majority of the homosexual men who live in San Francisco have achieved a level of education and income that is above the national average.[36] Of course, citing such data makes it difficult to argue that homosexuals are a discriminated group, deserving of affirmative action. Blacks and women, who do qualify for affirmative action, cannot marshal the same impressive figures that homosexuals can.

Of all the victories that homosexuals have scored, none has been as impressive as the change in attitude that many Americans have toward homosexuality. Although societal affirmation has not been forthcoming, there has been a marked increase in tolerance for homosexuals, one that has emanated from most every quarter of society. It is not just in municipal legislation where success has been achieved, nor is it accurate to say that only the medical, legal, and cultural elite have shown unprecedented tolerance: the average American is more tolerant of homosexuality today than at any time in the past.

But if ever there were a Pyrrhic victory, this is it. How much cause for celebration is there when tolerance for the life-style of promiscuous homosexuals becomes tolerance for the consequences of promiscuity, namely, death due to AIDS? For years the cultural elite has implored the public to be tolerant of homosexuals, hoping to convince them that what was going on in the orgy rooms of the bathhouses was nothing more than an "alternative life-style." For years the public has been told to be nonjudgmental, to presume that nothing more than a "victimless crime" between consenting adults was at play when homosexual masochists sought out homosexual sadists in the local torture chambers of urban America. And now, after all this, when public indifference to homosexual suffering is commonplace, the same people who sold the message of moral neutrality cannot understand why there isn't a greater sense of moral outrage over what is happening.

The message of tolerance has been sold so well that it has inured the public to the plight of homosexuals. If it is wrong to pass judgment on what people voluntarily do to themselves, then how much public outrage can realistically be expected when people learn that those who have abandoned all restraint have paid for their recklessness with their lives? It is to be expected that people will get indignant when they learn that an innocent person was pushed off a bridge, but not when they hear about someone who chose to jump.

So it appears that the goal of doing what one wants with his body has been achieved, but at a price that few anticipated and no one wants to pay. In typical new-freedom fashion, homosexual leaders want it all: they want to engage in suicidal behavior that doesn't result in suicide. They are insistent that what they are doing is none of the public's business, but they are equally insistent on making the public pay the bill for their behavior. They want society to be tolerant of their customs, but see no reason to respect in return the customs of society. They want to engage in deviant behavior without being labeled deviant. In short, they want rights but not responsibilities.

For the organized homosexual rights movement to succeed, victory in the courts must be forthcoming. That is unlikely, given the precedent set in *Bowers v. Hardwick*. It was in *Bowers* that the Supreme Court essentially ratified what had been the unwritten law of millennia, namely, that the right to commit sodomy is not a right that the public need endorse. Ever since Plato's *Laws* condemned sodomy as unnatural, it has been virtually impossible to change the accepted wisdom on this subject. What the Supreme Court did in *Bowers* was to say that engaging in sodomy is not a constitutional right, and that therefore it was up to the states to decide whether to legalize or proscribe the behavior.

In writing for the 5-4 majority, Supreme Court Justice Byron White argued that although there had been occasions when the high court had recognized rights that lacked textual support in the Constitution, those few cases shared characteristics that were lacking in *Bowers*. For example, for the court to accept sodomy as a fundamental right deserving of constitutional protection, it would have to be established that sodomy is "implicit in the concept of ordered liberty," such that "neither liberty nor justice would exist if [they] were sacrificed." Failing that test, it needs to be shown that the right to commit sodomy is a liberty that is "deeply rooted in this Nation's history and tradition."[37] It is not difficult to conclude that neither standard is met in *Bowers*.

Perhaps the most impressive finding in *Bowers* was the conclusion that to grant constitutional sanction to sodomy was to set the stage for unlimited court involvement in deciding the constitutionality of morally contentious acts. What about the right to commit adultery or incest? Justice White understood what that would mean: "We are unwilling to start down that road."[38]

Even the critics of *Bowers* must admit to the veracity of White's concern. For example, just one year after *Bowers* was decided, the New Hampshire Supreme Court upheld the constitutionality of a proposed state law barring homosexuals from becoming foster parents, adoptive parents, or operators of child care agencies. The significance of this decision lies in the fact that the court cited the ruling in *Bowers* as authority for its verdict.[39] In other words, had the decision in *Bowers* gone the other way, it is likely that homosexuals would have won, clearing the way for other rights, such as the right to marry.

Those who want to overturn *Bowers* need to make the case that the traditional nuclear family is undeserving of a privileged, elevated status. This they have not done. Incantations about rights are in abundance, but there is little discussion as to the social desirability of legally upending the nuclear family as the ideal family model. Every society discriminates in adopting a moral code; none can be neutral. Yet this is what gay rights ultimately tries to do: it tries to incorporate approval for every conceivable sexual expression, dissolving the very idea of a norm. It is a goal that runs counter to what the human condition is capable of achieving. And one that causes unnecessary havoc as well.

The sponsors of gay rights have made their goal clear. In the words of Sidney Abbott and Barbara Love, the movement will have succeeded when heterosexuality and homosexuality are regarded as totally equal moral choices, "a nonissue of no more importance than a person's preference for Swiss or American cheese."[40] It is for this reason that homosexual activist Tom Stoddard advises his followers to lobby hard, but to "*avoid discussions of morality*" at all cost, because once the debate moves in that direction, "you are in trouble."[41] Stoddard is correct, and that is why the homosexual rights movement is different from the civil rights movement of blacks and women. To win, homosexuals have to overthrow the moral order in which they live. That is a tall order, even in a society that is increasingly unprepared to defend the moral worth of its culture.

Notes

1. Dennis Altman, *Homosexual: Oppression and Liberation* (New York: Avon Books, 1971), p. 100.
2. William Masters and Virginia Johnson, *Crisis: Heterosexual Behavior in the Age of AIDS* (New York: Grove Press, 1988).
3. Quoted in *New York Times* editorial, "AIDS: Good News and Bad News," June 15, 1987, p. A16.
4. Michael Fumento, "AIDS: Are Heterosexuals at Risk?" *Commentary* (November 1987): 22–23.
5. Randy Shilts, *And the Band Played On* (New York: St. Martin's Press, 1987), pp. 251, 165, 200.
6. See the eye-opening article by John Adams Wettergreen, "AIDS, Public Morality, and Public Health," *Claremont Review of Books* (Fall 1985): 3–6. See, too, Wettergreen's rejoinder to his critics in the winter issue, pp. 24–31.
7. Alan P. Bell and Martin S. Weinberg, *Homosexualities: A Study of Diversity among Men and Women* (New York: Simon and Schuster, 1978), p. 69.
8. Ibid., pp. 85, 308.
9. Philip Blumstein and Pepper Schwartz, *American Couples* (New York: Morrow, 1983), pp. 195, 269, 270, 570.
10. Ibid., pp. 275, 298, 585–86.

11. Shilts, *And the Band Played On*, p. 39.
12. Ibid., pp. 19, 378.
13. Robert Lindsey, "Where Homosexuals Found Haven, There Is None Now with AIDS," *New York Times*, July 15, 1987, p. A16.
14. Shilts, *And the Band Played On*, pp. 154, 306.
15. Ibid., p. 491.
16. Ibid., pp. 454, 559.
17. Ralph Blumenthal, "At Homosexual Establishments, A New Climate of Caution," *New York Times*, November 9, 1985, p. 29.
18. Bruce Mailman, "The Battle for Safe Sex in the Baths," *New York Times*, December 5, 1985.
19. Ibid. (emphasis added).
20. *New York Times* editorial, "Morality, AIDS and the Bathhouses," October 19, 1985, p. 26.
21. Jane Gross, "Homosexuals Stepping Up AIDS Education," *New York Times*, September 22, 1985, p. 22.
22. Shilts, *And the Band Played On*, p. 260.
23. "40% of Single Men Are Found Homosexuals in San Francisco," *New York Times*, November 1984, p. B16.
24. "AIDS and the Education of Our Children," (Washington, D.C.: U.S. Department of Education, October 1987), p.7.
25. Shilts, *And the Band Played On*, pp. 414–15, 481, 492.
26. Ibid., p. 315.
27. Stephen Jay Gould, "The Terrifying Normalacy of AIDS," *New York Times Magazine*, April 19, 1987, p. 33.
28. Quoted in "Lavender Liberals," *Chronicles* (February 1988): 5.
29. Quoted by Lindsey Gruson, "Privacy of AIDS Patients: Fear Infringes on Sanctity," *New York Times*, July 30, 1987, p. D20.
30. Bruce Lambert, "Rise in AIDS Sparks Debate over Testing of Victim's Contacts," *New York Times*, January 27, 1987, p. B1.
31. Dr. Robert Mendelsohn made his remarks on "Crossfire," the CNN television show, November 19, 1984.
32. Quoted by Jane Gross, "New York Officials Brace for Conflict on Explicit AIDS Ads," *New York Times*, May 11, 1987, p. B1.
33. See Marjorie Rosenberg, "Inventing the Homosexual," *Commentary* (December 1987): 38.
34. The 1988 parade featured a float that showed an effigy of the pope sprayed with a swastika. This bigotry went unreported in the major media. See Chris Corcoran, "Gay Paraders Focus Their Anger on St. Patrick's and the Cardinal," *New York City Tribune*, June 27, 1988, p. 1.
35. Reported in "The Week," *National Review*, February 5, 1988, p. 14.
36. See the 1984 survey on homosexual men in San Francisco conducted by the Research and Decisions Corporation. The study, commissioned by the San Francisco AIDS Foundation, is one of the first reliable surveys conducted on this subject.
37. *Bowers v. Hardwick*, 760 F.2d 1202 (11th Cir. 1985).
38. Ibid.
39. The decision, *Opinion of the Justices*, N.H. Sup. Ct., No. 87-080, is cited in Bruce Hafen's unpublished paper, "Government Regulation of and for Family

Life,'' delivered at the Rockford Institute Conference on the Free Family and the Therapeutic State, October 15, 1987.

40. Sidney Abbott and Barbara Love, "Is Women's Liberation a Lesbian Plot?" in Vivian Gornick and Barbara Moran, eds., *Women in Sexist Society* (New York: Basic Books, 1971), p. 609.

41. Thomas Stoddard, "Gay Rights," in Kenneth Norwick, ed., *Lobbying for Freedom in the 1980s* (New York: Perigee Books, 1983), p. 163.

PART V

THE COLLAPSE
OF CONSTRAINTS

11

The Role of the Family

It has been noted since the time of Confucius that the family is the cornerstone of society. The family, together with the institutionalization of religion, has exerted the preponderant influence governing the nature of social relations. Whether a given society has a surplus or deficit of morally responsible individuals will in large measure be determined by the quality of family life. It is the key to social well-being.

By almost any measure, the quality of family life has deteriorated in the latter half of the twentieth century. Census Bureau data paint a bleak picture, revealing, for example, the decline of two-parent families and a concomitant increase in one-parent households. One in five families is now a one-parent family, and the figure for blacks stands at six in ten. There are now more childless couples, unmarried parents, people living alone, and unrelated people living together than ever before. The family, it is clear, has fallen on hard times.

Young people are hurt most when the family stumbles and falls. We know that children who are reared in one-parent families are more likely to live in poverty than children who live in two-parent families. They do less well in school, are more likely to exhibit discipline problems, and are more likely to become dropouts. They are more likely to have psychological problems, more likely to use drugs, and more likely to run afoul of the law.[1] It's not that the one parent who is at home, almost always the woman, is delinquent (it is the father who is typically delinquent), it's just that one person cannot be expected to do the job of two.

One-parent families are usually the product of divorce or illegitimacy, and on both counts the United States is in trouble. The hard reality is that the United States has the highest divorce rate in the world, and the highest teenage pregnancy rate in the industrial world. After looking at these figures, Cornell University psychologist Urie Bronfenbrenner exclaimed that the problems "are part of the unraveling of the social fabric."[2]

147

Though Bronfenbrenner's conclusion is entirely warranted, it is not universally held among specialists in family research. There are those who maintain that the family is simply changing, restructuring itself so as to keep pace with the realities of life in the modern world. These scholars, and they include family specialists Mary Jo Bane, Theodore Caplow, and Robert Bellah, do not accept the idea that the family is in trouble. They believe that many of the so-called problems that the family is experiencing are nothing more than temporary dislocations, adjustments that will work themselves out in due course. It is not without importance that such sociologists reject the position that there is one type of family that is preferable to others; their commitment to moral neutrality leads them to believe there are many "good" types of families but none that is ideal.

To say that the family is changing is to state the obvious: it is empirically verifiable. But just as we would want an evaluative report on a hospital patient's change in condition, we need to know whether the family's change in status signals health or illness. It is not enough to learn that the family is restructuring itself to meet contemporary demands. We ought to have some way of deciding whether more or less restructuring is desirable. After all, one of the functions of examining the family is to provide information on what should be done, if anything, and not simply to tally what's happened to it lately.

It is standard commentary among students of the family to proclaim that the family will not die. But what is the value of this popular assertion? What yardsticks do we have to measure its death? What would the corpse look like? Is it not the quality, and not the mere subsistence, of family relations that ought to concern us? If the family lives on as an institution, but is so drastically crippled that it cannot provide for the kind of psychological and social nourishment that only it can offer, of what utility is it to the ordering of a free society? These are the kinds of questions that deserve the attention of social scientists.

Margaret Mead was once asked whether the family will continue to exist in the future. Her answer was insightful: yes, because we know of no other way to live. Alternatives have been tried and all have been found wanting. Communes, for example, have often been launched with the noblest of ambitions, but before too long they usually descend into authoritarian and exploitative arrangements, just the opposite of the free and equal provisions they were supposed to be. Most of the other arrangements cited as alternatives to the family are merely relationships of convenience, of no lasting and widespread importance; in other words, they are not alternatives, as such.

The family is an enormously resilient institution, one that rebounds with high energy each time it's challenged. Even when an all-out assault is waged against it, it rebounds with vigor. If the family has survived the punishment it has had to endure in Stalin's Russia, Mao's China, and Pol Pot's Cambodia, it can safely be said that the family is indestructible. Even on the Israeli kibbutz, where with benign purposes men and women voluntarily sought the dissolution of the family, it reemerged as strong as ever.

So there is no comfort in learning that the family is "here to stay"; it has already proven that many times over. What we need to know is what particular family type is most desirable, and what can be done to support it.

More than any other factor, it is the widespread acceptance of the new freedom that explains our inability to reach consensus on what family type is most desirable. Nowhere was this point driven home with greater clarity than at the 1980 White House Conference on Families. Responding to growing concern about the status of the family, President Carter approved a national conference on the subject, looking for ways in which the government might alter social policy to buttress the quality of family life. All well and good, except that the conferees couldn't agree on what it was they wanted to help: assisting the family fast became assistance to *families*.

Peter and Brigitte Berger spotted the significance of using the plural (*families*) and not the singular: "It gave governmental recognition to precisely the kind of moral relativism that has infuriated and mobilized large numbers of Americans."[3] It also demonstrated the way in which the family was being perceived: through the eyes of the new freedom. So as not to offend those who either cannot or will not live within the confines of the nuclear family, new-freedom advocates chose to display their tolerance for alternative life-styles by refusing to give priority to the traditional family unit.

If the term *family* is to be redefined to mean any group of people "living together in a climate of caring," then there is no need to waste taxpayer dollars to rescue it. We are in no danger of running out of ways in which to live, and if every conceivable human arrangement passes as some form of the family, then there is nothing to save; there can be no solutions where there are no problems.

The idea that there is no single type of the family worthy of public policy preferences is held by senior officials in government. For example, it is the position maintained by Congressman George Miller, chairman of the House Select Committee on Children, Youth and Families. To Miller, there is no such thing as an ideal family model; the very thought that there is shows a "judgmental" attitude, one that unfairly "stigmatizes" children of divorce and those born out of wedlock.[4]

Notice how completely Miller's position expresses the new-freedom belief in moral neutrality and its characteristic rejection of constraints. The congressman is, of course, correct to assume that the defense of the traditional family is "judgmental." So, too, is his preference for moral neutrality, though he will not concede it. He is also quite right in his contention that the defense of the traditional family ''stigmatizes'' the children reared in other settings. By the same logic, it is also true that the defense of civility has the effect of stigmatizing the children of convicts. What should we do, then, abandon marriage, the family, and civility so that no innocent children will be stigmatized?

Despite what the critics say, the term *broken family* is a good one, that is, it accurately portrays what happens when one parent absents himself from the family: it breaks. No one knows this better than the children, and no amount of social acceptance of broken families can ever make up for this fact. Indeed, by lowering the social penalties for broken families, it is likely that there will be more such fatalities, thus making the situation worse for many more children. New-freedom thinkers hope to see the day when punitive measures and constraints of every kind are a thing of the past, but in the meantime their unrealistic conception of freedom unwittingly contributes to the very problems they want to eradicate.

The irony is that those who passionately want social and economic progress often work against what has proven to be its most natural generator, namely, the bourgeois family. As William J. Gribbin has noted, ''There is no engine of progress, security and social advancement as powerful as the family.''[5] Nothing that a department of labor or human services can do can match the ability of the middle-class family to provide for job training and care of the young and the elderly. There simply is no societal or state substitute for the traditional family.

Although it is true that there are other forms of the family that are better suited to the needs of premodern societies, it is nonetheless true that the bourgeois family best serves the needs of modern societies. Unlike the extended family, the nuclear family is small and relatively unburdened by responsibilities outside the immediate circle of relations. This enables individuals to develop their resources more fully than they would otherwise, and makes for positive contributions to the greater economic good of society.

The nuclear family allows for significant geographic mobility, freeing the individual to pursue his interests wherever opportunities exist. Significantly, it affords men and women unparalleled intimacy and emotional involvement, providing the kinds of traits that best complement the rational, impersonal workplace environment of advanced economies.

It is the bourgeois family that has undergirded Western societies for centuries. This child-oriented unit, based on heterosexual love, mutual obligations, and sex-role responsibilities, has served American society well since its founding (the extended family was never the norm in this country). Of critical importance has been the role that this family type has played in transmitting fundamental moral values.

Allan C. Carlson, one of the nation's most perceptive students of the family, has identified the values transmitted by the bourgeois family as "hard work, delayed gratification, and self-imposed restraints on personal behavior."[6] These are just the values that the new freedom discredits, holding as it does an animus against constraints. New-freedom celebrants find it difficult to believe that if constraints are levied in moderation they inexorably become liberating in their effects: it is the person who has developed his potential, through a life of self-discipline, who ultimately is the most free.

Self-discipline not only allows the individual to experience freedom but contributes to the production of a free society. "Self-government is not possible without self-discipline," exclaims Michael Novak, and it is to bourgeois values that we must turn if self-discipline is to be realized.[7] It is impossible to expect a free society to exist unless individuals take it upon themselves to attend to the needs of their local communities; individual initiative is the cornerstone of political freedom. If enough people prove to be incapable of doing their civic duties, then one of two things will happen: either certain necessities will go unattended or government will assume the mantle of responsibility. In either case, the loss to liberty is certain.

Brigitte and Peter Berger have also cited the link between the traditional family, the values it transmits, and the production and maintenance of a democratic society. They flatly state that "*the family, and specifically the bourgeois family, is the necessary social context for the emergence of autonomous individuals who are the empirical foundation of political democracy.*"[8] Put another way, there is no historical evidence that free societies have ever been associated with any unit other than the bourgeois family, making suspect arguments about the purported value of its contemporary alternatives.

The bourgeois family plays an important economic role, as well as a political one. Both critics and defenders of capitalism have uniformly acknowledged the invaluable role that the bourgeois family has played in the creation of a market economy. Marxists, for example, have accurately maintained that capitalism requires the bourgeois family, though they have inaccurately contended that under socialism it would disappear. Marxists hate the bourgeois family both for the life-style that it provides, and the privacy that it maintains. What they hate most of all is its ability to shield the individual from the reach of state, thereby blunting collectivist ambitions.

To the supporters of capitalism, it is precisely the kind of life-style that capitalism affords that makes it worthy of defense: In what other society has there been as much freedom of the individual and little real poverty? Certainly not in socialist societies. And is it not a strength, rather than a weakness, of the bourgeois family that it keeps the state at bay? Hasn't it been in those societies—they are called Marxist— where the state has penetrated the privacy of the family that unprecedented repression has resulted?

Joseph Schumpeter understood, in a way Marxists have not, that what made the bourgeois family so precious was its social function. Under capitalism, Schumpeter observed, men worked not so much to satisfy their own self-interest as to satisfy the interests of their wives and children. He was convinced that the bourgeois family was the engine of capitalism, given as it was to savings and investments.[9] More recently, George Gilder has made a similar argument, contending that under capitalism men work to satisfy others; family comes first. Capitalism, he says, is predicated on the kind of value structure that the bourgeois family encourages. He lists the bourgeois family as one of the "three pillars" (the other two being work and faith) of "a free economy and a prosperous society."[10]

It needs to be said that it is bourgeois values, with their emphasis on the positive role of constraints, and not the structure of the bourgeois family per se, that is of unsurpassed importance. There are plenty of examples of intact families where bourgeois values are absent, and conversely, there is no shortage of examples where middle-class values are present in one-parent families. Nonetheless, the most desirable structure wherein bourgeois values are transmitted remains the traditional father-mother-children arrangement; all things being equal, two parents are better than one.

Bourgeois values not only account for the political and economic success of American society but are functionally related to academic achievement. There is now overwhelming evidence that the children who do well in school exhibit a set of values and behavioral patterns that are quintessentially middle class in nature. Learning is not possible without a measure of self-discipline, and it is self-discipline that bourgeois values deliver.

The evidence presented by Reginald Clark offers exceptional insight into the factors governing academic success. He concentrated his research on poor black families, dividing them into four categories: two-parent families with at least one high-achieving twelfth-grade child; one-parent families with at least one high-achieving twelfth-grade child; two-parent families with at least one low-achieving twelfth-grade child; and one-parent families with at least one low-achieving twelfth-grade child.

Clark's initial assumption, that intact families do not necessarily make for academic success, was quite expectedly confirmed by the data. No one, of course, has ever suggested otherwise. That, of course, does not mean that children from from two-parent families do not generally do better in school than children from one-parent families. They do, and that is not something Clark tried to refute. What makes Clark's research so valuable is that he explored the reasons that some poor black children did well in school, and what it was that these children had in common, despite the fact that some came from two-parent families and others were raised in one-parent families.

According to Clark, it is the culture that the home affords that best explains educational outcomes. The children who were reared in homes where respect for authority was insisted upon, and where accountability was routinely enforced, tended to do well in school. "Sacred and secular moral orientations," Clark says, "are well developed in high-achieving students." He emphasizes that "one of the very first lessons taught to young children in these homes was the lesson of right and wrong, good and bad." Furthermore, in these homes, "parents declare a clear status hierarchy among family members with themselves at the top." The evidence shows that in these homes "the students' internal locus of control is firmly established and contributes to their willingness to assume personal responsibility for school outcomes."[11]

To be sure, Clark stresses that if these qualities are overdone, carried to excess, then the expected outcome may not occur. But consider the nature of the attributes that he ascribes to educational success, dispensed as they must be with moderation. "Moral orientations," lessons in "right and wrong, good and bad," "clear status hierarchy," a firmly established "internal locus of control," and a sense of "personal responsibility"—these are expressions of bourgeois values, the much-maligned characteristics that the new freedom assaults. Indeed, everything that Clark found that seems to matter (and if they matter to poor black kids, they matter to others as well), is exactly the opposite of the morally neutral, rights-without-responsibilities mentality of the new freedom.

The same values that provide for political freedom, economic prosperity, and educational achievement, account for law-abiding behavior as well. Although it is true that social compliance is no virtue in a dictatorship, it is important to the operations of free societies, and that is why it matters a great deal whether the norms and values that make for conformity are being successfully transmitted to young people. Once again, it is evident that the ability of the individual to practice a measure of constraint appears as a crucial variable in determining the desired outcome. A well-respected, and empirically supported, theory of antisocial behavior is control theory. There are many variants of this theory, but all have in common the understanding that if people are left to themselves, that is, if they are not properly socialized, they will naturally incline to antisocial behavior. It is premised on the idea that deviant conduct occurs when the individual lacks sufficient controls on his appetites. For Freud, this meant that norm violations would occur whenever there was an underdeveloped conscience or superego; if there were nothing to check the destructive capacities of the id, the result would be antisocial behavior.

The most convincing explanation of antisocial behavior comes from the work of Travis Hirschi.[12] Quite unlike most sociologists, Hirschi allows students of delinquency to test his ideas, putting forth as he does a true theory, one that is capable of being refuted by the evidence. That his psychosocial control theory has passed several tests is a tribute to Hirschi and a problem for those not ideologically prone to accept his explanation.

Hirschi maintains that the first line of inquiry relevant to understanding deviance should be to question why all people don't behave in an antisocial manner. At base, we are all animals, given to following our own needs and desires. What ultimately makes us moral beings is the process of socialization, the lifelong procedure whereby conventional norms and values are internalized and made part and parcel of our own personalities. In other words, we become moral when we submit to society, subordinating our own interests to the interests of others. This is the stuff that the social bond is made of, the ability of the individual to take into consideration the needs of others.

Hirschi identifies four components of the social bond, the realization of which is necessary to social well-being. The first part is attachment, the degree to which the individual is respectful of the interests of others. Those who are sensitive to the opinions and wishes of parents, teachers, and friends are tied to the social bond, and are unlikely candidates for delinquency. Commitment is the second element, a term used to describe the extent to which the individual has absorbed conventional norms, and is willing to pursue socially defined goals. Those who have little stake in society, and feel they have nothing great to lose by circumventing accepted codes of conduct, are much more likely to vent their noncommittal status through acts of delinquency.

Involvement is the third component of the social bond. It refers to the long-held belief that youngsters who have nothing to do are prime candidates for mischief. "Idleness is the devil's workshop" is not an adage without meaning, for it accurately conveys the idea that those not involved in such conventional activities as sports, games, homework, reading, and so on are likely to get into trouble. The fourth element is belief, a concept that expresses the individual's faith in the normative order of society. Those who feel no need to respect the law, and are not bothered by shedding their moral obligations, see little reason to conform; they generally do not.

Given what Hirschi has said, is it any wonder that incivility is so common in the United States? The new-freedom belief that there is nothing more important than to liberate the individual from all that limits, burdens, or in any way constrains him, is positively destructive to social well-being. The sky's-the-limit interpretation of freedom is a recipe for social disaster. The social bond requires that the individual accept his subordinate position in society and internalize conventional norms and values. When the dominant culture gives license to those who would unleash themselves from the social bond, it is to be expected that discord—and violence—will follow.

There is no question that the bourgeois family is best suited to the task of tying the individual to society. When people speak of a good family, they generally mean how cohesive it is, how integrated and anchored are its members. If the family falls on hard times, the social bond will be damaged. There's no getting around it. Even if all the other units of socialization maintain their verve, the social bond will not escape unscathed once the family has been wounded. Controls are necessary—they are not properties to be dispensed with at whim—and that is why the bourgeois value of self-discipline is indispensable to society, and most especially to the societies that struggle to be free.

It should be clear that it is in the communities where constraints are missing, where the value of self-discipline is in short supply, and where the social bond is weakest that the fewest success stories will be found. Individual initiative, as we have seen, is necessary in a democracy, and where it is lacking in certain communities, tasks that need to get done go undone. Self-reliance is also important to the work ethic, and where it has not been nurtured, there will be little prosperity.

Similarly, if great numbers of children have not been given the kind of home environment wherein self-responsibility is afforded, they will not possess the kinds of traits that make for success in school. And when large numbers of youngsters throw off their moral obligations, the community becomes a haven for crime and delinquency. Put all four together, and the result is a catastrophe.

There is really nothing mysterious about the utility of middle-class, or bourgeois, values: they make for middle-class people. It is their relative absence in lower-class communities that best explains the problems that inhere in them. When constraints are missing, the kinds of problems just discussed have a way of surfacing. That is as true for whites as it is for blacks, men as well as women; the social effects of the new freedom know no color or sex, nor any other background characteristic worth mentioning.

The new-freedom's animus against bourgeois values, and its relentless sabotage of the bourgeois family have created problems throughout every segment of society, but nowhere has the damage been greater than in the black community. Leaders in the black community are correct to argue that when things go bad for the country, they go doubly bad for blacks. And that is why the storm of problems unleashed by the new freedom hit blacks with the force of a hurricane.

It is by now generally acknowledged that the political and legal gains that blacks made in the 1960s were not matched by social and economic progress. Although it true that the fight against legal discrimination opened the door for many blacks, allowing them to take their rightful place in the ranks of the middle class, it is also true that many of those who were poor made no progress whatsoever. To make sense of this incongruity, consideration must be given to the context in which political and legal rights were achieved.

What happened in the 1960s was that the same government that awarded blacks their long-overdue rights, simultaneously socialized responsibilities for them as well, thus uncoupling the traditional relationship between rights and responsibilities. Within the space of just a few years, a large segment of the black population went from a position of many responsibilities and few rights to many rights and few responsibilities. This is exactly the logic of the new freedom, promoting as it does an inflation of rights and diminution of responsibilities. And as we have seen, when self-responsibility is lacking, social and economic problems multiply.

It is undeniably true that when blacks were burdened with the most onerous responsibilities (prior to the civil rights movement), and were the target of racism and discrimination, there was greater social solidarity and self-responsibility in the black community than has existed at any time since. Herbert Gutman, for example, has shown that the black family was relatively strong throughout slavery and the heyday of legal discrimination that followed. At the outset of the Depression, Gutman contends, the black family remained largely intact.[13] Noticeable changes were not detected until the 1960s, the decade of the new freedom.

At least one lesson can be drawn from this experience: there is no necessary relationship between oppression and family dissolution. In fact, as Eugene Genovese has suggested, the daily subjugation of blacks under slavery had the effect of strengthening the family: family members turned to each other for solace and psychological relief, driven as they were to mitigating the adverse conditions of life on the plantation.[14]

It should be clear, from the experience of blacks, as well as from the experiences of other minorities throughout the ages (Jews come quickly to mind), that the most horrid living conditions and hostile environment cannot deprive people of self-responsibility or a sense of social solidarity. For such deprivation to happen, something else must take hold: people must abandon constraint altogether. Why and how this occurs should be the first line of inquiry for public policymakers interested in undoing the damage done to blacks. Only then can sensible reforms be advanced.

Self-restraint is to some extent a function of demand, that is, the more people are required to exercise it, the more they do so. It is also a function of conditioning, meaning that the more it is reinforced, the more people are likely to practice it. Once self-restraint is successfully ingrained in a person's value structure, it becomes self-directing, capable of allowing the individual to bond with others, and to work toward the common good. It alone cannot save the individual from despair, but its absence positively assures desperation.

Self-restraint will atrophy once the demand for it declines and positive reinforcements dwindle. The best contemporary example of this can be seen in the nation's inner cities. The problems of the ghetto—illegitimacy, single-parent families, poor school performance, drugs, violence—are problems of impoverished character, the kinds of individual moral failings that have been socially produced and nourished. It cannot be said too strongly that these are not maladies rooted in race. On the contrary, these are ailments directly traceable to an enfeebled environment, one that was created in the 1960s and sustained in subsequent decades.

Beginning in the 1960s, millions of black youth were freed from the grip of family, school, church, and law. It was the combined effect of the dominant culture's embrace of the new freedom and large-scale government paternalism that worked to undermine the social bases of self-restraint in the black community. By unburdening the individual, culture and government lessened the demand for self-restraint and thus helped to erode bourgeois values, making it all but impossible to achieve upward mobility.

Charles Murray, best known for his trenchant analysis of the welfare system, captured what was happening. Murray contends that "the environment in which a young poor person grew up changed in several mutually consistent ways during the 1960s. The changes in welfare *and* changes in the risks attached to crime *and* changes in the educational environment reinforced each other. Together, they radically altered the incentive structure."[15] And together they helped entrap an entire generation, leaving them with crippled values and character disabilities.

Welfare hurt the family in many ways. One doesn't have to agree with everything that George Gilder says about men and women in order to appreciate his insights regarding the centrality of the male's role in the family. If a large number of men stop functioning as providers, for whatever reason, wives and children suffer, as does the community as a whole. No amount of outside help, Gilder contends, can make up the difference.[16] Perversely, welfare rules often entice men to leave their family, thus destabilizing the most crucial institution in society. If the state can provide at least as well (often better) than the father can, many men will yield to this kind of competition, escaping house and home for good.

The effect that welfare has on character is another source of contention. There are some, most notably Michael Harrington, John Kenneth Galbraith, and the U.S. Catholic bishops, who flatly deny that welfare has any bad side effects on character, but these voices are fast becoming a minority. To gauge the effects of welfare on character accurately, a few caveats are worth mentioning. First, there is a difference between noncontributory assistance, such as the welfare program, and contributory schemes, like Social Security. The former functions as a handout; the latter functions as a trust fund (at least as far as its effect on character is concerned). It is to be expected that when donor and recipient are one and the same, the concerns normally associated with welfare are moot.

Second, there is a difference between a welfare program that provides mostly noncash services, and one that directly offers the poor cash; a voucher system falls somewhere in between. It is the former system, the one we have now, that is the greatest cause for concern. Why? Because if people do not have to endure the burden of deciding how to spend their money, the disciplining effect that budgeting necessarily entails is lost. In other words, the all-important bourgeois value of self-restraint is undercut by eliminating one of the most important ways in which it is traditionally exercised. Extending in-kind relief to the poor assures their passivity, and with it, a dependent condition.

As has been repeatedly stated, when the need to practice self-restraint is lessened, prospects for antisocial behavior increase accordingly. It is not for nothing that teenage pregnancy, drugs, and violence are endemic in the welfare population. They are directly related to the absence of self-restraint, cultivated by a system that its defenders hail as social justice but that in effect promotes its opposite: social injustice.

It is the third caveat for assessing the effect that welfare has on the character of the recipient that is the most important: it is of monumental significance to discriminate between welfare programs that are interpreted as a privilege, and those understood as a right. The liabilities of the former are nothing compared to the disadvantages of the latter. Indeed, to make sense out of what has happened to the black family, and to appreciate what has been going on in the ghetto, primary consideration must be given to effects that the entitlement ethic has spawned.

Murray argues that it was between the years 1964 and 1967 that public policy objectives radically changed. It was during this "reform period," as he calls it, that the ethic of entitlement was born. Social policymakers pressed on blacks what was to become the dominant mantra of the ghetto: "It's not your fault."[17] Reflecting the power of the new freedom, welfare became a right, an entitlement to be insisted upon, instead of the privilege it had previously been. We are still living with the behavioral consequences of this ethos because it has yet to be rejected in toto.

When relief is interpreted as an entitlement, two status changes occur in the recipient: (a) he acquires newly awarded rights, allowing him to make claims on the earnings of others, and (b) he loses financial responsibility for himself, transferring that burden to the taxpayers. The net effect of this redistribution of rights and responsibilities is to nurture in the recipient an impoverished set of values: he learns to take, but not to give, expecting more from the community than he is willing to contribute. Not only are prospects for self-reliance dampened but the damage done to the social bond is incalculable.

In the end, what warps character most of all is not the sheer presence of being on the dole, it is the reasons that relief is sought in the first place that count. Those who are on the dole for relatively short periods of time—the majority at any given moment—are not the problem population. They seek relief out of need, as a means of tiding them over until unforeseen hardships pass. It is the long-term dependent poor who are the problem, and it is they who are most immobilized with the "It's-not-your-fault" mentality.

Another way of looking at it is this: twice in the twentieth century there has been a welfare explosion, once in the 1930s, and once in the 1960s. Only in the 1960s did the pathological conditions normally associated with public assistance evidence themselves. The difference is that those who sought relief in the 1930s did so for economic reasons; those who joined the dole in the 1960s did so mainly for political reasons. There was no "welfare rights" movement in the 1930s, even though 25 percent of the work force was unemployed. Significantly, there was one in the 1960s, even though the unemployment rate was only 3.5 percent (virtually no unemployment) at the start of the war on poverty (the figure for blacks was 4 percent).

Thanks to the efforts of the welfare rights establishment, the "It's-not-your-fault" attitude became pervasive in the ghetto. It would be difficult to think of a more disabling disease than this. It has done more to immobilize the resources of blacks than any other factor, including, certainly, the legacy of slavery. It, and not any structural defects in the economy, is what created the contemporary crisis in the black community.

If there is one area where there is increasing consensus among students of poverty, it is the conviction that indigence cannot be explained through economic analysis alone. Without addressing the norms, values, and behavioral patterns of the poor, students of poverty can make little progress in addressing present conditions. This is especially true when they study the underclass, the most recalcitrant segment of the poor.

The underclass constitutes the segment of the poor that has proven the least amenable to reform, whether it be in the nature of an expanding economy or government programs. Nothing, absolutely nothing, seems to affect it. Its members are largely illiterate, they have no work skills, no life skills of any sort. Self-restraint is so noticeably absent that it is perhaps their most defining characteristic. Two examples will suffice.

In 1984 New York City began the Young Fathers Program, an initiative designed to address the problems of unwed fatherhood. The program offers education, job training and placement, counseling, and virtually any other service that the young men request. It is a monumental failure. Of every hundred young fathers invited to an orientation session, only ten to fifteen show up on the average. And these represent the most-likely-to-succeed portion of the underclass: they were chosen because all have held jobs, have acknowledged paternity, and have in many cases had sustained relations with the mothers. Underclass women are just as hopeless: it is known that 40 percent of the women who weren't married when they began to receive welfare stay on the dole for ten years or more.

Ken Auletta, who has written a book on the subject, provides a graphic picture of this troubled population, effectively letting the underclass members and those who work with them, speak for themselves. Two aspects of underclass existence are revealed over and over again: the belief in entitlements, and the pervasiveness of the "It's-not-your-fault" mentality. As one member of the underclass said, "In a sense, welfare mentality is thinking you gonna get something for nothing."[18]

The "It's-not-your-fault" attitude, what columnist William Raspberry calls "victimism," is, in the words of Raspberry, devastating to young blacks: "There is no more crippling an attitude than to think yourself primarily as a victim. Victimism is a disease that blights our best-intended social programs . . . because it attacks the ability and the inclination of people to look after themselves. . . ."[19] Lawrence Mead, another astute student of the poor, agrees: "At the core of the culture of poverty is the conviction that one is not responsible for one's fate, what psychologists call inefficacy."[20]

It is this mind-set that must be changed if poverty is to be substantially reduced. Without doubt, the single most important cause of poverty in the United States is illegitimacy, a phenomenon itself caused by the crippled value structure that Raspberry mentioned. When young people are socialized to abandon both self-restraint and self-responsibility, there is little reason not to succumb to sexual temptation. The feminization of poverty that everyone deplores will not abate until the psychosocial dynamics that give rise to it are appreciated.

The role that constraints play in determining class is little understood. To be sure, the mere possession of self-restraint does not make one upwardly mobile, but it remains true that it is not possible to climb economically without its exercise (not legally, anyway). It is true, too, that many middle- and upper-class persons lack self-restraint, and they, as well as their families, suffer accordingly. The central point that needs to be made is that social constraints are necessary for mobility out of the lower class, and a public policy that does not address this issue is bound to be flawed.

Unfortunately, many of those most identified with understanding the plight of the poor often misinterpret the causes of poverty. When Dr. Kenneth B. Clark, one of the twentieth century's most noted students of the black poor, was asked in 1984 to explain the skyrocketing rates of illegitimacy among poor blacks, he confessed that he was "baffled," and then opined that it was largely due to the fact that "young people have practically nothing else to do."[21] Just as exasperating is Daniel Patrick Moynihan, another celebrated writer on the subject. Moynihan continues to resist the idea that the war on poverty triggered an increase in welfare dependency, family breakups, and illegitimacy. He laments the feminization of poverty, and is genuinely troubled by the increase in the proportion of children who make up the poverty statistics, but is without explanation why this should be so.[22]

It is not poverty, or even welfare, that causes illegitimacy, but the reverse; young unwed mothers go on welfare because it's available to them. Most don't plan to get pregnant so that welfare can be gotten, they get pregnant because they see little reason not to. To that extent, welfare plays a role, but its function is to reduce the penalties for irresponsibility; it does not *cause* people to act irresponsibly. The data tend to support this position. In a study of teenage pregnancy in Chicago, it was found that adolescent blacks reported far fewer unwanted pregnancies than their white peers. According to Dennis Hogan, the data suggest that "it is not so much that single motherhood is unwanted as it is that it is not sufficiently 'unwanted.' Women of all ages without a strong desire to prevent a birth tend to have limited contraceptive success."[23]

Although there is no one-to-one relationship between welfare and illegitimacy, it is also true that the two variables are not unrelated. For example, it is known that in the 1970s, real spending on welfare declined, as did the number of black children on Aid to Families with Dependent Children. However, during the same decade, there was an increase in the number of female-headed households, in illegitimacy rates, and in welfare rolls. In other words, more adolescent black girls got pregnant, went on welfare, and apparently decided against having another child. It is quite possible that the welfare system gave them little disincentive not to have the first child, but the inability of the benefit package to keep up with inflation had a sobering effect thereafter.[24]

Although it is still a matter of debate as to how welfare and poverty are related, the evidence is in on one important component of the relationship: when welfare is seen as a right, independent of any concomitant responsibilities, the effects on character are disastrous. This is nothing new. When England amended its Poor Law legislation to install the Speenhamland system in 1795, a system that established public assistance as a right, it took but a generation to discover what the system had wrought. By 1834 the law was reformed, having discoverd that the Speenhamland system "pauperized the poor."

Historian Gertrude Himmelfarb recounts what a government commission found at that time. Speenhamland destroyed independence, and "with that loss of independence came the familiar train of evils: the loss of self-respect, responsibility, prudence, temperance, hard work, and the other virtues that had once sustained [the poor]."[25] Alexis de Tocqueville uncovered the same phenomenon when he traveled about Europe in the mid-nineteenth century. Poor countries like Spain, which had no welfare, also had no paupers, no morally debased souls. But rich countries like England had plenty of paupers; it also had plenty of people on the dole.[26]

"The most vulnerable Americans," says Lawrence Mead, "need obligations, as much as rights, if they are to move as equals on the stage of American life."[27] And that is why workfare is a step in the right direction, though hardly a panacea. Others, such as Stuart Butler and Anna Kondratas,[28] are pointing the way out of the poverty trap with even more innovative ideas. These scholars recognize, as Harvard scholar Glen Loury surely does, that there is a major difference between fault and responsibility, that is, those who have created the problem are not always in a position to resolve it. As Loury has written, *"no people can be genuinely free so long as they look to others for their deliverance."*[29]

For a long time any discussion about the problems that inhered in the black family ran the risk of racist accusations. But in the 1980s, virtually every black organization has seen fit to address the issue, knowing full well that some will use the evidence against blacks for purely racist reasons. Regrettably, as long as there are racists, there will be those who will distort the truth, but the alternative to frank discussion is stasis, and that is not something the country can afford. Now that family issues and character questions can be discussed openly, there is a need to understand the psychological and social mechanics of poverty, and the problems attendant to it.

Howard Smith, one of the teachers of the underclass mentioned by Ken Auletta, hit on the principal reason that so many of his black brothers and sisters are in the condition they are in: "We have a generation of people coming up now with no family structures. The traditional institutions that taught them what was good and bad, church, schools, the family unit itself— there's an entire generation out there that has not had the benefits of family, church, school."[30] The same can be said of whites, rich or poor. Poor blacks have certainly fared the worst, but the problem identified by Smith is nation-wide, knowing no status boundaries of any kind.

The solidity of the family, just as Confucius said, is the key to social well-being. That the bourgeois family has been impaired is beyond dispute; even those who think the family is merely changing do not deny that it's changing *away* from its traditional form. But despite the many problems that the nuclear family is faced with, it is not likely to be eclipsed by another model. It is becoming increasingly apparent that the number of alternatives is really quite limited. The real question is whether consensus can be reached on the desirability of the nuclear family as the model social unit in society.

Everyone, or nearly everyone, is for strong families; few are for weak families. But not everyone wants to pay the price that is necessary to restore the family to its previous vigor. And that is because good families require greater submission of the individual to the collective interests of the family than most are prepared to bear. Indoctrinated with new-freedom thinking, it is difficult for most persons to see the social value of self-denial. We are so used to junking constraints, so accustomed to equating liberty with the absence of limits, that commitment, sacrifice, and compromise—the very heart of any long-lasting human relationship—become weighty and problematic.

A society that defines freedom the way we do—negatively, as freedom *from*—will inevitably come to think of the family as an obstacle to individual liberty. The family has always functioned as a source of constraint, that being one of its prime purposes. It is the duty of the family to introduce the individual into society, to integrate him into the social web. That takes work, and lots of it. And that is why attempts to portray the family as the enemy of freedom are ignorant of social reality. Worse than that, they are counter-productive to the process of freedom as well.

Notes

1. See the findings of a 1980 study, "The Most Significant Minority," conducted jointly by the National Association of Elementary School Principals and the education branch of the Charles Kettering Foundation. See also William Bennett, "The Importance of the Family to Society," a Family Research Council reprint of a June 1986 address by the Secretary of Education before the Fourth Annual Meeting of Networking Community Based Services, Washington, D.C. The most thorough report remains the volume by Irwin and Sara McLanahan, *Single Mothers and Their Children: A New American Dilemma* (Washington, D.C.: Urban Institute Press, 1986). Sara McLanahan received a $600,000 grant in 1988 from the National Institutes of Health to conduct further research on this subject, the results of which should shed greater light on the problem.
2. Urie Bronfenbrenner, "Alienation and the Four Walls of Childhood," *Phi Delta Kappan* (February 1986): 434.
3. Brigitte Berger and Peter Berger, *The War over the Family: Capturing the Middle Ground* (Garden City, N.Y.: Anchor Press, Doubleday, 1984), p. 59.
4. Congressman Miller debated the issue with Family Research Council President Jerry Regier. See "Miller, Regier Debate Family Issues," *Family Research Today* (July/August 1987): 1.
5. William J. Gribbin, "The Family in Public Policy," *Journal of Family and Culture* (Spring 1985): 29.
6. Allan C. Carlson, "Families, Sex, and the Liberal Agenda," *Public Interest* (Winter 1980): 72.
7. Michael Novak, *The Spirit of Democratic Capitalism* (New York: Simon and Schuster, 1982), p. 168.

8. Berger and Berger, *The War over the Family*, p. 172.
9. Joseph A. Schumpeter, *Capitalism, Socialism and Democracy* (New York: Harper, Torchback, 1962), p. 160.
10. George Gilder, *Wealth and Poverty* (New York: Bantam Books, 1981), p. 94.
11. Reginald M. Clark, *Family Life and School Achievement* (Chicago: University of Chicago Press, 1983), pp. 120–21, 125; see also p. 200.
12. Travis Hirschi, *Causes of Delinquency* (Berkeley: University of California Press, 1969).
13. Herbert G. Gutman, *The Black Family in Slavery and Freedom, 1750–1925* (New York: Vintage Books, 1977).
14. Eugene D. Genovese, *Roll, Jordan, Roll* (New York: Pantheon, 1974).
15. Charles Murray, *Losing Ground* (New York: Basic Books, 1984), pp. 167–68.
16. George Gilder, *Visible Man* (New York: Basic Books, 1978).
17. Murray, *Losing Ground*, pp. 24–25, 191.
18. Ken Auletta, *The Underclass*, (New York: Vintage Books, 1982), p. 60.
19. Ibid.; the Raspberry quotation appears on p. 38.
20. Lawrence Mead, "Jobs for the Welfare Poor," *Policy Review* (Winter 1988): 66.
21. Quoted by Joseph Berger, "Unwed Mothers Accounting for Third of New York Births," *New York Times*, August 13, 1984, p. B4.
22. Daniel Patrick Moynihan, *Family and Nation* (New York: Harcourt Brace Jovanovich, 1987), p. 69 and *passim*.
23. Quoted by William Julius Wilson, *The Truly Disadvantaged* (Chicago: University of Chicago Press, 1987), p. 73.
24. The literature in this area is rich and complex. See especially: David Ellwood and Mary Jo Bane, "The Impact of AFDC on Family Structures and Living Arrangements" (Washington, D.C.: U.S. Department of Health and Human Services, 1984); David Ellwood and Lawrence Summers, "Is Welfare Really the Problem?" *Public Interest* (Spring 1986): 57–78; Charles Murray, "How to Lie with Statistics," *National Review*, February 28, 1986, pp. 39–41 (see also, "Erratum," in the March 28, 1985 issue, p. 20; Gregory Christiansen and Walter Williams, "Welfare, Family Cohesiveness, and Out-of-Wedlock Births," in Joseph Peden and Fred Glahe, eds., *The American Family and the State* (San Francisco: Pacific Research Institute for Public Policy, 1986), pp. 381–424.
25. Gertrude Himmelfarb, *The Idea of Poverty* (New York: Knopf, 1984), pp. 162–63.
26. Alexis de Tocqueville, "Memoir on Pauperism," *Public Interest* (Winter 1983): 102–20.
27. Lawrence Mead, *Beyond Entitlements: The Social Obligations of Citizenship* (New York: Free Press, 1986), p. 17.
28. Stuart Butler and Anna Kondratas, *Out of the Poverty Trap* (New York: Free Press, 1987).
29. Glenn C. Loury, "The Moral Quandary of the Black Community," *Public Interest* (Spring 1985): 11.
30. Quoted by Auletta in *The Underclass*, p. 67.

12

The Role of the Schools

The production of morally responsible individuals can never be the job of the family alone. Other institutions must be actively engaged as well. The role of the schools is central, insofar as it is to the schools that much of the teaching of norms and values is entrusted. It stands to reason that if the schools become disabled, the shock waves will be felt far beyond the domain of scholarship. Literacy can be restored relatively easily; good character cannot.

There is by now abundant evidence that the schools are in trouble. In the 1980s one report after another has been issued detailing the poor condition of the public schools. From the much-celebrated report "A Nation at Risk," we learned that American students ranked last among twenty-one industrial nations on seven of nineteen academic tests. Some 13 percent of all seventeen-year-olds, and better than 40 percent of minority youth, are functionally illiterate. Illiteracy in mathematics and science is particularly bad, and when the subject switches to history and literature, the results don't get any better. Knowledge of elementary geography is so bad that James Vining, director of the National Council for Geographic Education, has said, "We have a situation where Johnny not only doesn't know how to read or add, he doesn't even know where he is."[1]

That's not all of it. The decline in academic performance has been accompanied by a decline in manners and morals, as the incidence of teenage pregnancy and violence in the schools makes clear. Reports of teachers, as well as students, who have been beaten, robbed, and raped—although not a daily occurrence—are nonetheless more prevalent now than at any time in our history; some schools are no more safe than the streets on which they are situated. Drugs are commonplace, in rich as well as poor neighborhoods, and the data on alcohol abuse are not encouraging. To top it off, the number of incompetent teachers, as judged by the easiest of tests, is shocking, and the quality of college graduates going into the education profession is a disgrace.

The recommendations of the many reports issued on the schools have centered on matters of curricula and teacher effectiveness. The National Commission on Excellence in Education said that "the rising tide of mediocrity" that threatens American education can be reversed by doing such things as tightening standards, developing a core curriculum of academic courses for all students, assigning more homework, and raising teacher salaries. The Twentieth Century Fund Task Force focused on the establishment of a master-teacher program, one that would financially reward excellence in teaching; it also recommended that mastery of English be given priority, arguing that federal funds for bilingual programs be used only for teaching English to non-English-speaking students.

The Carnegie Foundation for the Advancement of Teaching, under the leadership of Ernest Boyer, has turned out three reports: one on secondary education, one on higher education, and one on the status of urban schools. High schools, Boyer said, need to clarify their goals, pay more attention to English, develop a core of academic courses, lighten teacher load, and reward teacher excellence. He urged the colleges and universities to rethink the emphasis on careerism and to restructure curricula toward a more defined liberal arts orientation. These ideas found support from such authorities as the National Institute of Education and the Association of American Colleges.

The problem with the urban schools, Boyer contended, was that they were largely untouched by the reform movement of the early 1980s. He urged greater accountability and, reflecting the influence of an earlier report by John Goodlad, called for building smaller schools, capping enrollment around five hundred students; the anonymity of large schools has clearly had a negative effect on academic achievement and discipline.

A report issued by education specialist Theodore Sizer stressed basic skills, teacher autonomy, and greater teacher accountability for the performance of students. Once high school students have proven to be literate in English and math, Sizer concluded, they should no longer be required to stay in school. Philosopher Mortimer Adler's Paideia Group called for extensive reform, with all students assigned to a single track, allowing of no electives (save choice of foreign language); courses should be selected from the traditional liberal arts areas. Adler's contribution is perhaps the most tightly woven proposal of all the reports on the schools.

The common assumption that undergirds these recommendations is that the key to better education is more student exposure to quality educational opportunities. It assumes that test scores, as well as other measures of educational success, will increase once a core group of traditional academic courses are offered by highly trained and motivated teachers. No doubt these aspects of reform would go a long way to improving the schools. But at best these reforms address only half the problem.

Better curricula and better teachers do not, by themselves, make for better students. Curricula and teachers are to education what training and coaches are to sports: they constitute program development, properties that are necessary but not sufficient conditions for success. For success to be achieved, something must be done to insure that the individuals who are subjected to quality programs are themselves able and willing to benefit from these opportunities. And that means that character development must be stressed as much as program development; if the requisite personal traits that make for success are lacking, all the techniques and instructors in the world won't make a young person a good student or a good athlete.

The kinds of personal traits that are necessary for success in school are the same ones necessary for success in any endeavor, be it on the playing field or in the office: hard work, determination, sustained effort, practice, and so on. Yet as obvious as this should be, many educators still undervalue the role that character development plays in determining academic achievement. That is why they concentrate their time on program development, concocting new teaching techniques and the like. It's as if the recipient of their innovations, namely, the student, will somehow take to whatever it is that's offered. But as we should have learned by now, if students don't possess the kinds of character qualities that allow for progress, it is not likely that being exposed to even the most effective pedagogical resources will make much of a difference.

There are some educators, like former Secretary of Education William Bennett, who clearly understand the relationship between character development and academic achievement. Bennett has consistently emphasized the importance of "the three C's," namely, content, character, and choice [of schools]. It needs to be said that good personal skills are not only critical to learning but important to the maintenance of discipline in the classroom as well. Indeed, the problems of the schools in general—poor academic performance, teenage pregnancy, violence, and drugs—are ultimately a reflection, if only in part, of flawed character development. It is to this aspect of education that attention must be given if progress is to be achieved.

The really good schools, and there are many of them, play close attention to character development. A good school can be defined, in part, as a place where the values of self-discipline and hard work are consistently nurtured by both teachers and administrators. Studying is not possible without sustained effort, and that is not a quality that most of us just happen to possess. It needs to be demanded of us regularly, and induced through daily routines. Experience shows that holding students to high standards is perhaps the best way to inculcate desirable character traits. The evidence is pretty clear on this matter, as a look at the best schools in the country supports. Not surprisingly, the same traits appear in Japanese schools, arguably the best in the world.

We have known since the 1960s that money, teacher credentials, quality of learning facilities, and student-teacher ratio are not the key variables explaining academic achievement. That was one of the major findings of the Coleman Report (formally known as "Equality of Educational Opportunity"), a comprehensive study of the schools conducted by a team of researchers led by University of Chicago sociologist James S. Coleman. The evidence collected since that time is supportive of Coleman. For example, between 1960 and 1980, the amount of money spent per student each year more than doubled in constant dollars. The average class size shrank considerably, and the percentage of teachers with master's degrees rose from one-quarter to one-half. Yet SAT scores dropped by eighty five points during those years.

Further support for the Coleman Report's findings can be ascertained from educational data collected by the states. New Hampshire typically has the highest average SAT scores of any state, yet ranks in the bottom half in expenditures per pupil. In terms of graduation rates, a state like South Dakota, which ranks eighth on this measure, is forty-second in expenditures per pupil and dead last in average teacher salary. On the other hand, the District of Columbia has the worst graduation rate in the country, but is near the top of the chart on both expenditures per pupil (second only to Alaska) and teacher salaries (fourth overall). Money, then, is not the great elixir.

The Coleman Report's basic conclusion was that the quality of the family that a child was reared in proved to be a major determinant of educational success. In other words, it was the resources that a child took to school, and not what he acquired in the classroom, that seemed to matter most. Other researchers later came to similar conclusions, including those who, like Christopher Jencks, were not ideologically disposed to accepting such findings.

And what individual traits seemed to matter most? Coleman found that the strongest single determinant of academic achievement was self-responsibility. The students who took responsibility for their performance, although more burdened than those who did not, were also more autonomous and more successful.[2] Obviously, the schools that actively sought to develop self-responsibility had a better track record than those that did not. But as good as a particular school might be, nothing could quite substitute for the primacy of the family.

Twenty years after the Coleman Report was issued, the U.S. Department of Education released a study entitled "What Works: Research about Teaching and Learning." It underscored Coleman's emphasis on the family, maintaining even further that it was not the income level of the family that mattered most; it was what parents actually did to help their children academically that was of unsurpassed significance. Schools did matter, the report said, and those that did the most effective job were the ones that had a safe and orderly environment, stressed daily homework, had high expectations of students, and held them to rigorous standards of accountability.[3]

In 1987 the Department of Education issued a sequel to its "What Works" report, this time focusing on the needs of disadvantaged students. Its recommendations included such things as building character and instilling the values of hard work, self-discipline, and self-responsibility. Building character and teaching values, the report stressed, is every teacher's business, not just those assigned to teach specialized courses. By doing such things as giving students responsibilities and insisting on daily homework, teachers help to develop in students such habits as persistence and self-control, thus enabling them to do better in school and ultimately in life. Accountability is critical, for when students are trained to assess the future consequences of their behavior, such problems as teenage pregnancy, drugs, and dropping out of school are minimized.[4]

Many of the same conclusions are evident when comparisons are made between private and public schools. As sociologists like Andrew Greeley and others have long maintained, the relative success of Catholic schools, especially when compared to their public school counterparts in ghetto neighborhoods, is largely a function of the demands that parochial schools place on their students. A 1981 study published by the National Center for Education Statistics confirmed Greeley's research. On the basis of data from tests given to nearly sixty thousand high school students in over one thousand schools, the study, conducted by James S. Coleman, Thomas Hoffer, and Sally Kilgore, found that the reason that the average public school did not do as good a job as the average private school (many of them Catholic) was due to the lack of an orderly environment, relatively easy demands placed on students, and absence of school spirit.

With regard to Catholic schools in particular, Coleman found that students did better than their public school peers in math, vocabulary, and reading comprehension. Catholic schools also insisted on more discipline, and dispensed with it in a fairer manner than was true of public schools. The overall level of problems, as reported either by students or principals, was much less in the Catholic schools. This clearly accounts for the dramatic increase of non-Catholic enrollment in Catholic schools in recent years, especially in ghetto areas. In fact, in many of the Catholic schools in ghetto neighborhoods the majority of the students are now non-Catholic. Parents are investing in better education and stricter discipline.[5]

There is no mystery as to why Catholic school students do better: (a) more is demanded of them, and (b) the overall climate of discipline is conducive to learning. Indeed, as anyone who has ever attended a Catholic school will confirm, compared to the average public school, the Catholic school's teachers typically have fewer credentials, its classes are larger, its facilities are inferior, and the amount it spends per pupil is small. With regard to finances, in fact, without candle and cookie sales, bingo, and the like, many would simply not survive at all. As Coleman found, good schools, whether they be public or private, have in common what good Catholic schools have: "Schools which impose strong academic demands, schools which make demands on attendance and on behavior of students while they are in school are, according to these results, schools which bring about higher achievement."[6]

Perhaps the most revealing aspect of the study done by Coleman and his associates was the analysis of the data by Amitai Etzioni, a distinguished sociologist at George Washington University. Etzioni secured access to the computer tapes of the Coleman study and, after careful analysis, concluded that self-discipline was the variable that most prominently figured in accounting for academic success. It was the internal attitudes and motivations of students, Etzioni said, that best explained school performance. That is why he recommended that more homework be given to students: it nurtured self-discipline. Just as important, Etzioni said, was prompt and detailed feedback on homework assignments; teachers, as well as students, need to be held accountable.[7]

What all this boils down to is what Barbara Lerner aptly calls "the hard work variable." To be specific, Lerner says that an analysis of the research literature consistently reveals that four factors are central to good school performance: amount of homework; amount of class time spent directly on relevant school work; frequency of class attendance; and textbook demand levels.[8] None of these factors, it should be noted, costs a great deal of money to implement. It is commitment, not money, that spells the difference.

Further proof that "the hard work variable" is the key to academic achievement can be found by studying the tremendous success of Japanese education. Merry White, in her splendid book *The Japanese Educational Challenge: A Commitment to Children*, details the role that hard work and character development play in accounting for the unparalleled success of Japanese education. Mothers are dedicated to instilling the value of self-discipline in their children and do not hesitate to place strong demands on them. Mothers typically work at home, attending to their children's needs, offering "quality time" all day long, and not just for half an hour after supper. Moreover, the culture supports the kinds of constraints that allow for success and reinforces self-discipline through a variety of social techniques.

The Japanese schools are goal-oriented. In the lower grades, White reports, children learn to bear hardships and to behave unselfishly. Once in the middle grades, they learn to persist to the end with patience and to live a life of moderation. Learning to be steadfast and to live an orderly life is emphasized in the upper grades. This is part of the moral education program that all

Japanese children experience. Hardship, White informs, is not only accept-able to Japanese culture but extolled: "Hardship builds character, which is not innate, and anyone, the Japanese believe, can acquire the habit and virtue of self-discipline."[9]

It should be obvious by now that self-discipline and "the hard work variable" are strongly related to academic achievement. It should be equally obvious why American schools are in trouble: our culture nourishes habits and values that are directly contradictory to the very qualities that make for success. Quite simply, the new-freedom appeal to self-indulgence works to undermine the social basis of academic excellence. It is just not possible to import the value of sustained effort in a culture hell-bent on immediate gratification and the abandonment of constraint. By fixing our eyes exclu-sively on the merits of unburdening the individual, we find it culturally impossible to comprehend the Japanese celebration of hardship. We pay a heavy social price for our idea of freedom, one that shortchanges us in many ways.

It was the education elite, not parents, principals, or teachers, who adopted the ethos of the new freedom and turned the schools upside down. What makes the story so tragic is that the radical reforms that took place in the 1960s were so unnecessary. In the two decades that followed World War II, SAT scores and other measures of academic achievement improved steadily. Elementary codes of conduct were regularly followed and problems of drugs and violence were mild compared to the near-out-of-control situation that exists in many schools today. Then, about midway through the decade, a series of untested assumptions and unrealistic theories were put into practice, devastating the progress that had been made and turning the clock backward on an entire generation of students.

The score is in on this one: progressive education, as interpreted since the 1960s, has yielded regressive results. Traditional education, with its emphasis on daily homework, structured learning, and discipline in the classroom, has delivered far more progress than progressive education ever hoped to achieve. And if further proof is needed, consider the results of an Abt survey con-ducted in 1977 for the U.S. Office of Education. A total of 9,200 third graders were divided into two groups: one was taught the traditional way, with highly structured lessons and lots of homework; the other was subjected to the progressive ideal of "informal and innovative" techniques, representative of the "open-classroom" ideal. Tested after three years, the traditional approach won hands down, and at a lower cost than its progressive rival.

It is results like this that have prompted educators like Theodore Black to sound the alarm on the liabilities of progressive education. Black, an eleven-year veteran of the New York State Board of Regents, the last as its chancel-lor, has seen firsthand the different outcomes that the two opposing strategies yield. For him, the results of the Abt survey prove what should be common knowledge among educators but sadly is not: competition, self-restraint, and accomplishment produce better educated students than egalitarianism, self-expression and test-bashing. "Modernism," he says, has typically led to a deterioration in quality wherever it has succeeded in supplanting traditional education.[10]

What has happened, as Joseph Adelson has said, is that both civility and competence declined once authority was attacked. "The loss of authority is felt most strongly," he says, "at the secondary-school level, and its effects are seen most clearly in the area of discipline." But the effects, he adds, go even deeper than this: "The weakened authority of teachers and principals also led to a weakening of academic demands."[11] And we have seen what happens when "the hard work variable" is not in force.

It was the radical reformers of the 1960s who junked "the hard work variable" and led the attack on authority. Those who brought the new freedom to the schools were the proud intellectual descendants of John Dewey. The highly structured approach that the traditional education model espouses was declared—without supporting evidence—to be unfit. Following Dewey, the new-freedom advocates sought to usher in a neoprogressive agenda, one featuring "open education" and undirected learning. But in fairness to Dewey, the education gurus of the 1960s went far beyond anything he counseled. They took his ideas to extremes and thereby corrupted any value they might have had.

Dewey fairly criticized the often taut and antiindividualistic approach of traditional education. By concentrating so heavily on structure, the methodology of traditional education helped to stifle individual creativity and to bore many students, especially the brighter ones. Dewey sought to open things up a bit and move away from the mechanical-skills approach so commonly employed. Throughout his work, he maintained a serious, realistic stance, quite unlike the utopian visionaries of the 1960s. Dewey was content to be a reformer; his new-freedom heirs wanted nothing less than revolutionary politics, played out in the theater of the nation's classrooms.

Perhaps the most important difference between Dewey and the radical reformers of the 1960s was the way in which they defined freedom. For Dewey, "freedom from restriction . . . is to be prized only as a means to a freedom which is power: power to frame purposes, to judge wisely, to evaluate desires by the consequences which will result from acting upon them; power to select and order means to carry chosen ends into operation." As to the proper meaning of freedom, Dewey said, "The only freedom that is of enduring importance is freedom of intelligence, that is to say, freedom of observation and of judgment exercised in behalf of purposes that are intrinsically worth while." And the purpose of education was clear: "The ideal aim of education is creation of power of self-control."[12]

New-freedom educators not only did not share these ideals but explicitly rejected them and actively worked against them in practice. For them, freedom from external constraint was not a means to an end, it was an end in itself. The new-freedom approach to education was essentially nihilistic, and that is why very few of the self-styled radical reformers had much interest in promoting a conception of freedom that served inherently good purposes. And it was self-expression, not self-control, that they valued.

One of the most tenaciously held beliefs of the radical reformers was, and still is for many new-freedom eduators, the conviction that the schools are oppressive institutions. Charles Silberman, one the most respected new-freedom students of education, helped set the tone of the discussion by maintaining that most Americans were ignorant as to the despotic quality of the public schools. He lampooned Americans for failing to appreciate "what grim, joyless places most American schools are, how oppressive and petty are the rules by which they are governed," and so on. What was it that he found so offensive? The answer: the practice of insisting on peace and quiet in the classroom. Silberman berated teachers for being "obsessed" with peace and quiet, charging that such concerns were "unnatural."[13]

Charles Reich came to the same conclusion as Silberman, arguing that the sheer existence of classroom rules proved that teacher authority was "in the purest sense lawless." He said students were no more free than prisoners in a penitentiary, and maintained that "an examination or test is a form of violence."[14] Jonathan Kozol, the well-known social critic and former teacher, opined that all students were subjected to a certain "intellectual and custodial Hell within the public schools." Kozol called for change, sponsoring the Free School movement, but was quick to warn that reform should not be limited to white rich kids from rural areas, likening such a prospect as being "a great deal too much like a sandbox for the children of the SS Guards at Auschwitz."[15] It is this kind of hysteria that makes any comparison with Dewey seem unthinkable.

The ideas of the new freedom—that anything that constrains is necessarily bad—permeated the writings of the radical reformers. Their vision of reality was so affected by new-freedom consciousness that had the average person actually read what they said, the most logical conclusion would have been that these people are delirious. For example, most people believe in compulsory education, on the grounds that if a child is deprived of schooling by neglectful parents, he will forever be disabled. But educator John Holt concluded that this was the same as saying, "If you don't go to school, we are going to put you in jail—a real jail with bars on it." Yes, he thought the analogy was just that close.

Most people understand that in the course of going to school, a selection process of sorts takes place, as young men and women find a match between their abilities and aspirations. For Holt, this quite natural process is nothing more than "meat stamping." What about the perfectly normal practice of teaching students values, including the value of patriotism? Holt objects, screaming "indoctrination."[16] In other words, such perennial functions of the schools as socialization, selection and allocation of human resoures, and social control are all seen as being hostile to freedom and destructive to the mission of education.

So what should we do? According to Free School enthusiast Allen Graubard, we need to develop a "libertarian pedagogy," one that will contribute to the larger process of building "a truly humane and liberating social order."[17] And where should we look for inspiration? To the work of English educator A. S. Neill. Neill's Summerhill school was widely touted by new-freedom thinkers of the sixties and seventies as a place where freedom without repression reigned. Neill hated authority of any kind, and that is why he insisted on participatory democracy in his school, holding, for example, that if students wanted to use profanity, they had a perfect right to do so. Reflecting the sentimentalism of the times, Neill believed that love was all that children needed to set them free.

One of the working assumptions of these writers is the belief that everyone quite naturally wants to learn, and were it not for the methods of traditional education, everyone would. Psychologist Carl Rogers, for instance, spoke for many when he confessed, "I become very irritated with the notion that students must be 'motivated.' The young human being is intrinsically motivated to a high degree."[18] Ergo, there is no good reason that a student should ever be bored or dislike school. If such a situation does arise, it is proof not of any defect in the student but in the teacher or the school. The whole notion of self-directed learning assumes this to be true, holding as it does to a quixotic picture of the human condition.

Some of the most specific suggestions to overhaul the schools came from Herbert Kohl. Kohl developed a guide for teachers, instructing them on the merits of the "open classroom." His how-to approach includes such advice as doing away with the practice of assigning seats to students, allowing school kids to hang their coats wherever they choose, abolishing the requirement that students should raise their hands before asking questions, ending the tradition of lining up before entering or exiting the building, and doing away with prohibitions against talking in class, chewing gum, and wearing sloppy clothes. As far as instruction was concerned, Kohl said that students should be taught such things as "conventional" spelling, but that "once they know about the rules of uniform spelling, they should be free to accept or modify them as they please."[19]

Neil Postman and Charles Weingartner implored teachers to subvert openly the tenets of traditional education, and even offered ways in which this goal might be achieved. Included in their recipe for action were such nuggets of advice as teaching without textbooks; having students learn from teachers not trained in the field in which they are teaching; fining teachers twenty-five cents if they used more than three declarative sentences per class; limiting teachers to asking only those questions they know they cannot answer; making every class an elective; requiring all graffiti accumulated in school lavatories to be reproduced on large paper and hung in the school halls; and banning the use of such terms as *teach, syllabus, I.Q., makeup, test, disadvantaged, gifted, accelerated, course, grade, score, human nature, and dumb*.[20]

It might be objected that such absurd notions as these would never be taken seriously by educators. Wrong. The praise heaped on these savants came from the most respected, mainstream institutions and critics in the country—from the experts at Ivy League colleges to the education specialists at the *New York Times*. No, most schools did not implement some of the sillier proposals that were made, but collectively the new-freedom educators had the effect of discrediting the value of traditional education and substituting in its place some ersatz version of their own offerings.

All of the reform efforts, be they called "free school," "open classroom," "alternative education," or the "deschooling movement," had in common certain presuppositions governing the worth and value of American society. "None of these movements," writes Diane Ravitch, "was isolated from the others; they shared certain assumptions about the failure of the existing public schools, the corruptness of American society, and the need to adopt radical changes in school and society."[21] Ravitch is exactly correct: it is impossible to understand the mentality of those who wrecked the schools without referencing the profound contempt they had for American society. It was alienation from society, coupled with utopian visions of a new social order, that energized their thoughts and fueled the movement.

If there was one flaw that both Dewey and the new-freedom educators of the 1960s and 1970s had in common it was their unwarranted assumption that most students came equipped with a minimum level of self-discipline. Dewey's oversight was somewhat more understandable, given the many social and cultural inducements to self-discipline that existed in the first half of the century; it was more natural that he would take self-discipline for granted. But the radical reformers in the second half of the century should have known better; a "libertarian pedagogy," if it can work at all, must have as a base a society wherein self-discipline is carefully nurtured. The 1960s was not such a time, as should have been evident to everyone.

The curriculum reformers not only took self-discipline for granted but did much to undermine its development. But it was the other wing of new-freedom educators—the ones dedicated to students' rights—that made discipline of any kind almost impossible to achieve. Much, though certainly not all, of the breakdown in discipline in the schools is an outgrowth of moving the rights movement into the classroom.

Beginning in the 1960s, proponents of children's rights made the seemingly innocuous case that students are human beings like everyone else, and are therefore entitled to the entire panoply of rights extended under the Constitution. Rights advocates worked hard to remove what they saw as the second-class status of students, and found cause for celebration in *Tinker v. Des Moines*. It was in that 1969 decision that the Supreme Court proclaimed that students do not "shed their constitutional rights to freedom of speech or expression at the schoolhouse gate." Though the high court has more recently taken a less expansive interpretation of the Constitution as it applies to students, it cannot easily undo the social effects of decisions like *Tinker, Gault, Winship*, and *Goss*, cases that in one way or another extended due process rights to students.

The fundamental problem with extending rights to students is that it inevitably becomes a zero-sum operation because every gain in students' rights must result in a proportionate loss of rights to principals and teachers. The net social effect of this redistribution of rights is a decline in both teacher authority and principal autonomy. This outcome is not lost on students, as many begin to sense that teachers have limited rule, meaning, naturally, that the cost for misbehavior diminishes with every new round of court-awarded rights. But if it can be said that this is a zero-sum exercise in rights distribution, it surely is a net overall loss to the goals of education because both students and teachers lose. And no one loses more than students.

No student can learn without a modicum of order in the classroom, and for this to be achieved, teachers must have the authority to maintain it. It is not easy to see how this can be done when the right to punish a student for misbehavior has been called into question, subjected to scrutiny by the court, and ultimately made into a rebuttable presumption. The greatest irony of all is that in the name of rights, students have a hard time learning anything, including learning how to read and write at a minimal level, thereby depriving them of taking full advantage of their First Amendment right to freedom of speech.

A California study demonstrates the changing nature of discipline problems in the schools. In the 1940s the most common complaints centered on such things as talking, chewing gum, running in the hallways, getting out of place in line, and not putting paper in the wastebaskets. In the 1980s the most common complaints centered on such things drug abuse, pregnancy, suicide, rape, robbery, and assault.[22] The difference: in the 1940s students came to school more well-behaved than they do today, the authority of teachers was more widely respected, and principals had more control over disciplinary procedures. The new freedom changed all that, relaxing constraints on young people and stripping authority and autonomy from teachers and principals.

Gerald Grant, a sociologist who has conducted his own field studies in this area, maintains that "the new adversarial and legalistic character of urban public schools" would be the most noticeable change "to an observer who had not visited a public school since the mid-1960s." The bottom line, he says, is "a shift of profound dimensions" as "adult authority is increasingly defined by what will stand up in court."[23] Again, students are not unaware that the tide has shifted their way, and that is why the most reckless among them exploit their "rights" to the hilt.

By teaching students they have rights but not responsibilities, new-freedom lawyers, judges, and educators have literally perfected a blueprint for flawed character development. To give one instance, beginning in 1980 students in the Boston public schools received a twenty-five-page pamphlet called "The Book." In it they learned all about their rights, culled from such sources as the ACLU, but practically nothing about their responsibilities (there were eleven lines of type devoted to this side).[24] Now, young people being young people, what lesson in morality are they likely to draw from "The Book"? Have they been given an incentive to conform to the rules of classroom decorum, or have they been presented with a case for challenging rules that strike them as disagreeable?

The problem of discipline in the schools is not wholly the result of the rights-without-responsibilities craze. It is due to something much larger: it is due to the new-freedom's fixation on moral neutrality as the governing ethos in society. It reflects, at bottom, a crisis of confidence, an uneasiness with the defense of the dominant norms and values of American society. The problem is that many new-freedom educators have psychologically divorced themselves from American society, thus making it impossible to endorse programs designed to defend the moral worth of the social order. The consequences of this alienation are still with us, and show no signs of abating.

It would be wrong to suggest that most of today's teachers and administrators are alienated from society, or that they are not committed to its defense. But it is nonetheless true that most of them are still reluctant to accept their duty as moral educators, influenced as they have been by new-freedom thinkers. Yet from the ancient Greeks down to recent times, it has been a staple of the schools to provide moral education.

The notion that a young person should not be trained for citizenship—to accept obligations to the community—is an outgrowth of 1960s excess, an idea so bizarre as to be outside the historical parameters of discourse on education. The purpose of the schools has always been, first and foremost, instruction in morality. A school that turned out academically prepared but morally underdeveloped students would historically have been judged a failure. Until the advent of the new freedom, that is.

Whether or not virtue can be taught is still debatable, but what is not debatable is that most people think it should be. Traditionally, it has been true that most parents want the schools to teach virtue, with the expectation that what is being taught in the classroom is consistent with what is being taught at home. No one contends that the schools can be an adequate substitute for the authority of the family, but few will deny that teachers can play a supporting role to that of parents. At the center of the controversy is not whether teachers can assist in teaching virtue, it is the proposition that they should refrain from doing so altogether.

"To suggest that a society lacks the right to teach children the basic morality on which its very existence depends," notes philosopher Andrew Oldenquist, "is tantamount to suggesting that it has no right to exist."[25] How true. Oldenquist reminds us that there is nothing exceptional about a people teaching its morality and culture to its young. Indeed, quite the contrary; it is the exception to the rule—in defiance of all the anthropological literature—to find a society determined to deprive its members of its heritage and mores. Yet this is what new-freedom educators have sought to do. They do not want to allow the schools to act as cultural depositories of American norms and values.

The standard new-freedom response to the question of teaching values in the schools is that not everyone agrees on what values should be taught; therefore, all that should be done is to allow teachers to facilitate students in the clarification of their values. But to insist on a standard of unanimity is to obscure the issue. There is consensus, a general agreement, on what values should be taught, and that is all that is needed. How many people, for example, would protest that it is wrong to teach students the values of hard work, self-discipline, honesty, fidelity, and so on? Not many, as even those who dissent must admit.

Those who insist on the "value-neutral" approach hold a deep-seated hostility to traditional authority. They assert, without offering any proof, that traditional religious and cultural norms and values have proved to be unsatisfactory in modern societies. Of course, the same people who commonly make such pronouncements think it a good thing that it is illegal for teachers to lead their students in prayer. So what do they offer? A "value-neutral" approach that seeks to help students clarify their values.

Should teachers begin a class in values clarification by informing their students that the Judaeo-Christian tradition, of which they are a part, holds to a core set of moral values, or should teachers just allow the boys and girls to state whatever values come to mind, and then help them to clarify those values? The latter is the prescribed course of action. What if students ask for help by asking their teachers what values they hold? According to the Sidney Simon school of values, the teacher should say nothing, unless such questions come at the end of the exercise. At that point, "the teacher should present himself as a person with values (and often with values confusion) of his own.''[26] He can then share his values, confusion and all, with his students, making sure, however, to state that his values are no better than anyone else's.

It would be interesting to see how these students, indoctrinated as they have been with the doctrine of moral neutrality, would respond to the same teacher, who, in a history class, were to say that slavery is evil. To begin with, would a teacher who taught the Simon method be likely to make such a "value judgment" in the first place? If so, what moral authority could he summon if a student challenged him? Having just told the students in a values clarification class that all values are morally equal, how could he now start by making exceptions? More important, why should anyone bother to listen?

The new freedom emphasis on individual rights is also evident in the value-neutral approach. Lawrence Kohlberg, in particular, was quite fond of insisting that moral claims could be impartially resolved by considering individual rights. Like Simon, Kohlberg came to the question of values formation and maturation from a decidedly asocial position. Traditional figures of authority—parents, teachers, clergy, and police officers—carried no special weight with Kohlberg. What Kohlberg tried to do was to assess the merit of moral claims wholly outside the real world context of social roles and status groupings. Whatever the philosphical value of such a method, it is sociologically suspect, thereby stripping it of useful purposes.

To get an appreciation for how the values-clarification approach plays itself out in real life, consider its application in sex education classes. Ever since values clarification became the predominant orientation in sex education, there has been no shortage of textbooks and teachers' guides aimed at teaching moral neutrality. As Jacqueline Kasun's analysis of the literature shows,[27] one of the most popularly used books explicitly states that "we must finish the contemporary sex revolution . . . . our society must strive to sanction and support various forms of intimacy between members of the same sex." Another widely used text advises first-grade teachers to lead their students on a mixed-group "bathroom tour," the purpose of which is to acquaint boys and girls with the proper names for male and female genital parts.

Other exercises favored by the values-clarification approach to sex education include dividing the class into boy-girl pairs so that they can work on "physiology definition sheets." In this session, high school students are instructed to define such terms as "foreplay," "erection," "ejaculation," and so on. Included in the curriculum is the recommendation that teachers should encourage students to discuss whether they are satisfied with the size of their sex organs. To what end it is not clear, for those who feel cheated are apparently left without solace, counsel, or hope.

Perhaps the most offensive aspect to using the model of values clarification in sex education classes is that it purports to be value free. Nothing could be further from the truth. By instructing students to make up their own minds regarding the moral worth of premarital sex, abortion, adultery, sodomy, and so on, teachers are imposing a value judgment on them, leading students to the conclusion that it is perfectly acceptable to ignore the tenets of established religions, community standards, and social norms. Such a value preference has defined behavioral consequences as young people resolve to follow their own dictates, guided more by passion than by wisdom.

The American people have made it clear that they do not want sex education shorn of moral values. Indeed, seven in ten want abstinence to be stressed. Yet organizations like Planned Parenthood continue to support relaxed sexual mores and openly reject traditional moral standards.[28] And some sex education experts have now gone beyond the values-clarification strategy by implicitly sanctioning promiscuity. For example, in the "Pennsylvania Health Curriculum Guide" prepared by that state's Department of Education, the following is one of the questions that students are asked: "Is sexual abstinence beneficial to a person's health, strength, wisdom or character?" The right answer, as the students quickly learn, is no.[29]

When students are told by their teachers, in defiance of community norms, that they should make up their own minds regarding the merits of abstinence, or, worse still, are told that abstinence is not a good thing, why is it surprising that young people are more sexually active than ever before? Isn't it just plain common sense that what has stopped adolescents from being sexually active throughout the ages is fear? Fear of shame and stigma, of poverty and disgrace, of ostracism and abandonment—isn't this what adolescents have always dreaded? It only makes sense that once cultural prohibitions on sexual expression have been lifted, adolescents will do what comes natural to them: engage in sex. Indeed, to think that an increase in dead fetuses and bastards wouldn't result from this kind of "moral education" would be truly astonishing.

Fear, of course, is anathema to the new freedom. Fear constrains, and the new freedom will have none of it. Yet as child psychologist Bruno Bettelheim has long argued, desirable moral development is not possible without a healthy dose of fear. Those who doubt this to be true need to explain the relatively low rates of teenage pregnancy in the 1950s. It certainly wasn't due to sex education, for there was very little of it back then. In fact, most adolescents were quite ignorant about the subject of sex in the 1950s, making absurd the popular notion that the way to stem the rise in unwanted pregnancies is to have more sex education. As the record shows, when young people knew the least about sex, they engaged the least in it.

It is well known that when teenagers learned about sex "in the street," instead of the classroom, they were less likely to become sexually active. And for good reason: learning about sex covertly—"in the street," so to speak—

made it clear to everyone that sex outside marriage was wrong. Once legitimate authority figures like teachers invited "open" and "honest" discussions about sex, the stigma was removed, making it difficult, if not impossible, to brand adolescent sex as illegitimate. Add to this the Dr. Ruth phenomenon of counseling teenagers to have "good sex," and the result is predictable. Telling teenagers to have "good sex" is analogous to telling fat people to have "good food"; it only makes it easier for them to indulge their appetites.

Despite the popularity of the new-freedom approach to morality, there are some signs that things may be turning around. There has been unexpected help from organizations like People for the American Way, which has drawn attention to the near-absence of any mention of religion in the nation's textbooks. The research of New York University psychologist Dr. Paul Vitz has documented this neglect, making it intellectually indefensible for publishers to continue to deprecate the positive role that religion has played in American history. The National Education Association has stated its misgivings over the value-neutral approach to moral education, as has New York Governor Mario Cuomo. And leading the way in this area has been California Schools Superintendent Bill Honig, one of the nation's most tireless campaigners for reform.

But for genuine reform to take place, there needs to be consensus on the kind of moral vision that we want to import, and that goes well beyond deciding which values are good for character formation. There also needs to be an understanding that schools that turn out academically literate but morally illiterate students are a disservice to the mission of education. That may sound like a tall order, but in reality all it calls for is a restatement of the founding principles of education. And the will to complement them.

Notes

1. Quoted by Solveig Eggerz, "Emphasis on Social Studies Leaves Students Ignorant of History and Geography," *Human Events*, June 21, 1986, p. 12.
2. James S. Coleman, "Equal Schools or Equal Students?" *Public Interest* (Summer 1966): 75.
3. "What Works: Research about Teaching and Learning," (Washington, D.C.: U.S. Department of Education, 1986).
4. "Schools That Work: Educating Disadvantaged Children," (Washington, D.C.: U.S. Department of Education, 1987); see especially recommendation 3, "Building Character," p. 23.
5. See Hilary Stout, "More Non-Catholics Using Catholic Schools," *New York Times*, November 28, 1987, p. 25.
6. James S. Coleman, "Private Schools, Public Schools, and the Public Interest," *Public Interest* (Summer 1981): 25.
7. Edward B. Fiske, "Etzioni Wants to Shift Focus to the Students," *New York Times*, November 1, 1983, p. C1.

8. Barbara Lerner, "American Education: How Are We Doing?" *Public Interest* (Fall 1982): 72.
9. Merry White, *The Japanese Educational Challenge: A Commitment to Children* (New York: Free Press, 1987), pp. 17, 30.
10. Theodore M. Black, *Straight Talk about American Education* (New York: Harcourt Brace Jovanovich, 1982).
11. Joseph Adelson, "How the Schools Were Ruined," *Commentary* (July 1983): 46.
12. John Dewey, *Experience and Education*, (New York: Macmillan, 1938), pp. 69, 74, 75.
13. Charles Silberman, *Crisis in the Classroom* (New York: Random House, 1970), pp. 10, 90.
14. Charles Reich, *The Greening of America* (New York: Random House, 1970), pp. 136–37.
15. Jonathan Kozol, *Free Schools* (Boston: Houghton Mifflin, 1972), pp. 11, 118.
16. John Holt, *Freedom and Beyond* (New York: Dutton, 1972), 243, 247, 251.
17. Allen Graubard, *Free the Children* (New York: Pantheon Books, 1972), pp. xi, 10.
18. Carl Rogers, *Freedom to Learn* (Columbus, Ohio: Charles E. Merrill 1969), p. 131.
19. Herbert Kohl, *The Open Classroom* (New York: Vintage Books, 1969), pp. 22–30, 111, 112.
20. Neil Postman and Charles Weingartner, *Teaching as a Subversive Activity* (New York: Dell, 1969), pp. 137–40.
21. Diane Ravitch, *The Troubled Crusade* (New York: Basic Books, 1983), p. 238.
22. Reported in "Getting Tough," *Time*, February 1, 1988.
23. Quoted by Bruce Hafen, "Developing Student Expression through Institutional Authority: Public Schools as Mediating Institutions," *Ohio State Law Journal* 48, (1987): 685–86.
24. Gerald Grant, "Children's Rights and Adult Confusions," *Public Interest* (Fall 1982): 91.
25. Andrew Oldenquist, " 'Indoctrination' and Societal Suicide," *Public Interest* (Spring 1981): 86.
26. Sidney Simon, Leland Howe, and Howard Kirschenbaum, *Values Clarification: A Handbook of Practical Strategies for Teachers and Students* (New York: Hart, 1972), p. 26.
27. Jacqueline Kasun, "Our Erogenous Zones," *Crisis* (March 1988): 30–34. An earlier version of this article, "Turning Children into Sex Experts," appeared in *Public Interest* (Spring 1979): 3–14.
28. See the article distributed by Planned Parenthood and written by Marie Patten, "Self Concept and Self Esteem: Factors in Adolescent Pregnancy," *Adolescence* (Winter 1981): 765–78; especially p. 776.
29. I am indebted to Jo Ann Gasper of the U.S. Department of Education for bringing this to my attention. See "Pennsylvania Health Curriculum Guide: Family Health" (Pennsylvania Department of Education, 1984), p. 34, question 89. This is not an isolated question, as the guide makes clear. Fortunately, some responsible parents brought this publication to the attention of Governor Robert Casey and it has since been retired.

13

The Role of Religion

Throughout the ages most students of society have remarked on the strong association between religion and freedom. There have been important exceptions, as the Marxists make clear, but generally speaking most of the great thinkers have commented on the centrality of religion to freedom. However, ever since the 1960s, it has become increasingly apparent that many of today's thinkers no longer hold to this conception, preferring instead to question whether freedom can survive religion. They are wary of religion in general, and distrustful of its public role, in particular.

Those who look askance at the relationship between religion and freedom typically cast religion in an extremist light, making generalizations about its societal contribution from its worst excesses. Of course, any good value can be corrupted when taken to extremes, but for some reason religion seems to be singled out for radical diagnosis. If we perceived equality in the same way—in its most radical manifestation—we no doubt would want to curtail it, associated as it is with totalitarianism. But to judge a value by what it might become, instead of what it more typically becomes, is to obscure its essence and deprecate its meaning.

Despite some contemporary misgivings, religion remains what it has always been, one of freedom's best allies. The founding fathers understood this lesson well, including those who, like Jefferson, were deists. When John Adams said that the Constitution was made "only for a moral and a religious people,"[1] he had in mind the role that moral responsibility plays in the exercise of freedom. Without men and women of good character, without a measure of restraint in the conduct of human affairs, human passions would dominate and liberty would be abused. It was this that Adams feared most.

"Despotism may be able to do without faith," Tocqueville counseled, "but freedom cannot."[2] Under despotism, there was nothing incongruous about the societal need for order's being met by the state. Free societies, however, could afford no such option, dependent as they were on social institutions to meet that test. Clearly, one of the institutions that is supposed to do the job is the church. If it falters, so too does character development, impairing prospects for social cohesion and beckoning the hand of the state. To think that the family and the schools can pick up the slack, when they are already burdened, is wishful thinking.

For Tocqueville, religion steadied the individual, allowing him to set anchor in society. This was especially important in democratic societies, given as they were to change and instability. The human condition required a set of dogmatic beliefs, Tocqueville reasoned, and nothing was more suitable to democratic society than religious dogma. Religion offered a degree of certainty, supplying answers to ontological questions. "When a people's religion is destroyed," the French sociologist said, "doubt invades the highest faculties of the mind and half paralyzes all the rest."[3] Next to illness and death, Tocqueville listed doubt as the greatest of all human miseries.[4]

Religion humbled the individual, fixing his eyes on something other than himself. Tocqueville saw this as functional to democractic societies, given their propensity to individualism and material pursuits. "Every religion also imposes on each man some obligations toward mankind," Tocqueville said, "to be performed in common with the rest of mankind, and so draws him away, from time to time, from thinking about himself."[5] Religion, then, was a strong antidote to narcissism, a trait commonly found in every society; just as important, it countered the effects of individualism, a characteristic more typical of democratic societies. By inspiring the individual to participate in the affairs of his community, freedom was served and the state was held at bay.

If there has been one trait of religion that has been universally recognized by sociologists, it has been its ability to promote social solidarity. Durkheim spoke favorably of this characteristic, appreciative as he was of any social force that induced social cohesion. Marx gave religion many a backhanded compliment, criticizing it for sustaining bourgeois society and inhibiting revolutionary appeals. Weber understood religion's stabilizing influence, but wanted also to demonstrate its dynamic potential in fostering social change. All of them saw religious institutions, traditions, and values as being constitutive of society, independent of whether they approved or not of its role.

The psychological effects of religion have also drawn the attention of social scientists. Quality-of-life surveys and studies of psychological well-being reveal that adults who take their religion seriously tend to score well on measures of self-esteem, individual integration, and personal happiness.[6] For youngsters, the benefits are manifold. Adherence to religion is a deterrent to delinquency; adolescents who report strong religious orientation have relatively low rates of antisocial behavior.[7] There is even a link between academic success and the presence of a strong religious-spiritual orientation in the home, at least as far as the lower class is concerned.[8] And for people of all ages, the therapeutic effect of religion has long been noted, being in service in times of bereavement as well as in times of personal reform.

The weight of the evidence suggests that religion enhances both civility and community, benefiting the individual as much as society. It is not surprising, then, that the religious upheavals of the past few decades have been accompanied by increasing levels of psychological and social disorders. Indeed, given the gravity of the religious tumult, it would have been contrary to virtually everything we know about the human animal to find that the side effects were few.

There was no way that the established, mainline religions could have escaped the fury of the new freedom. Once the dominant culture embraced the idea of total emancipation from constraint, it was inevitable that religion would be targeted for assault. It has always been one of the most defining characteristics of religion—any religion, Eastern or Western—to place demands on the individual, subordinating personal desires to otherworldly ends. Religion denies, and there is nothing in the repertoire of the new freedom that gives sanction to denial. Just the opposite.

It was the new-freedom's espousal of moral neutrality that put it on a collision course with religion. To understand how this happened, the roots of moral relativism in the modern world need to be acknowledged. As Leszek Kolakowski has said, the ascendancy of moral relativism dates to the seventeenth and eighteenth centuries, when, during the Enlightenment, the claims of religious absolutists were vigorously challenged. The idea that no religion was the carrier of absolute truth had, at first, a meliorating effect, putting an end to the religious fanaticism that colored sectarian strife. But, as Kolakowski warned in his Jefferson Lecture of 1986, the triumph of moral relativism succeeded to such a point that the very ideas of pluralism and tolerance were made as relative as their opposites.

The nineteenth century saw the social sciences add to the problem as anything other than provable "facts" were declared irrelevant to the search for truth. In an attempt to mirror the precision of the natural sciences, social scientists of the late 1800s abandoned all interest in evaluating moral claims, arguing that to do so was simply an expression of one's value judgments, an inherently subjective, and therefore unfruitful, thing to do. So in the interest of science, the line between good and evil was reduced to the level of a parochial quarrel, having no special meaning to students of human behavior.

The consequences of moral neutrality were felt in the twentieth century, most specifically in Stalin's Russia, Hitler's Germany, Mao's China, and Pol Pot's Cambodia. When good and evil become unrecognizable, there is virtually no act of human barbarism that can go unchallenged. The loss of values, of a moral center, is inextricably linked to totalitarian conquest, as scholars such as Eric Voegelin and Paul Johnson have made clear. Skepticism and doubt cannot turn to nihilism without claiming victims along the way. That is one of the most fundamental lessons of the twentieth century, one still resisted by many segments of society.

And so the new freedom has a rich pedigree. Nonetheless, it was the special contribution of the new freedom in the 1960s that elevated moral neutrality to the status of an absolute, creating the kind of moral confusion that is everywhere apparent. In 1968, Will Herberg put his finger on the problem when he commented, "Today's culture comes very close to becoming a nonmoral, normless culture."[9] In the words of Kolakowski, we have now descended so far that it is possible to ask, "To put it crudely, shall we say that the difference between a vegetarian and a cannibal is just a matter of taste?"[10]

The social legacy of moral neutrality is the legitimation of immorality. Tolerance has been pushed to such an extreme that even those who commit the most obscene acts can expect to escape repudiation. Religious proscriptions have lost their traditional weight, having been cast aside as unnecessary and unfair baggage. It is by now quite certain that moral neutrality cannot reign without eroding the very meaning of sin. "What has happened to sin," notes William F. Buckley, Jr., "is the evanescence of the religious sanction."[11] Proponents of unbounded liberty may think this a good thing, but even they have to cope with the moral debris of the new freedom.

The fact that there has never been a single society in all of history that did not sport a religion should give new-freedom advocates pause. Religion is universal because religion answers universal questions and provides for universal needs. But for it to work, it must be genuinely received, and not simply grafted onto society by an elite group of social engineers. When taken seriously, religion allows society to cohere without resort to force. There being no alternative to consensus than force, and there being no consensus without the existence of a moral code of some kind, it stands to reason that a role for religion cannot be denied. Moral codes are never made out of whole cloth; they are always stitched from the fabric of some religion.

When religion loses its elasticity, the binding of society comes undone. But it rarely comes undone altogether because the pain that is induced by religion's unraveling proves intolerable to almost everyone. In the end, there is no psychological, nor sociological, antithesis to religion; as soon as a spiritual void is reached, the demand for replenishment proceeds automatically. But not before great harm has been done.

There is plenty of evidence to suggest that those who got caught up in the throes of the new freedom quickly found themselves without anchor, harriedly searching for relief wherever they could find it. Some turned to drugs, others to pop, quasi-religions, while still others enlisted in cults. All sought a sense of incorporation, a feeling of connectedness, grasping at anything that promised attachment and wholeness. Ever since the 1960s, ersatz religion has been booming, thanks largely to the effects of the new freedom. It's proven to be a flourishing market, with new recruits produced each day.

Had Jim Jones randomly chosen nine hundred people to walk with him to their altar of death, he would not have been successful. Had he given his instructions in the 1950s, he would not have been successful. Had he set up shop somewhere in America's heartland, he would not have been successful. He was successful because he drew on nine hundred fully atomized, rootless souls, all of whom had gravitated to San Francisco, the contemporary mecca for the estranged in the age of the new freedom. The script was perfect, and the outcome, if not predictable, was certainly understandable. Jones owned his victims—financially, physically, psychologically, and spiritually. But it was they who put themselves up for sale.

Those who rode the waves of the new freedom found themselves unhinged, so thoroughly liberated from society that they wound up psychologically and spiritually emaciated, in desperate need of community. They no sooner approached their destination of unrestricted freedom than they started out again in quest for society. To their chagrin, they discovered that there is no escaping the magnetic field of society; its reach is infinite, and no one feels its force more than those who try to desert it.

Those who most fully experienced the new freedom soon learned that it was possible to reject religion, but it was not possible to reject its appeal. It is important to note that the growth of alternative religions began the moment conventional religions lost their sway. Many young people, in particular, found that although the established churches no longer spoke to their needs, there remained an appetite for spiritual nourishment that begged to be fulfilled. Over the past few decades there have been several orchestrated attempts to meet the demand, as charlatans and gurus have surfaced along the way, offering their services and collecting their fees. That they have enriched themselves is not in dispute; that they have enriched their customers is.

Those who were drawn to alternative religions were people in search of moral meaning in their lives. Having immersed themselves in the new freedom for a number of years, and having rejected as artificial the utilitarian qualities of "get-ahead" individualism, millions of men and women were looking for a cultural outlet that could sustain their need for self-actualization while at the same time allowing them to function according to societal expectations. It was never difficult to find ephemeral relief; one could always escape to Vermont for a weekend or, barring that, simply hallucinate at home. What was difficult was to find an experience that enabled them to live by the norms and values of the society, without accepting as valid the tenets upon which the norms and values were based. Enter the human potential movement.

Perhaps the most successful human potential spinoff has been the Erhard Seminars Training (*est*) program developed by Werner Erhard. What has made *est* so lucrative is its ability to marry new-freedom individualism to the normative order of society, answering the call for self-actualization within the context of the dominant culture. True to its new-freedom heritage, *est* has a strong egocentric appeal, teaching conformity to social rules as a means of pleasing oneself. "*est* justifies following rules and keeping agreements," writes social observer Steven Tipton, "because these practices produce good consequences for the agent, not because they obey God or conform to reason. This constitutes 'rule egoism': compliance with rules is being justified on egoistic grounds."[12]

est has been so well received that it has been assimilated to the flourishing New Age subculture of the 1980s. The idea of self-empowerment, that each individual is capable of controlling his own destiny, is central to New Age belief. Being in charge resonates well with those who reject wholesale the constraints of conformity. New Age thought, a curious blend of Eastern and Western religions, is laced with mysticism and the promise of self-salvation. With its adamant rejection of sin, guilt, sacrifice, and self-denial, New Age belief has little in common with the traditions of either Eastern or Western civilization, but has much in common with the tenets of the new freedom. In a very real way, the New Age movement is the spiritual axis of ascendant new freedom culture.

It is by now a common observation that many of the hippies of the 1960s became the yuppies of the 1970s and 1980s, looking for a legitimate, new-found way to bask in their wealth without the pretense of materialism. New Agers sought and found a way to enjoy the best of the good life without having to endure the hardship of guilt. Making money was okay, just so long as it wasn't being done out of slavish conformity to the status quo. There was virtually nothing in bourgeois culture that New Agers couldn't indulge in, providing it wasn't done in deference to cultural expectations.

Sociologicially, New Age culture is an attempt to reject bourgeois values while maintaining bourgeois comforts. The bourgeois condemnation of self-gratification is seen as impractical, and without value to the individual. That is because New Agers believe they can have it all, finding intolerable the notion of limits. Theirs is a world wherein each individual is a deity, capable of creating reality according to personal choice or whim. The degree of autonomy that New Agers impute to the individual is unparalleled, having no basis in either psychology or sociology.

It is the self-help aspect of New Age mysticism that has attracted the attention of the corporate community. Plagued by an increasing number of employees in need of spiritual guidance but who reject the aid of priests, ministers, and rabbis, many of the blue chip firms have enlisted New Age gurus as a means of coping with their personnel problems. What they buy are the services of people like the Reverend Terry Cole-Whittaker, a chic New

Age evangelist from California, and a self-confessed veteran of new freedom experiences: "I rebirth, do yoga, gesalt therapy." She adds that "I have had my primal scream. I'm an explorer. I'm a metaphysical, evangelical, pentecostal space cadet."[13] These are the kind of people who are being recruited by such companies as AT&T, General Motors, Ford Motor Company, Calvin Klein, and IBM. Psychic healing is big business; it's also quite respectable among the cultural elite.

As the heir to the counterculture of the 1960s, the New Age movement is only one of two developments that has made its mark on American social and cultural life in recent years. The other development is the rise of the evangelical and fundamentalist religions, a phenomenon that began in the mid-1970s and hit stride in the 1980s. Opposite in content, both cultural changes were nonetheless weaned from the same source: a disaffection from the status quo. Though only a minority of the population is associated with either development, their combined effect has proven to be significant to the larger society.

Perhaps the most cogent analysis of these cultural changes has come from the work of Wade Clark Roof and William McKinney. Roof and McKinney note that the counterculture, which emerged from the fringes of society, and evangelical revivalism, which arose from the bottom of society, have much in common, despite their outward appearances. "Both challenged the religious establishment as well as modern secularity with which it is often comfortably allied. And both were expressions of a search for spirituality and inner truth, one drawing off Eastern themes and the other off older, more indigenous elements of the American religious heritage."[14] It could be added that both were responses to a culture that had grown numb from moral relativism and indifferent to the psychic needs of the individual.

The biggest losers, without a doubt, were the mainline religions. They lost because they gave up too much: in their attempt to appease the rampant individualism evident in the culture of the new freedom, mainline churches sought to adapt to the ruling winds of change, absorbing so many elements of the dominant culture that they lost their distinctiveness in the process. As a result, many people left their religions, shopping around for membership in an organization that gave some reason for belonging. The big winners were the more conservative churches, those that demanded from the rank and file a measure of commitment in order to remain in good standing.

Dean Kelley was one of the first writers to analyze the rise of the conservative churches and the decline of the liberal ones. Writing in the early 1970s, Kelley noted that the more ecumenical the church, the more likely it was to see its rolls decline. Conversely, the more exclusive the church, the more likely it was to witness an increase in membership. Among the big winners were the Black Muslims, Mormons, Southern Baptists, Pentecostals, Jehovah's Witnesses, Assemblies of God, and Orthodox Jews. The big losers were the Episcopalians, Presbyterians, Methodists, Unitarians, and Reform Jews. Catholics, Lutherans, and Conservative Jews occupied the middle ground.[15]

After studying the data, Roof and McKinney concluded that ''Almost all the churches that retained distance from the culture by encouraging distinctive life-styles and beliefs grew; those most immersed in the culture and only vaguely identifiable in terms of their own features suffered declines.''[16] It is fascinating to note that it was precisely the churches that opened their doors to everyone that fared the worst; few walked in but many walked out. In the end, it was the radical ecumenical spirit of the mainline religions that did them in.

The problem with ecumenism is sociological, not theological. Only non-believers would challenge the ecumenical spirit behind the proposition that we are all God's children and should therefore not erect artificial barriers that divide one from another. Problems begin, however, when attempts to implement ecumenism run afoul of the sociology of community building. The fatal flaw in the ecumenical mind-set, at least in its more radical manifestation, is the assumption that ecumenism is best served by trying to create an all-inclusive community, one that is capable of bringing everyone into the same religious tent. That's where it fails. Radical ecumenism fails because it violates the cardinal principle upon which all communities are based: exclusivity.

Communities are never open-ended affairs, that is, they never include everyone, for that would necessarily mean the loss of any genuine commonality. Communities are in-groups and thus are incapable of accommodating everyone equally. If some are included, others must be excluded; there is no getting around it. The conservative churches understood this lesson well, and that is why they prospered while the more inclusive churches did not. By trying so hard to embrace everyone equally, the mainline churches left themselves without anything to embrace. People belong to communities because they want to be a part of something special, and there is nothing special about a community to which everyone belongs.

What attracted many people to the conservative churches was the restrictive criteria for membership. By placing demands on the individual, these churches were able to extract something from the faithful, making participation a worthwhile exercise. And given the fact that these churches were embedded in a culture lacking in moral constants, the concreteness of the religious experience proved to be a welcome antidote to prevailing cultural vacillations.

Those who accepted the cosmopolitan thinking of the mainline churches found it difficult to understand why their churches lost ground in the age of the new freedom. From their perspective, it made no sense that anyone would want to submit to the constraints of a conservative church when the dominant culture allowed for license. But as we know, it was the conservative churches that grew commensurately with the rise of the new freedom. Dean Kelley's understanding of this apparent paradox is enlightening: "Strict moral requirements are part of what makes a religion work. What makes a religion convincing is not so much the content of the religion as what it costs to belong. Not what it costs in money, but the discipline that is required to gain membership."[17]

It is ironic to note that the more "relevant" a church tried to become, the less relevant it became. For example, while the conservative churches were preaching salvation, speaking to the timeless concerns of the human condition, the mainline churches were preaching politics, speaking to temporal events of the here and now. What happened to the Episcopal church is a case in point.

Beginning in the 1960s, the Episcopal church moved decidedly to the center of culture, embracing all the causes of the day. First it was the endorsement of "black power," then it was the ordination of female priests, and more recently it has been the cause of homosexuals. Having forfeited whatever unique claims it once had to speak as an authoritative voice in matters of morality, the Episcopal church has faded into the cultural landscape, showing more interest in promoting the platform of the Democratic party than in teaching Christian dogma. Its politicization has not been lost on the faithful. Given fewer and fewer compelling reasons for staying the course, many have decided to jump ship, entering the ranks of the "switchers." The result: membership fell 25 percent between the midsixties and the mideighties.

The Catholic church also got hit hard, though not nearly so badly as the mainline Protestant churches. If it weren't for the sizable increase in the Hispanic population over the past few decades, the number of reported Catholics would have shown a decrease, and not an increase. Fully one in five persons reared a Catholic no longer belongs to the faith, and the number of "lukewarm" Catholics is surely higher now than ever before; only 53 percent of Catholics attend mass on a weekly basis. Most of these former Catholics and part-time members of the church are drawn from the most-well-educated and wealthy segments of the population; they are also the most liberal in their politics.

There are two opposing schools of thought among Catholics who profess to understand why the church has floundered in recent decades. Both target the Second Vatican Council (1962–1965) as being the key event: one side says Vatican II didn't go far enough; the other argues it went too far. Not at issue is the number of priests and nuns who have called it quits: between 1965 and 1985, the number of priests declined from 59,193 to 57,183; among nuns, the decline went from 181,421 to 113,658. The figures on seminarians are even more dramatic: there were 48,046 seminarians in 1965, but just 10,440 twenty years later.

Those who think the Church didn't go far enough in its reform efforts are typically unfazed by the declining number of priests, nuns, and seminarians. To these progressive-minded persons, Vatican II simply cleared the dead wood from the church, emptying the rectories and convents of priests and nuns who blindly followed preconciliar teachings, never showing an ounce of independence nor a good reason for having adopted a collar or habit in the first place. Those who accept this line of thinking usually rejoice at the sight of dissenting priests and nuns, scoring such departures from authority as a victory for a reinvigorated church, one more authentic, alive, and real than the church of old. They would rather see one progressive-minded priest or nun serve a thousand people than see a hundred traditional priests and nuns tend to the same flock.

One of the most popular explanations among the progressives is the one afforded by the Reverend Andrew Greeley, sociologist and novelist. Greeley is convinced that Vatican II was pure gold, yielding nothing but positive results. He lays blame for the church's decline squarely on the shoulders of Pope Paul VI, holding the pope accountable for issuing the encyclical "Humanae Vitae," the document that reaffirmed the church's teachings on birth control.

Greeley accuses the pope of reversing the progressive tide unleashed by Vatican II, thus alienating to the point of no return the Catholics who wanted even more changes in the church. With the assistance of "sophisticated mathematical models," Greeley professes to have settled the issue once and for all: it was the encyclical that "shattered the euphoria that had flourished after Vatican II" and "sent the Church into a sudden and dramatic decline."[18]

There are several problems with Greeley's thesis. First, if Greeley really thinks that the fallout in the church was due to the encyclical, then his complaint is not with Pope Paul VI but with Vatican II. Nowhere in the sixteen documents of Vatican II is there any hint that traditional church teachings on birth control should be changed. All the pope was doing was restating the conventional view, much to the chagrin of Father Greeley to be sure, but faithful to tradition, and to Vatican II, nonetheless. Greeley might just as well have blamed Pope John XXIII for not rescinding the church's teachings on birth control than take aim at his successor for reaffirming tradition.

The "euphoria" that allegedly took place after Vatican II was lodged mostly in the minds of the progressives, those priests, nuns, and laypersons who wanted to depart from the constraints of pre-Vatican II days. Most of the Catholic community not only did not share in this euphoria but, it would be more accurate to say, were more confused than convinced by what was taking place. It is a matter of record that Catholicism peaked in 1965, the very year Vatican II ended, and declined thereafter; the encyclical was issued in 1968, three years after the decline had begun.[19] In addition, many of the changes that took place during this period did not come all at once. The change from the Latin Tridentine Mass to the vernacularized version (Novus Ordo Missae) did not become mandatory until 1971, making it difficult to determine the effect that any one change might have had, even with the help of "sophisticated mathematical models."

It was so obvious that Vatican II unleashed turmoil in the Church that almost a year and a half before he issued the encyclical on birth control, Pope Paul VI asked Catholics to join him in a "year of faith." At about the same time Emmet John Hughes wrote: "From Boston to Bombay, the Catholic world has entered upon a time of tension without parallel since the age of Luther."[20] In 1968, before the consequences of the encyclical could have taken hold, Philip Deasy was able to note that "since the end of Vatican Council II there have been at least sixty-nine books, not to mention countless articles in Catholic periodicals and diocesan papers, all designed for general reader perusal, on the subject of change, crisis, and revolution in the Catholic Church."[21]

This is not to say that "Humanae Vitae" had no effect. It did have an effect on the minority of progressive-minded reformers for whom any tie to the past was unacceptable. They had their hopes kindled by Vatican II and then doused by the encyclical. But in no way can it be said that "Humanae Vitae" began the church's decline; it simply accelerated the decline among a small segment of the faithful. Protestant theologian Martin Marty captured what was happening to the church better than the progressives did, when in 1968 he wrote: "Catholic renewalists engage in overkill when their attempt to reform the Church leads to their removal from it."[22]

Another favorite argument advanced by the progressives is that the decline in the church would have been even greater had it not been for the saving grace of Vatican II reforms. Of course, there is no way to know for sure, but from what we know about the rise of the conservative churches and the collapse of the progressive ones, it would be more accurate to suggest that the reforms contributed to, instead of thwarted, the decline.

But no amount of data will convince those who, like Greeley, are determined to rescue Vatican II. After noting the defections from the church that have taken place in the first two decades after the Second Vatican Council, Greeley still holds to the belief that "Catholicism in America is more healthy today than it was before Vatican II. And alive. In truth, never more alive."[23] For Greeley, the degree of aliveness in the church is judged by the amount of chaos, confusion, dissent, and discord that exists: the more, the better. Nothing else matters, not even the loss of clergy and laity.

It is not uncommon to hear rabid supporters of Vatican II speak contemptuously about the preconciliar church and those who still defend it. Straight out of the pages of new-freedom thought, the progressives continue to lament the constraints that the preconciliar church levied on clergy and laity alike. Following the trajectory of change in the culture at large, the progressives think that traditional church strictures were too rigid, and that everything from what constitutes sin to what is appropriate attire at mass should be reexamined with an eye toward relaxing constraints. Their conception of freedom is so contemporary that it is fair to say that progressive postconciliar thought is the Catholic expression of new freedom ideology.

Those who trace the church's decline to Vatican II do not uniformly reject everything the council did; much of what was done was long overdue. Their complaints focus more typically on the extent and abruptness of the reforms, with special attention to the changes that are without basis in the actual council proceedings. Members of any organization tend to resist change, and this is especially true of those who belong to traditional institutions. Had the laity been better prepared for the reforms, much of the discontent could have been mitigated.

The Catholic church violated two of Tocqueville's admonitions when it embarked on Vatican II: it diminished the role of symbols and weakened the certainty of its teachings. "I do not imagine that it is possible to maintain a religion," Tocqueville exclaimed, "without external observances." A practicing Catholic, Tocqueville was especially concerned about his own religion: "In all religions there are ceremonies which are inherent in the very substance of belief, and one must take care not to change anything in them. That is especially seen in the Catholic religion, where form and substance are so closely united that they are one."[24]

In the aftermath of Vatican II came the disappearance of many external observances. Eating meat on Friday was no longer proscribed, St. Christopher was stripped of his sainthood, the Latin mass was replaced by a demystified English rendition, the rosary became near obsolete—as did benediction—and nuns shed their habits, as well as their residences, for modern clothes and apartments of their own. The church was becoming modern, so modern, in fact, that it lost its uniqueness and relinquished its authority. In the words of Tocqueville, form was split from substance, having exactly the negative effect he thought it would.

Tocqueville also warned that the human need for answers to primordial questions had to be delivered by religious bodies in a language that was "clear, precise, intelligible to the crowd, and very durable."[25] This the church has not done, thanks largely to the forces that were set in motion as a result of Vatican II. No one has realized these changes more than students in Catholic schools.

Whatever failings the Baltimore catechism had, it nonetheless grounded the student in his religion, providing for the kind of certainty that is indispensable to any faith. That it was too rigid and too doctrinaire is true. But it was at least able to introduce the student to his religion, which is more than can be said of contemporary religion texts. The typical book used in religion classes since Vatican II has little in the way of religion in it: recitations on peace and justice are fine, but if they're not tied to church teachings, then religion and ethics merge as one, making it easy for students to slide away from their religion later in life. It needs to be remembered that aside from the first three Commandments, there is nothing in the Ten Commandments that wouldn't be acceptable to any atheist, and religion textbooks that overlook this point are unwittingly greasing the slide, making it difficult to hold onto what is special about Christianity.

The durability of Catholic thought is being challenged almost daily, by clergy and laity alike. We now have the spectacle of Catholic bishops, armed with degrees in theology, proclaiming their authority on everything from macroeconomics to space defense systems. Proabortion groups have arisen among nuns (National Coalition of American Nuns) and the laity (Catholics for a Free Choice), and there are even prohomosexual groups (Dignity) that seek church approval of sodomy. Theologians at Catholic universities insist on reinventing the church, and administrators back them up, citing their newfound allegiance to the principle of academic freedom. And to top it off, church "peace groups" have emerged all over the country, sponsoring a liberation theology that is a close cousin to Marxism, an ideology most known for its promotion of slavery, not liberty.

The net result of these changes is a kind of do-it-yourself, on-the-job approach to Catholicism, and to the mainline religions in general. Roof and McKinney speak to the new voluntarism that has developed among the organized religions, meaning that increasingly people of all but the most conservative religions are picking and choosing which strictures they want to obey and which ones they want to discard. Religion has become personalized, tailor-made to individual interests. Nowhere is this more apparent than among those who are classified as "unchurched," that is, those who are merely nominal members of a religion. Sheila Larson, one of the persons interviewed by Robert Bellah and associates, epitomizes the new voluntarism: "I believe in God. I'm not a religious fanatic. I can't remember the last time I went to church. My faith has carried me a long way. It's Sheilaism. Just my own little voice."[26]

As Roof and McKinney point out, there has been a marked increase in the number of "unchurched" Protestants, Catholics, and Jews over the past few decades. There has also been a sharp increase in the number of Americans who report having no religious preference: in 1952, 2 percent of the population classified themselves as having no preference; by 1985, the figure reached 9 percent, an increase of 350 percent. These two segments of the population have much in common. They are largely young, white, well-educated, middle-class persons from metropolitan areas, all of whom have found the three major religions wanting and some of whom have searched for alternatives. Reportedly, they are the most "tolerant" segment of the population.[27]

One of the greatest myths perpetrated in the study of civil liberties is the notion that there is an inverse relationship between religious commitment and tolerance for the rights of others. Yet this oft-repeated myth continues to gain currency, even with responsible scholars like Roof and McKinney.

The typical way tolerance is measured, by asking respondents whether they approve or disapprove of the right of others to be nonconformists, is wholly inadequate to the task. Before any such question is asked, data need to be collected on both the behavioral practices of the respondents and the intensity of their commitment to an entire range of values. For example, if tolerance for drug use is the issue, it should first be known whether the respondent is, or ever was, a drug user. Second, it needs to be known what values, if any, the respondent holds dear, and how he feels about those who trash them. Absent this information, measures of tolerance are soft and misleading.

Using the same data provided by Roof and McKinney, it is possible to derive an entirely different set of conclusions about those least religiously inclined. They collected information on what they call attitudes toward "the new morality," or what could easily be referred to as a new-freedom index. What they found was that those who professed no religious affiliation were very accepting of the new morality: a clear majority believed that (a) abortion was okay, for any reason, (b) extramarital sex was not always wrong, (c) premarital sex was not wrong, (d) homosexuality was not always wrong, (e) divorce should be easier to obtain, and (f) marijuana should be legalized. As Roof and McKinney note, most Americans oppose each of the new-morality positions, putting those without religious preference in a distinct minority.[28]

Notice what is going on here. Those who are reportedly the most tolerant of nonconformity are also the most accepting of the new morality. This is, of course, as it should be. Is it any wonder that those who favor the new freedom are also the most tolerant of those who practice it? How deserving of our applause are they? Is it to their credit that they are tolerant of immorality? Do they even regard adultery as immoral? Are they disturbed by the explosion in teenage pregnancy and illegitimacy of the past few decades? If so, do they think there is no connection between tolerance for promiscuity and record-level rates of abortions and illegitimate children?

Further evidence that studies of tolerance often reveal moral lassitude, more than any other attitude, is borne out in the Middletown (Muncie,

Indiana) research of Theodore Caplow and associates. "The new tolerance is the most striking change in Middletown's religion in the past half century," writes Caplow.[29] But is it tolerance for other people's religion that Caplow found, or indifference to one's own?

According to Caplow, there was a "significant and consistent" difference between religious commitment in Middletown and the rest of the nation. For example, compared to the national average, a significantly higher percentage of the residents of Middletown express no religious preference. In addition, those who belong to a church are much less likely to attend services on a weekly basis, and the percentage of residents who never pray is considerably higher than found elsewhere.[30] Is it surprising that greater tolerance for other people's religion should be found among those for whom religion is of declining significance?

It is absurd that the bearers of the new freedom should be touted as a model for the rest of society; they are deserving of no emulation. There is nothing admirable about practicing moral truancy, nor is it at all virtuous to be tolerant of vice. Only those who have biases, as the Catholic philosopher Etienne Gilson once said, are capable of toleration. And that is why new-freedom moralists are undeserving of praise: there is so little that they hold sacrosanct that they are singularly incapable of demonstrating true tolerance.

Most disturbing to American culture, however, is the extent to which those with little or no religion have seen their idea of moral neutrality infuse the law, especially First Amendment law. It deserves to be said that they are not alone in championing this idea; the most liberal members of the mainline religions, and in particular the clergy, have also supported a strict separationist approach to the establishment clause. Together, these persons have worked to limit the role of religion in American public life, while furthering what they see as tolerance for individual rights and pluralism. This belief, at one with new-freedom thought, holds that nothing is more central to liberty than the right of the individual to be totally unaffected by religious thought or observances. It is this idea that stands behind the privatization of religion, a process in evidence since the 1960s.

There are many examples of the new-freedom attitude toward religion. This can be seen in the staunch opposition that is shown to any religious display on public property, be it a creche at Christmas or a menorah at Hanukkah. Religious hymns cannot be sung in the schools at Christmas, nor can pop-religious plays be performed, such as "Jesus Christ Superstar," without the threat of an ACLU lawsuit. The inscription on coins, "In God We Trust," and the words "under God" in the pledge of allegiance, have also merited court challenges. Even the tax-exempt status of churches and synagogues has drawn fire, the Catholic Church being singled out most recently because of its antiabortion position. This is how exponents of the new freedom practice their tolerance. What they have bequeathed is what Richard John Neuhaus aptly calls "the naked public square."

Most disturbing is the growing tendency to exclude religious institutions from any public role in attending to the nation's multiple social problems. At a time when every part of the country is being burdened with unprecedented psychological and social disorders, public policy is bent on curtailing the influence of both the parochial schools and the churches. For instance, poor blacks who attend parochial schools in the inner city are literally forced to receive remedial education in vans parked across the street from their Catholic school. They must attend school in vans because the Supreme Court has decided that publicly paid remedial-education teachers cannot dispense their services on the premises of a sectarian school, though not a single teacher in history ever registered a complaint.

There have been many other such attempts to weaken the public role of religious institutions. Civil libertarians have challenged proposals to allow every institution, public or private, the right to receive public monies for the purpose of teaching abstinence to teenagers in sex education classes. The alleged offense? Some religions promote abstinence as a matter of doctrinal belief, therefore any revenue they might receive would necessarily be advancing their religion. In a related matter, day care centers and foster care homes run by religious institutions have been told to remove all religious symbols from their premises, and to keep to themselves their own peculiar religious ideas and practices about child rearing, if they want to qualify for public financing.

It is a tribute to the age of the new freedom that although we are besieged with all sorts of social problems, we define liberty as the absence of religious institutions from the workings of public policy. Instead of summoning the good deeds that the churches are capable of providing, especially in a time of overwhelming need, we act as though involvement of religious institutions in solving social problems would be a greater threat to liberty than allowing moral depravity to go unchecked. It is because religion constrains, and constraints are labeled taboo, that the policy to limit the public role of religion in American life goes almost unchallenged.

The problem goes well beyond a fradulent interpretation of the original intent of the First Amendment. It goes to the heart of what freedom means. Religion and freedom, in the eyes of the new freedom, are incompatible. The new freedom sees religious ideas and practices as a form of pollution, requiring constant surveillance. If they are allowed free expression, if they get into the atmosphere and affect the public, the cost to individual liberty will be great. Such is the new freedom mind-set.

Even those who, like Michael Harrington, are themselves without religious affiliation or belief have come to understand that society needs a set of core moral values, grounded in transcendentals. Though Harrington awaits the promise of democratic socialism, he does not deny that the established religions of Western civilization have traditionally filled this human need. There is little doubt that the churches are capable of doing the job; the only question that is outstanding is whether they are prepared to do so. One thing is certain: If the challenge is to be met, it will take a fresh look at the positive contribution that religious institutions can make—and have already made—to the cultural bases of individual freedom.

Notes

1. Quoted in Richard John Neuhaus, *The Naked Public Square* (Grand Rapids, Mich.: William Eerdmans, 1984), p. 95.
2. Alexis de Tocqueville, *Democracy in America*, ed. J. P. Mayer (Garden City, N.Y.: Anchor Books, 1969), p. 294.
3. Ibid., p. 444.
4. Alexis de Tocqueville, *Journey to America*, ed. J. P. Mayer (New Haven: Yale University Press, 1959), p. 155.
5. Tocqueville, *Democracy in America*, p. 444.
6. For a good overview of the literature in this area, see Donald Capps, "Religion and Psychological Well-Being," in Phillip E. Hammond, ed., *The Sacred in a Secular Age* (Berkeley: University of California Press, 1985), pp. 237–56.
7. See Charles Peek, Evans Curry, and H. Paul Chalfant, "Religiosity and Delinquency over Time: Deviance Deterrence and Deviance Amplification," *Social Science Quarterly* (March 1985): pp. 120–31.
8. Reginald Clark, *Family Life and School Achievement* (Chicago: University of Chicago Press, 1983), p. 62.
9. Will Herberg's article was later reprinted in the same journal that carried his 1968 piece. See "What Is the Moral Crisis of Our Time?" *Intercollegiate Review* (Fall 1986): 9.
10. Leszek Kolakowski, "The Idolatry of Politics," *New Republic*, June 16, 1986, p. 31. This article is a slightly different version of Kolakowski's 1986 Jefferson Lecture.
11. William F. Buckley, Jr., "Thou Shalt Not," *New York Times Magazine*, April 6, 1986, p. 36.
12. Steven Tipton, "Conversion and Cultural Change," in Robert Bellah et al., eds., *Individualism and Commitment in American Life* (New York: Harper and Row, 1987), p. 354.
13. Earl C. Gottschalk, Jr., "The Rev. Terry Has a Gospel to Cheer the Me Generation," *Wall Street Journal*, August 23, 1984, p. 1.
14. Wade Clark Roof and William McKinney, *American Mainline Religion* (New Brunswick, N.J.: Rutgers University Press, 1987), p. 4.
15. Dean Kelley, *Why Conservative Churches Are Growing* (New York: Harper and Row, 1972), pp. 88–90.
16. Roof and McKinney, *American Mainline Religion*, pp. 20–21.
17. Dean Kelley's response appeared in an interview published in the *National Catholic Register*, July 28, 1985, p. 6.

18. Andrew Greeley and Mary Greeley Durkin, *How to Save the Catholic Church* (New York: Viking, 1984), pp. 6–7.
19. See the data on the decline of the church marking 1965 as the peak year in Charlotte Low, "A Flock at Odds with Its Shepherds," *Insight*, July 28, 1986, p. 11.
20. Emmet John Hughes, "The Catholic Crisis," *Newsweek*, March 6, 1967, p. 21.
21. Philip Deasy in a review of *The Catholic Revolution*, by Douglas J. Roche, *Commonweal*, December 20, 1968, p. 411.
22. Martin Marty, "A Warning to Catholic Extremists," *America*, August 31, 1968, p. 122.
23. Greeley and Greeley, *How to Save the Catholic Church*, p. 4.
24. Tocqueville, *Democracy in America*, p. 447.
25. Ibid., p. 443.
26. Robert Bellah et al., *Habits of the Heart* (Berkeley: University of California Press, 1985), p. 221.
27. Roof and McKinney, *American Mainline Religion*, pp. 16–18.
28. Ibid., pp. 209–21.
29. Theodore Caplow, "Religion in Middletown," *Public Interest* (Summer 1982): 84.
30. Ibid., p. 85.

14

The Role of the Law

Free societies rely on the family, schools, and churches to levy constraints, socialize children, introduce them to the unwritten laws of society, and provide for value formation. In addition, all three institutions are key agents of social control, and are in fact more important to order maintenance than the role played by law. The law's role is always ancillary, and can never be a substitute for the efforts of the three major social institutions. But that is not to say that the law's role is unimportant: it is just to say that a society that increasingly relies on the state to maintain social control is a society headed for trouble.

There is plenty of evidence to suggest that the legal system is currently overburdened, carrying a disproportionate share of the societal responsibility for social control. From overworked police to overcrowded prisons, every segment of the legal system is stretched to capacity, trying to pick up the slack of failed families, schools, and churches. Had these social institutions done their job, and not yielded to the pressures of the new freedom, antisocial behavior would have been checked and the burden on the legal system would have been manageable. The reality, of course, is that the idea of unrestricted liberty won out, leaving a trail of incivility in its wake.

The most conspicuous proof that social control has broken down lay in the crime statistics. Rates of crime and delinquency exploded in the 1960s and 1970s, reaching a peak in 1981. Between 1960 and 1980, the juvenile delinquency rate rose by 130 percent, while the number of juvenile arrests more than doubled. The death rate among adolescents due to violent causes tripled during the same period; murders of ten-year-olds to nineteen-year-olds rose 200 percent. There was a decline in the overall level of crime in the 1980s, though this was hardly the result of a newfound respect for civility: almost the entire decrease was due to a decline in the teenage population, the segment of society most responsible for the lion's share of crime in any era.

And the downturn may prove to be short-lived, for the crime rate in 1987 and 1988 inched upward once again.

It remains true that the crime rate in the United States is much higher than exists in Western Europe. For example, a 1988 report by the Justice Department's Bureau of Crime Statistics said that homicide, rape, and robbery were four to nine times more frequent in the United States than in Western Europe. Another Justice Department study disclosed that an estimated 83 percent of twelve-year-old children in America will be victims or intended victims of violent crimes at least once in their lifetimes. No matter what technique is used to measure crime—official FBI statistics, victimization surveys, self-report studies, or some other measure—no serious criminologist doubts the accuracy of saying that America is the most violent place to live in the modern world.

The extent to which young kids are involved in serious crime is perhaps the most disturbing indicator of the breakdown in civility. Kids are not only responsible for an increasing share of the overall level of violent crimes, the age at which they are getting involved is dropping. "Without question," says Hunter Hurst, director of the National Center for Juvenile Justice, "all the biggest increases are in the younger ages. Once you pass 13, all the increases begin to drop."[1] What makes matters worse is that chronic delinquents typically become chronic adult offenders.

The most comprehensive work on the subject of chronic offenders has been done by sociologist Marvin Wolfgang and his associates at the University of Pennsylvania. The first of Wolfgang's studies collected information on all males born in 1945 who were residents of Philadelphia from their tenth to eighteenth birthdays. By examining police files and school records, Wolfgang was able to conclude that of the nearly ten thousand boys in his study, fully 35 percent had a delinquent record. But his most important finding dealt with the chronic offender: 6 percent of the entire cohort accounted for over half the total number of offenses, making it plain that a small proportion of the population is responsible for the bulk of offenses.

Two subsequent studies were done. One was a follow-up to the original; it traced a 10 percent sample of the 1945 group through adulthood to age thirty. The other was a replication of the first study; it examined all persons who were born in 1958 in Philadelphia and who lived there from 1968 to 1975. Both research projects were supportive of the findings of the original study, offering further validity to the contention that most serious crime is committed by a small and identifiable part of the population, a segment that is discernible by age thirteen or fourteen. As was reported in the follow-up study, "Subjects with long and serious juvenile careers are likely to have long and serious adult careers."[2] This is one area of research where there are few dissenting voices: frequency and seriousness of juvenile arrest is the best predictor of adult criminal behavior.

That chronic juvenile offenders graduate to the status of chronic adult offenders has long been true, but what is different about today's young criminals is the utter lack of feeling they have for their victims. It is the unbelievable degree of casualness that juveniles display in the commission of their crimes that is new, not the number of offenses they commit. With characteristic aplomb, today's delinquents dismiss any suggestion that they ought to feel guilty about their behavior, and look askance at inquiring psychologists who think otherwise. The so-called "wilding" episode in New York's Central Park—where a gang of teenagers brutally assualted, raped and sodomized a woman jogger—may be unusual for its viciousness, but not for the total lack of guilt that the boys displayed: such insouciance is characteristic of thugs in the age of the new freedom.

Claude Brown, author of the 1960s classic *Manchild in the Promised Land*, understands better than most the changing nature of life in the ghetto. As one who grew up in Harlem in the 1940s and 1950s, before the civil rights movement began, Brown is disturbed by what he sees in his old neighborhood. "Today's manchild," Brown observes, "is an enigma to his predecessor of 30 years ago. He obtains the biggest gun he can find—usually a sawed-off shotgun or a .45—sticks it in the face of some poor working person and takes all of $5 or $10 *and* his life—a maniacal act." The word on the street, Brown says, amounts to this: "Murder is in style now."[3]

As anyone who lives in suburbia will testify, high levels of of crime and delinquency are not exclusively inner-city problems. It is worse in the inner city, but it is bad all over, making unpersuasive sociological theories that focus on poverty, discrimination, and urban anomie. The problem is national in origin and national in scope: it represents nothing less than a collapse of constraints, beginning with the family, schools, and churches, and extending to the panoply of agencies that constitute the legal system. "The criminal," as Michael Novak perceptively notes, "is an underdeveloped moral being."[4] And the reason that we have so many underdeveloped moral beings is because the social institutions whose duty it is to provide for character development have dropped their guard, thereby weakening the mechanisms of social control.

Social control is maintained through varying degrees of formality, extending from such informal means as guilt, shame, stigma, ridicule, and ostracism, to more formal mechanisms like imprisonment. It is safe to say that, across the board, we have sorely underutilized these resources, and as a result are forced to endure incredibly high levels of crime and delinquency. It is a needless endurance, for no nation is destined to self-immolation; likewise, no nation that has adopted a reckless idea of freedom can escape its consequences.

The law has not escaped the effects of the new freedom. The cultural relaxation of constraints that is evident in the value-forming institutions of family, schools, and churches is equally apparent in the value-affirming institutions that make up the legal system. The rejection of punitive sanctions, the acceptance of moral neutrality, and the societal embrace of excessive individual rights has worked its way into the criminal justice system with as much ardor as found in any institution of society. It would be hard to find a veteran cop or prison guard in the entire country who would disagree with this assessment.

The new-freedom's rejection of punitive sanctions is based on the belief that the carrot is mightier than the stick. Moreover, even when the evidence is clear that sometimes it is necessary to change strategies, new-freedom believers remain unmoved, convinced of the moral superiority of the carrot to the stick. That is why restraint, coercion, stigma, guilt, and punishment are spurned, while tolerance, communication, reward, inducement, and understanding are espoused. Punishment is inhumane, to be avoided at all cost, even when it is clear that the failure to punish results in greater inhumanity; it is the intent that counts, and nothing more. Not only is it wrong to punish the wrongdoer, it is right that he or she be given amnesty. Hence the pleas in recent years for amnesty for draft dodgers, tax dodgers, illegal aliens, and so on. Some have even demanded amnesty for spies![5]

As Ernest van den Haag has shown, the reluctance to punish criminals is a twentieth-century phenomenon, having no counterpart in history. Most societies, he says, never had a need for prisons, other than to detain those awaiting trial. Upon conviction, the guilty were "fined, pilloried, flogged, mutilated, or put to death."[6] Not any more. Today they typically plea bargain their way out of prison, or wind up with reduced sentences. Even that's unusual; the vast majority of criminals never get caught in the first place.

It is a canon of the new freedom that retribution and vengeance, being essentially the same thing, have no legitimate role to play in a decent and humane society. But as van den Haag points out, they are neither synonymous nor morally equal. Vengeance is unregulated retaliation, carried out by private persons against alleged wrongdoers. Retribution is legal reprisal, imposed by a court of law according to existing scales of justice. Vengeance is street justice; retribution is justice according to law. There is a difference.

To do away with legal retribution not only would be foolish but would needlessly induce a passion for revenge, resulting in vigilante-style justice. Indeed, it has been the reluctance to punish criminals that has made heroes out of people like Bernhard Goetz, the New York subway rider who shot his young assailants when accosted for money. The root cause of Goetz's popularity, and of movies like *Rambo* and *Death Wish*, as well as television programs like "The 'A' Team" and "The Equalizer," is directly attributable to the public's outrage at a society that treats criminals with kid gloves. It is no wonder that the Guardian Angels and Black Muslims are welcome in high-crime areas: they are doing the job the criminal justice system refuses to do.

Punishing criminals is proper for two reasons: (a) it is only just that those who violate the rights of others be punished for their wrongdoing, and (b) it has, or may have, a deterrent effect. A by-product of punishing criminals, and one of no slight importance, is the solidifying effect it has on society. Emile Durkheim knew of what he spoke when he maintained that a certain amount of crime was necessary in any society, for when those who violate the laws of society are punished for their infraction, the social effect of punishment is to clarify the norms, reinstill their importance, and enhance a sense of community. The collective conscience of society is strengthened when those who trespass against its precepts are punished for doing so. In short, both civility and community are served when the guilty are punished. Conversely, both are undermined when the guilty get off scot-free.

There has been a movement over the past decade to imprison more of the guilty, but it is still resisted by those who think punishment is wrong, and would not have occurred at all had it not been for public outcry. In 1988, there were 228 persons in prison per 100,000 in the population, up from 138 in 1980. The increase has occurred at a time when the crime rate has been falling, a fact often cited as proof of how irrational public policy is in this area. Of course, it is entirely possible (no one knows for sure) that the decline in the crime rate throughout most of the 1980s is partially due to the greater likelihood of being sentenced to prison. One thing is certain: in the decade when the new freedom flowered—the 1960s—the crime rate went up 144 percent, while the number of persons in prison went from 118 per 100,000 at the beginning of the decade to 96 at the end of the decade. One would have to be awfully naive to think that the reluctance to punish was unrelated to the increase in crime.

From corporal punishment to capital punishment, the argument has been the same: a civilized society does not resort to punishment as a stratagem for social control. But can a society be called civilized when criminals punish the innocent and then go unpunished for doing so? Is it the mark of a civilized society that storefronts are covered with metal gates, bars are put on apartment windows, garbage-can covers are chained to poles, kids carry three keys to get in the front door, locks are put on the gas tanks of cars, subways are underutilized, and cab drivers refuse to travel to certain neighborhoods? Finally, is capital punishment really more barbarous than allowing urban barbarians to go undeterred? The public doesn't think so, as every survey confirms, but that matters little to those who reflexively denounce punishment, nestled away as they usually are in some low-crime, high-priced ghetto.

"It is disturbing to consider that murder is the style among young muggers," comments Claude Brown, "and that the style among the New York political establishment is anti-capital-punishment-liberalism, and how well the two styles complement each other."[7] Brown has identified an important link. The most illiterate mugger is capable of reading the writing on the wall, that is, he intuitively comprehends when the authorities have lost their nerve. For example, is it a matter of coincidence that between 1966 and 1980, only six persons were executed in the United States while more than a quarter million murders were committed? How many innocent lives might have been saved by executing even 10 percent of the murderers cannot be known, though it is unlikely that it would have had no effect. It is understood by criminals, if not by criminologists, that respect for human life deteriorates as society's will to avenge those who wantonly take it diminishes.

The reluctance to punish goes hand in hand with the new freedom's desire for a morally neutral, nonjudgmental ethos. It is expressive of the new-freedom's priorities that rights take precedence over responsibilities, so it should come as no surprise that holding individuals accountable for misconduct is not of striking importance. What often happens is nothing less than wholesale exculpation of the guilty, relieving offenders of any responsibility for their behavior. The system did it, the environment did it, he was insane, he was driven to do it, poverty perverted him, society alienated him, he had a rotten upbringing, and so on and so forth, these are the familiar explanations that sociologists advance to understand the nature of crime. Correction: these are the familiar explanations sociologists use to explain lower-class crime. When the subject switches to upper-class crime, tolerance for deviance ends, as calls for law and order echo from the strangest places.

If it is true that a commitment to moral neutrality makes it difficult to establish guilt, it is not impossible to do so; the collectivization of guilt shows no sign of abatement. Violence by black males, for example, is not only understood but often justified. It is justified as a response to violence-inducing situations created by society. But the proponents of this view have unwittingly laid their own trap: if society is to blame, then no particular individual is guilty. And so life goes on.

The impulse to exculpate the guilty is strong, so strong in fact that those who challenge contemporary deterministic theories of crime are often seen as disloyal to the profession of the social sciences. James Q. Wilson and Richard Herrnstein, for instance, were met with a storm of criticism, much of it vitriolic and vituperative in nature, simply because they maintained that there were biological predispositions to criminality. Their masterful examination of the literature led them to conclude that crime was an interaction between social factors and certain biological factors, a finding that challenged prevailing sentiments.[8] That was all they needed to do to be regarded as heretics by their peers, so strong is the element of ideology in the so-called social sciences.

The new-freedom's moral relativism is not accepting of the idea that crime may be the result of a defect in the individual. The defect, if such an admission is granted at all, is in the nature of the economy, or the social structure of society; the individual would naturally incline to doing good if it were not for man-made institutions that have corrupted his nature (but if the corrupting institutions were made by man then isn't it proof that man is corrupt?). Above all, no individual is evil. Really bad people, if they exist at all, are insane, and they are not responsible for their behavior. No one is.

When a person commits a crime of passion, such as belting a bully, or breaks the law out of need, such as robbing the rich so as to feed his family, the criminal act is entirely understandable and readily explained. When a teller steals money from a bank, we do not approve, but again we find it easy to comprehend; all of us have yielded to temptation. But when a person commits a crime that we ourselves could never fathom committing, such as raping an old person, we immediately conclude that the person must be crazy. But why don't we immediately conclude that he must be evil? The point of departure is critical, for if it is assumed that those who do evil things are not evil, but are instead insane, then it follows that explanations of insanity will be forthcoming. Why not assume that evil deeds are done by evil people, unless there is proof to the contrary?

The idea that some people are inherently evil does not sit well with the cultural elite. But that is a philosophical preference, and not a conviction rooted in scientific research. Science has not settled the matter either way, and may be incapable of ever doing so, but one thing is sure: there has been very little interest in even raising the issue, much less investigating its plausibility. Yet there is no reason for this state of affairs, other than politics; it is offensive to modern sensibilities to suggest that there are individuals who are beyond repair. However, there is some criminological research that should give pause to those who cling to the accepted wisdom.

For a decade and a half, psychiatrist Samuel Yochelson and psychologist Stanton Samenow studied hard-core repeat offenders in maximum security prisons, searching for data that might explain their common condition.[9] What they found was a set of personal traits that separated these criminals from the general population. They were compulsive liars, lying about matters of no consequence or value to them. They were evasive, manipulative, paranoid, cunning, and secretive. What Yochelson and Samenow concluded, after looking at the evidence, was that some people were simply wicked. The reaction of their colleagues was revealing: the armchair psychiatrists and psychologists, that is, those who never set foot in a prison, were generally negative, while those who worked with repeat offenders generally felt that the findings confirmed their own experiences.

There is one school of thought in sociology, what is known as labeling analysis, that does not seek to relieve the individual of responsibility for his behavior. But neither does it endorse punishment for untoward behavior. It recommends tolerance. Labeling theorists provide a good example of how the doctrine of moral neutrality has found its way into the sociology of deviance.

Most theories of deviance seek to explain why the offender did what he did, looking for meaning in behavioral patterns that were antecedent to the misconduct. This approach takes for granted that (a) what the deviant did was wrong, (b) something other than the will of the miscreant was operative, and (c) something must be done either to him or to his environment to alter his behavior. Labeling theorists reject all three assumptions as false.

To begin with, labeling theorists believe that there is no intrinsic meaning to any behavior; society assigns meanings to behavior, and we then act accordingly, either positively or negatively, as the case may be. For example, we have a drug problem in this country only to the extent that we think drugs are bad; if we altered our perspective, the seriousness of drug use would abate. Second, individuals determine their own behavior. This does not necessarily mean that all behavior is the product of conscious design—many young people sort of drift into situations where "delinquent" opportunities (drug use at a party) are present. But it does mean that the individual determines his actions, and not some mysterious psychological, social or economic force. Last, it is society that needs to be changed, and not the "deviant"; more tolerance is needed.

What the labeling theorists do is to turn on its head the question most sociologists like to ask. They seek to know why society reacts the way it does to people who do not accept its norms, rather than question why people do not accept the norms of society. Students of the labeling perspective are interested in uncovering what happens to people once they are labeled as deviants, in other words, they want to learn how the individual copes with the problems that society has created for him. Unlike other sociologists, labeling theorists assume that delinquency is widespread, a condition that most youngsters experience at one time or the other. What separates the delinquent from the nondelinquent is that the former got caught; it's all a matter of contingencies, some persons are luckier than others.

Here's how it works. Johnny goes to a rock concert at the local civic arena. Like many others, Johnny is high on drugs, but unlike the others, he is unfortunate enough to be nailed by the cops, processed through the system, and written about in the neighborhood newspaper. The parents of Johnny's friends tell their kids (who are also into drugs) to stay away from him, Johnny being a no-good, drug-abusing delinquent. Johnny is stigmatized, and begins to impute to himself the negative self-image that has been foisted on him by others. In addition, Johnny's ostracism has made him uneasy, inducing him to find a new set of friends. Lo and behold, the only ones available to him are those who have been similarly stigmatized and ostracized. It doesn't take long before the company Johnny keeps transforms him into a serious delinquent, graduating as he does to hard drugs and a career of crime. All this could have been avoided had society acted with greater tolerance in the first place.

That, in essence, is how labeling theorists reason. So what should be done? Edwin M. Schur, one of the more prominent advocates of this approach, argues for a policy of "radical non-intervention," by which he means "policies that accommodate society to the widest possible diversity of behaviors and attitudes, rather than forcing as many individuals as possible to 'adjust' to supposedly common societal standards." This does not mean that "anything goes," but it does mean that the basic injunction for public policy ought to be "*leave kids alone wherever possible.*"[10]

Now, it is true that some of the strategies used to control delinquency have been misguided. It is also true that overreaction by parents and police to ordinary youthful misconduct can cause more problems than it solves. But is not true that even ordinary youthful misconduct should go unattended. It made more sense in the 1950s to counsel parents not to overreact if their son or daughter ran away from home, or was truant from school. In all likelihood, the youngster ran away to a friend's home or cut school to see a ball game. But this is not the 1950s, and Johnny is far more likely to hop on a bus to Times Square, or absent himself from school for antisocial purposes, than he is to copy the misconduct of his father's generation.

The strong denunciation of stigmatization is consonant with the new-freedom's aversion to punitive sanctions, as well as its commitment to moral neutrality. To label someone negatively is to stigmatize; it also suggests wrongdoing, and these are two heretical beliefs in the mind-set of the new freedom. But why? If a particular kind of behavior can reasonably be interpreted as being so self-destructive that it burdens others, is violative of social norms and the collective conscience of society, and is found to be damaging to the public interest, then why should those who misbehave be spared the penalty of social stigma? What the advocates of tolerance really want is for society to alter its norms and values so as to be in compliance with the norms and values of deviants. To put it plainly, they are more interested in accommodating society to the interests of deviants than in accommodating deviants to the interests of society.

Behind the rhetoric of labeling analysis stands the core of the issue: Should society have the right to proscribe legally the behaviors that violate its moral precepts? The question needs qualification because stated this way it makes debatable the Thirteenth Amendment, which bars slavery; forbidding slavery is the kind of legislation of morality that virtually everyone agrees is a good thing. But what about private vices, should they be legislated against? There are a number of so-called victimless crimes that are relevant to this issue, among them, pornography, prostitution, homosexuality, gambling, and narcotics.

Those who seek the decriminalization of "victimless crimes" maintain that consenting adults should be free to do as they please, providing no unconsenting person is harmed. But few people really mean what they say. Dueling, for example, is outlawed (the exception being when regulated as a collegiate or amateur sport). Why not legalize it altogether? Why not allow two consenting adults to duel it out in an arena, stadium, or park in a fight to the finish? The reason we do not allow dueling is because it egregiously offends our concept of morality; it degrades the community in which it occurs. That the participants may not agree is interesting but not persuasive, for there are many deviant acts that are not regarded as deviant by the deviants.

There is a legitimate public interest in seeing to it that the behaviors that appeal to the worst in us, that is, behaviors that are debasing to the human spirit, do not flourish unencumbered by law. What pornography, prostitution, homosexuality, gambling, and narcotics have in common is their appeal to the worst in us: they are dehumanizing because they are so auto-erotic in nature as to be antisocial in practice. If morally responsible individuals form the basis of a free society, then it is morally irresponsible to lift legal prohibitions against acts that constitute and induce morally irresponsible behavior.

It cannot go unnoticed that the increase in blatantly pornographic material has occurred at a time when traditional sex roles have been changing. A phenomenon that needs explaining is why the rise of the women's movement, which has generally been opposed to pornography, has coincided with a rise in the pornography market. The common answer has it that men oppose women's rights, are insecure, and have engaged in a backlash. But if this were true then why is it that survey data show that throughout the campaign for the Equal Rights Amendment, more men than women were in favor of the ERA? A more reasonable explanation is that once the new freedom blew the roof off traditional forms of etiquette governing relationships between the sexes, there was little constraint left in the culture to inhibit male hedonism.

The other wing of the new freedom—rights without responsibilities—is abundantly in evidence throughout the entire criminal justice system. It is the duty of the legal system in a free society to strike a balance between order, without which there can be no freedom, and the rights of the individual, without which there can be no prospect for liberty. Judging from studies done on the degree of confidence the American people have in their criminal justice system, it is clear that an obsessive fixation on the rights of the accused, and especially prisoners, has blinded us to the morally prior rights of the lawful, rights that at base include life, liberty, and the pursuit of happiness.

Much more can be learned about the quality of life in urban America by strolling through a neighborhood park than by reading the latest crime statistics. What one is likely to find is the near-absence of families, or of women and children, despite the fact that structural provisions have been made for them. This is due not to disinterest but to fear; most urban families know that urban parks are not for everyday folk—they are for junkies, degenerates, and thugs. And that is why the lawful stay away: urban parks are practically owned by the lawless.

It is strange that decent people who pay for parks cannot use them, but indecent people who do not pay for them are allowed to abuse them. All this is known to fathers and mothers, teachers, children, criminals, police, politicians, and judges, yet no one seems prepared to challenge the status quo. It is a vivid commentary on urban America that most decent people have simply given up, surrendering to offensive young males the control of its parks. If most of these parks were converted into parking lots tomorrow, almost no decent person would be inconvenienced, so bad is the condition in most areas.

There are many reasons for this state of affairs, not the least of which is the contemporary severance of rights from responsibilities, a phenomenon that is demonstrative of the new-freedom's ascendancy in American culture. Park bums are simply not held responsible for their behavior. More than that, they are defended as exercising their own rights, that is, their "homeless" condition (which includes using public parks as bathrooms and bedrooms) is seen as expressive of their "alternative life-style," and not as a violation of elementary codes of decency. The same ACLU lawyers who defend the right of the homeless to refuse mental health services are never seen demanding responsible behavior from their clients. It is a sad statement on life in big cities that dog owners who do not clean up after their pets are fined, but human beings who defecate in public are excused.

As legal scholar Richard Morgan says, "It is clear that the rights industry generally, and those in the law schools who most prominently carry its colors, continue to be obsessively preoccupied with defendants' rights even though the trial load is now elephantine, and the criminal justice process is dealing with only a fraction of those who commit offenses."[11] But why is this so? It's the new-freedom's equation of rights with freedom that stands behind such thinking. And it is because responsibilities weigh on rights that civil libertarian lawyers eschew much interest in them. Thus the microscopic examination of a defendant's rights, even to the point of making absurd the practical workings of the criminal justice system.

The *Miranda* decision, which afforded the accused his rights prior to securing a confession, and the finding in *Mapp*, that evidence obtained illegally is inadmissible in court, have been the subject of much controversy. Supporters have argued that overzealous law enforcement is as much a danger to liberty as street crime, and critics have contended that the rights of the accused have hamstrung the cops from doing their job. Both sides are right, up to a point. Unrestrained police powers are indeed a threat to liberty, and court-ordered rights for the accused do inhibit law enforcement.

The question that needs to be asked is whether the good that *Miranda* and *Mapp* sought to do could have been done without the costs they incurred on crime control? Why, for example, isn't it possible to punish the policemen who overreach their authority while holding for trial any evidence obtained in the course of interrogation? Why is it necessary for the public to lose each time the accused wins? Because everyone in society could arguably be the subject of an encounter with the police, why not adopt measures which the public is willing to live with, that is, law enforcement practices that afford the maximum degree of safety consistent with a minimal degree of protection for the rights of the accused? It is not clear why the public interest is best served by granting maximum rights to the accused consistent with minimal respect for law and order.

Defenders of the exclusionary rule assert that only a small percentage of cases are actually thrown out of court or result in acquittal because of improper searches. But no one knows just how many policemen have been discourged from pursuing a case to trial for fear of its being thrown out on a technicality. What can never be measured in quantitative terms is the effect that court-awarded rights of the accused have had on police morale, especially given the social context in which they were granted. Had defendants simply been given their rights, the effect on morale would have been minuscule. But what happened in the 1960s, when these rights were being awarded, was a revulsion on the part of many elite segments of American society to police work in general. Cops were "pigs," and were told so to their faces: ironically, the last thing insulting youths feared from the "pigs" was reprisal, so intimidated had cops become of court-initiated reprisals against them for striking back.

The real problem, then, was that beginning in the 1960s, the combined effect of more rights for defendants and more responsibilities for the police occurred at a time of unprecedented hostility to peace officers and equally unprecedented sympathy for the accused. To veteran cops, it seemed as though the courts had gotten their priorities mixed up, so obliging had judges become of the rights of the accused and so demanding had they grown of police compliance with the latest round of rulings from the bench. A "let-'em-kill-each-other" code of conduct was adopted as cops counted the years or months to retirement, blissfully observing street warfare on the job.

And for this they were congratulated by the media because doing absolutely nothing was interpreted as a decline in police brutality. That the streets became more brutal as a consequence barely seemed to matter.

Even more controversial than the rights that defendants have received since the 1960s are the rights that the convicted have won. Because the accused are assumed innocent until proven guilty, it is eminently reasonable that they be accorded certain fundamental rights, debatable though the extent of these rights surely is. But no such conflict of rights exists in the case of prisoners' rights, making appeals for all but the most minimal rights unpersuasive. Indeed, there are cases in which even the right to life can justifiably be abridged.

A decent and humane society should make provisions accommodating the most basic needs of prisoners, but there is no reason that such provisions should spring from a corpus of law specifying prisoners' rights; it is sufficient that the state recognize its own self-imposed duties to the incarcerated. Another way of looking at it is this: Because rights are claims made on others by the claimant, it makes no sense to extend to those who have violated the rights of others the right to make claims on them.

The dominance of new-freedom thinking in the area of penology is readily apparent. Many criminal justice specialists have practically given up, so convinced are they of the inhumanity of prison life. Horror stories are routinely reported in the press, or made the subject of a lawsuit citing overcrowding, though relatively little is heard about the bereavement that crime victims and their families are forced to endure. There is a selective moral outrage at work here, one that strangely sees the guilty as more persecuted than their innocent victims.

Prisons exist for four purposes, depending on the viewpoint of the advocate: incapacitation, retribution, deterrence, and rehabilitation. All but the last function are violative of new-freedom thinking.

In 1988 there were about 600,000 prisoners in state and federal penitentiaries, all of whom served the purpose of incapacitation. If there is one thing that proponents of incapacitation have going for them it is the virtue of having the most modest justification for imprisonment: the goal of getting criminals off the street is accomplished simply by putting offenders behind bars. It is also fairly effective, in light of the fact that a small proportion of the population is responsible for a large part of the problem.

If recidivists were to remain in prison for a truly long stretch of time (those sentenced to life imprisonment in Texas serve eight years on the average), incapacitation would prove to be even more beneficial because the pool of prospective crime victims that these criminals could victimize would shrink to those already in prison. But the new-freedom objection is that incapacitation is just an easy way for society to get rid of its most undesirable elements. There is a great deal of truth to this observation, though it is puzzling why it should be regarded as objectionable. Should society choose the most difficult way to remove the guilty from its midst?

The primary objection to retribution is that it is a primitive tool, an eye-for-an-eye mentality sorely out of date in a civilized society. This view reflects the modernist objection to traditional sanctions, a belief that advanced societies should be able to develop more scientific and efficacious ways of dealing with antisocial behavior. But what if they can't? It is true that a civilized society should not be persuaded to adopt *any* tried-and-true measure, for some are not consistent with basic standards of human decency (torture, mutilation, and so on), but it is also true that a civilized society should not turn its back on all traditional techniques of social control just because they have been used before. To do so is irrational.

Another objection to retribution is that it usually punishes people who already have been victimized by society. The prototypical example is the ghetto kid who steals. But whom does he steal from? Neighbors, which is to say other poor people, persons for whom it is no relief to learn that the person who victimized them lives in a ghetto. So do they. Most people in any neighborhood are law-abiding, and that is why those who try to justify crime by blaming social factors—and not the offender—find little support for their ideas, even among those who live in high-crime areas. Telling a black welfare mother that the person who robbed her was a poor black man, and that therefore she should be understanding of his condition, is likely to be greeted with derision, if not outrage. She quite understandably reads such sentiments as showing more compassion for the guilty than for the innocent.

Still others object that there are many cases where retribution makes no logical sense. For example, it is often said that about half the murders in the United States are committed not by strangers but by family members, loved ones, and friends. That is why the murder rate goes up each year between Thanksgiving and New Year's Day; the holidays provide opportunities to visit with relatives, and some take the occasion to kill their least-favorite cousin. It is true that in most of these cases the murderer is not a threat to society—it was a one-time loss of control. If he or she were simply left alone, there is good reason to believe that he or she would never kill again. But it does not follow that no punishment is necessary. The fact remains that an innocent person is dead, and justice demands that society not overlook that fact. The guilty must pay.

There are two types of deterrence, both of which are found wanting by those who resist the idea of punishment generally. Specific deterrence refers to methods of deterrence that seek to deter the convicted criminal from committing crime again; general deterrence has as its goal dissuading would-be criminals that the costs of imprisonment are not worth the crime.

It is never easy to know how many potential crimes have been deterred by punishing the perpetrators of actual crimes, but it is likely that the number is dependent on the arrest and conviction rate. It stands to reason that if most criminals go unpunished, as is now the case, then relatively few prospective criminals will be deterred. For example, critics of capital punishment are famous for citing figures that indicate that states that have capital punishment on the books are no more successful in stemming serious crime than states that have abolished it. But what they fail to mention is that the majority of the states that allow capital punishment do not invoke it regularly enough to make a difference, and some haven't used it in decades. A punishment not enforced obviously carries no deterrent effect.

Figures on specific deterrence are more readily obtainable. The recidivist rate is the best indicator, and for some time now it has hovered at about 70-75 percent, meaning that better than seven in ten persons in prison have been there before. The actual number of former convicts who commit another crime is probably higher than what the recidivist rate indicates because it cannot be assumed that the other three in ten went straight; they might have been able to beat the system by not getting caught. Now, some look at these numbers and conclude that prisons manufacture criminals, making them more depraved than before they went in. But there is more to it than this.

To say that prisons manufacture criminals is to suggest that something ther than criminals enter prison, which of course is untrue; every rookie inmate became a criminal prior to being imprisoned. However, it is true that most criminals exit the penitentiary more depraved than before, such are the consequences of confining deviants together for an extended period of time. But because it is constitutive of prison life that the most undesirable persons in society be forced to live with one another, and because there is no way to stop them from sharing one another's vices, there isn't much value in registering these kinds of complaints. If anything, recognition of this fact argues for longer sentences and not, as some contend, for the abolition of prisons.

The one justification for imprisonment that does not run counter to the tenets of the new freedom is rehabilitation. Unlike the other three rationales for imprisonment, the thinking behind rehabilitation does not accept the need for punishment. The rehabilitation model presumes that punishment is counterproductive and that anything short of positive reinforcements is unlikely to work. Rehabilitation has as its overriding goal the restoration of the individual, and as such does not subscribe to the notion that some people are beyond hope. In this respect, proponents of rehabilitation share with progressive-minded educators the assumption that there is no such thing as a person who does not want to better himself. Those who fail, it is believed, are failed by society.

The biggest problem that advocates of rehabilitation have is finding evidence that supports their claims. Aside from a few spot success stories here and there, the literature on rehabilitation is not very encouraging. Social scientists Robert Martinson and James Q. Wilson are arguably the nation's leading experts in the field of rehabilitation studies, and neither of them can cite more than a handful of studies that showed rehabilitation to have had any demonstrable effect.[12] Just as important, neither can point to a single rehabilitation effort as a model program. Both do not rule out the possibility that a model rehabilitation program may yet be devised, but as of right now there are none, not in the United States, not anywhere. Not even in Sweden, which despite its progressive system, is an absolute failure, having recidivist rates that approximate our own.

It is not hard to understand why rehabilitation has proven to be so unsuccessful. Change, as married couples will testify, does not come naturally to any of us, and the kinds of changes that rehabilitation seeks to accomplish are so dramatic that it is bound to be almost impossible. To reorient one's lifestyle fundamentally, after years of habitual deviance, is not easy. That is why after decades of rehabilitation efforts, and countless studies, all the therapy, counseling, vocational programs, tutoring, and job training in the world cannot equal the success rate of the one thing that has proven to be a deterrent to crime: age. When young criminals become middle-aged, most of them—including drug addicts—straighten up, having become too old to mess around any more.

Those who embrace the new freedom must concede the failure of rehabilitation, but that hasn't stopped them from urging prison reform. Even if rehabilitation doesn't work, their revulsion from punitive measures demands that they push for more extensive prisoners' rights. Punishing criminals is not acceptable, even though there is good reason to believe that the old-fashioned authoritarian prisons of the past yielded far more humane conditions than the progressive, rights-laden ones favored by new-freedom advocates.

Prison reform over the past few decades has come to mean three things in particular: more court control of the prisons, more prisoners' rights, and less-humane conditions. Not until the mid-1960s, just as the new freedom was setting sail, did the courts become active in setting prison policy. And what the judges dealt were more prisoners' rights, saying barely a word about prisoners' responsibilities, that being someone else's job, as they blithely informed their critics.

Before the reforms began, it was not uncommon to have overcrowded prisons, undereducated prison guards, and other conditions said to cause much of the violence in today's prisons. Therefore, the cause of today's prison problems must be ascribed to something else. And that something else is this: the unprecedented number of murders, assaults, drug dealings, and gang rapes that now take place in federal and state penitentiaries is a direct consequence of progressive prison reform. That is the conclusion of Kathleen Engel and Stanley Rothman, as well as of John J. DeIulio, Jr., a Princeton social scientist who disagrees with much of Engel and Rothman's work, but not on this count.

Engel and Rothman maintain that where prisons were once run by authoritarian administrators, they are now run by aggressive inmates, with the result that order has broken down and violence is rampant. What has happened is that court-ordered reforms have led to more inmate councils, grievance boards, and the like, which offer the appearance of greater democracy but in reality are nothing more than new opportunities for the most aggressive inmates to assume leadership. Not only are they not representative of inmate interests but they have grown in power, physically asserting themselves whenever necessary, going largely unaccountable for their actions. The biggest losers are the most nonviolent prisoners; they are the ones preyed upon with abandon.

Engel and Rothman concluded that "the loss of custodial power today *is* the result of humanitarian reforms and court decisions."[13] DiIulio agrees, saying that " 'participative prison management' [has] turned higher-custody cellblocks into versions of Hobbes's state of nature in which the inmates' most basic right—the right to safe incarceration—has been forfeited."[14] All this was unnecessary, DiIulio asserts, had more attention been given to effective prison governance and less to sociological theory.

DiIulio points out that Texas, for instance, was until the 1980s a model of prison excellence, before court-ordered reforms came into being. It is now a disgrace, having gone the way of California and other states that experimented with prisoners' rights. The problems began once Texas moved away from its "control model" of penal administration and assumed the mantle of progressive reform. The "control model" stressed "inmate obedience, work, and education, roughly in that order"; it was run along "strict paramilitary lines." But the more relaxed set of procedures that new-freedom judges ordered into being have since turned Texas prisons into a showcase of violence and inhumanity. After looking at the history of what works and what doesn't, DiIulio finds it indisputable that "especially in higher-custody prisons, those prison managers have governed best who have governed most and most formally."[15]

The reason that prisoners' rights lead to violence and inhumanity is because granting rights to inmates necessarily undercuts the authority of prison officials. Prisoners cannot be awarded rights without altering the relationship between inmate and guard, as well as warden. Awarding rights to prisoners is a redistributive effort, one that has dire consequences for everyone, save the most depraved, for they are the only winners.

If the law is to do its job of assisting families, schools, and churches in the nurturance of morally responsible individuals, then the present hostility to social constraints will have to end. In a free society, it is the duty of the law to insure rights and to provide for order. Doing half the job is not good enough, not even if the half that is addressed is rights.

Notes

1. Quoted in Peter Applebome, "Juvenile Crime: The Offenders Are Younger and the Offenses More Serious," *New York Times*, February 3, 1987, p. A16.
2. Marvin Wolfgang, Terence Thornberry, and Robert Figlio, *From Boy to Man, from Delinquency to Crime* (Chicago: University of Chicago Press, 1987), p. 36.
3. Claude Brown, "Manchild in Harlem," *New York Times Magazine*, September 16, 1984, pp. 44, 54.
4. Michael Novak, "Crime and Character," *This World* (Spring/Summer 1986): 51.
5. See Alton Frye, "To Smoke out Spies, Offer an Amnesty," *New York Times*, March 21, 1986, p. A35.
6. Ernest van den Haag, *Punishing Criminals* (New York: Basic Books, 1975), p. 6.
7. Brown, "Manchild in Harlem," p. 44.
8. James Q. Wilson and Richard Herrnstein, *Crime and Human Nature* (New York: Simon and Schuster, 1985).
9. Samuel Yochelson and Stanton Samenow, *The Criminal Personality* (New York: Jason Aronson, 1977).
10. Edwin M. Schur, *Radical Non-Intervention* (Englewood Cliffs, N.J.: Prentice-Hall, 1973), pp. 154–55.
11. Richard Morgan, *Disabling America* (New York: Basic Books, 1984), p. 103.
12. See Robert Martinson, "What Works?—Questions and Answers about Prison Reform," *Public Interest* (Spring 1974): 22–54; James Q. Wilson, " 'What Works?' Revisited: New Findings on Criminal Rehabilitation," *Public Interest* (Fall 1980): 3–17.
13. Kathleen Engel and Stanley Rothman, "Prison Violence and the Paradox of Reform," *Public Interest* (Fall 1983): 100.
14. John J. DeIulio, Jr., "Prison Discipline and Prison Reform," *Public Interest* (Fall 1987): 77.
15. Ibid., pp. 72–74.

PART VI

CONCLUSION

15

Where Do We Go from Here?

The defining mark of contemporary American culture is the celebrated idea of liberty without limits. Freedom is cast in purely individualistic terms, there being no notion of, nor respect for, the common good. The individual is entitled to do exactly as he pleases, short of the most blatant and egregious violation of another person's rights. There is endless talk of the rights of the individual, but nary a word spoken of any concomitant responsibilities. Right and wrong are relative, having no discernible objective reference or content. That which burdens the individual is seen as unfair, and anything that restricts choices is condemned. This is the heart and soul of the new freedom. It is also the heart and soul of our psychological and social disorders.

Though the ideological origins of the new freedom can be traced to many and diverse sources, it would not have succeeded without the sponsorship of the cultural and legal elite, the men and women who are the decision makers in the media, academy, mainstream churches, and legal profession. It is they who are the carriers of the new freedom, and it is they who most approximate a power elite in the United States, to the extent that one exists at all.

For far too long social scientists have equated power with wealth, thus overlooking the independent role that ideas, values, sentiments, and belief systems play in shaping society. When values are discussed, it is assumed that the values of the wealthy determine the values of society, setting the standard by which deviance is judged. Although this formulation bears much truth in describing preindustrial and early industrial societies, its explanatory powers are nugatory in understanding a modern, complex, postindustrial society like the United States. This is especially true in an age of mass communications and judicial activism.

One of the main reasons that it will be hard to supplant the new freedom from its preeminent status is because those who keep it afloat are largely unaccountable to democratic checks and balances. Judges, academicians, and professionals in the media are among the least answerable segments of the population. The judiciary is the least democratic branch of the government; college professors are protected from accountability through tenure and academic freedom; reporters invoke special immunities under the First Amendment; and the media subject every institution in society to critical examination, save themselves.

From the ranks of the legal elite we get activist lawyers and judges who understand little about freedom except the rights of the individual, and from the opinion makers who constitute the cultural elite we get the nonjudgmental, morally neutral mind-set that has become so popular. This is the one-two punch of the new freedom, delivered by those almost impervious to retaliation.

And yet there is reason for optimism. When the 1980s began, just about the only people who spoke to the question of moral irresponsibility were conservatives, epitomized by the Moral Majority. Because of the stridency of some of these voices, its authoritarian imagery, and plainly sectarian appeal, the Moral Majority inhibited many others from joining the fray, fearing that expressions of discontent with the prevailing moral abyss would be seen as right-wing reactionism. But events got so bad by the end of the decade that the silence in the liberal camp was beginning to break. It promises to continue.

American culture has experienced several sharp turns during the past quarter century. The new freedom exploded with the counterculture of the 1960s and then developed into the dominant culture of the 1970s and 1980s. It now appears, however, that a reassessment of our cultural norms and values is taking place, occurring, significantly, in some of the very places where it counts most: among the cultural and legal elite. To be sure, the new freedom has not lost its grip on American culture, and most of those who constitute the cultural and legal elite are just as addicted to liberty without limits as ever before, but nonetheless there are enough unmistakable voices of concern to warrant hope. Despite the popular folklore, much of it a product of the academy, there is nothing inevitable about the direction of cultural change.

Michael Walzer and Christopher Lasch, both men of the Left, have been open in their denunciation of the hedonistic strain in the dominant culture. Harvard philosopher Michael Sandel has urged fellow liberals to give up their fixation on rights and start addressing issues of community. Allan Bloom has eloquently stated the problems of higher education, complete with a searing analysis of the emptiness of the "open-mind" approach to culture. Within the feminist movement a gulf has arisen between those who still believe in the primacy of the autonomous self and those who prefer a more "we-centered" approach to human relations. And blacks are more willing than ever to demand better police protection, insist on punishment of criminals, and push for discipline in the schools.

Columnist Meg Greenfield is symbolic of the reassessment that is going on in the quarters of the cultural elite. "As a guide and standard to live by," says Greenfield, "you don't hear so much about 'right and wrong' these days. The very notion is considered politically, not to say personally, embarrassing, since it has such a repressive, Neanderthal ring to it."[1] Instead of right and wrong, Greenfield points out, we have developed a number of shorthand substitutes. There is right and stupid, right and not necessarily unconstitutional, right and sick, right and only to be expected, and right and complex, everything but right and wrong. This is the vocabulary of the new freedom.

In the pages of *Time* magazine, journalist Roger Rosenblatt writes about the strange sense of freedom that we've created for today's young people, a phenomenon he aptly calls "The Freedom of the Damned." "Over the past 20 years," Rosenblatt observes, "the idea of freedom has evolved like a mutated animal, involving the absence not only of significant choice but of moral or rational restraints. Without a context of limitations, freedom has become dangerous and meaningless." Parents, he chides, are most to blame for this cultural slippage, for it is they who make provision for everything but what really matters. "The only things missing," Rosenblatt says of the typical American family, "are the essentials: authority, responsibility, attention and love."[2] Notice that Rosenblatt did not include individual rights as being essential to strong families. He is correct: rights are claims that people make on others, and the family is the one institution in which duty, not claims, should take priority.

In 1988 the editors of the *New Republic*, the nation's most influential and repected liberal journal of opinion, wrote a lead essay identifying the problems that have beset "The Culture of Apathy." Our cities, they noted, "have fast become centers of barbarism," and by barbarism they meant "the exacerbated cultural degradation of man and environment." Drugs and sex have been engaged in with such abandon that it took death due to AIDS to change life-styles. "Lives are ruined," the editors proclaimed, by the ethos of 'anything goes' just as surely as they are lost." It is the new freedom that is to blame: "Contemporary liberalism is so intellectually and psychologically invested in the doctrine of ever-expanding rights—the rights of privacy, the rights of children, the rights of criminals, the rights of pornographers, the rights of everyone to everything—that any suggestion of the baleful consequences of that doctrine appears to them a threat to the liberal idea itself."[3]

And so there are signs that we may be turning the corner. To be successful, however, we need to give due recognition to the perennial problem of reconciling individual interests with the interests of society. "Seeing no essential tension between interest and virtue," says historian John Patrick Diggins, "liberalism and conservatism alike seem to want to deny the reality of moral conflict and the grandeur of its responsibilities."[4] The Calvinist ethic that once undergirded liberalism, Diggins argues, has lost its resiliency, leaving "naked liberalism" behind. This is an environment that is ripe for a license-as-freedom ethos.

Robert Bellah recognizes the problem between interest and virtue, but like so many other social scientists, he sees self-reliance and community as opposites. In its most extreme form, self-reliance is certainly hostile to community. But to judge a value by its most extreme manifestation is patently unfair, for no value stands well once driven to extremes. The kind of "connectedness" that Bellah properly holds as desirable, and that is sorely missing in today's society, cannot be built on a foundation of anything but self-reliant and mutually interdependent individuals. There is nothing inherently contradictory about self-reliant, competitive individuals who cooperate with others to serve the common good. The pages of history are filled with such examples.

Behind the association of self-reliance with radical individualism stands the conviction that capitalism induces greed and narcissism, thus destroying all prospects for community. But the sleaze on Wall Street that has been so apparent in recent years, and the profiteering that former government insiders traffic in so casually, is more a function of a culture gone wild with irresponsibility than a reflection of market economics. Yuppie materialism owes more to a culture that refuses to acknowledge moral restraints than to any design of Adam Smith's. That some demonstrate their irresponsibility by being promiscuous with money and others manifest their recklessness by being promiscuous with sex and drugs is hardly astonishing. A promiscuous society allows for diverse demonstrations of promiscuity.

Bellah has done as good a job as anyone in describing the problems of community that face American society. Unfortunately, his prescriptions are not as convincing as his diagnosis, lacking as they do the authority of experience. By proposing that we follow the thinking of "democratic planners," mapping society according to the principles of so-called economic democracy, Bellah is willing to put his faith in an idea that has historically yielded neither economic prosperity, social solidarity, nor individual liberty. To think that bureaucracy can answer the problems of community, after the painful lessons of the twentieth century are considered, is astounding. What is even more confounding is Bellah's admission that the proponents of the new social order have nothing to offer but a vision, lacking in detail as to how the culture is to be transformed.[5]

The reader searches in vain for Bellah to advocate the importance of a moral hierarchy. He understands what the new freedom has done, but is equally opposed to traditional normative structures: "Our present radical individualism is in part a justified reaction against communities and practices that were irrationally constricting."[6] Is it? It is one thing to understand why an overly constricting environment might engender a backlash, quite another to justify the present binge of self-indulgence as a response to it. Indeed, the case could easily be made that today's radical individualism carries no justification whatsoever, in that it denies both community and freedom; at least the "irrationally constricting" societies of the past made good on community.

Those who promote the new freedom are the problem, and not the communities and practices of previous generations. There is never any justification for license. Though no one will admit to sponsoring license, those who think the road to liberty is paved with nothing but rights, embedded in a climate of moral neutrality, are necessarily contributing to license, whether they intend it or not. It is not surprising that those who place so little value on the responsibilities of the individual should themselves fail to accept responsibility for the consequences of their ideas.

The restoration of civility and community, and the return to a tolerable level of psychological and social disorders (having a zero level is neither possible nor desirable), requires first and foremost a reformulation of what it means to be free. It should be clear by now that having too few constraints on the individual is just as inimical to liberty as having too many. Therefore, the first step to progress means accepting some constraints, how many it is hard to say, but certainly many more than what we've grown accustomed to. Just as critical is the realization that we cannot have it all; choices are available, but choosing some inescapably excludes others. Once the idea of unconditional freedom is recognized for what it is—a fraud—the first step to recovery is over. But giving it up requires the willingness to sacrifice, and that is a tall order in a culture that views sacrifice as an unfair imposition on the freedom of the individual.

A sociologically realistic understanding of freedom does not pit the individual against society. Because freedom is not possible except within the confines of society, it makes little sense to treat as objectionable those constraints on the individual that are indispensable to the functioning of society. Civility and community both require the subordination of individual interests to the common good. It is only in a civil society, and through the context of community, that individual liberty becomes meaningful. The key is to construct a society wherein an optimal level of individual autonomy and societal needs can coexist.

A free society is predicated on liberal theory, that is, freedom exists in a society where the rights of the individual are respected by law, where pluralism flourishes and where government is restrained in size and scope. But a free society also needs to rely on what conservative thought emphasizes, namely, respect for tradition, custom, and social convention. Though the right blend cannot be calibrated with precision, attempting to do so promises to deliver the best of all possible worlds.

Achieving moral consensus is just as important to a free society as attainment of political consensus. Without a moral nucleus, without a hierarchy of values, no society is possible. It is subversive of the sheer existence of a social order to maintain that each individual should be allowed to pick and choose precisely which norms and values he finds acceptable, discarding those he finds disagreeable. A moral smorgasboard is a moral disaster, subverting all prospects for freedom. Yet we continue to travel down this road, practically oblivious to the sociological consequences. Harry Jaffa has shed some light in this area: "A free society is undoubtedly 'pluralistic.' But pluralism implies diversity *within* unity. It cannot be an unbounded diversity."[7]

It is in constitutional law that the idea of a moral smorgasboard has been most trumpeted. In the name of the rights of the individual, there have been countless instances where defense lawyers have pressed the majority to accommodate the idiosyncrasies and eccentricities of their clients. Although the damage that each victory inflicts on the viability of shared norms and values is slight, the cumulative effect is devastating. In a democracy the majority is obliged to respect the rights of the minority. But that doesn't mean that the majority must yield each time someone dissents. If a consensus of values is to be upheld, then those who dissent from the norm cannot be allowed to veto the will of the majority whenever they like. A tyranny of the minority is just as bad as a tyranny of the majority.

The focal point to any meaningful discussion of liberty is the character of freedom's subjects. It needs to be restated that only morally responsible individuals are capable of exercising liberty—morally irresponsible individuals exercise license. That being so, it is incumbent upon students of freedom to detail how morally responsible individuals are to be nurtured in society, that is, it behooves them to be specific as to how their conception of liberty provides for the promotion of desirable character traits. Put another way, the sociology of freedom is every bit as important as its philosophical foundation.

Among the character traits that may be deemed important in a free society are honesty, loyalty, commitment, willingness to sacrifice, hard work, persistence, sobriety, and responsibility. These are the virtues that give strength to social relationships. They are the glue that fastens one individual to another, weaving in practice what constitutes the social fabric. All of them exact a measure of constraint, the very attribute most warred on by the new freedom. And that is why they are in short supply: bourgeois values have no role to play in a society that sees the limitations of the human condition as the enemy of liberty.

There are some things that can be done to ameliorate present conditions, but not among them is the prospect of social engineering. When Dr. Kenneth Clark, the famous psychologist and New York educator, says that ''I'm convinced that social engineering is no more difficult than space engineering,''[8] he speaks for many social scientists. He sincerely believes that putting a man on the moon is no more difficult than making the unambitious ambitious. And that is why we constantly hear how America has the ability but not the will to solve social problems. It is one of the most fantastic ideas ever entertained by social scientists, for nothing could be further from the truth: there is no such thing as corrective surgery for those unwilling to alter their behavior. Positive and negative sanctions can make a difference in affecting behavior, but there is little that can be done to abet fundamental behavioral changes in those unwilling to change.

Short of social engineering, there is much that can be done to reorient people's behavior. A good place to begin is with the nation's law schools. Law schools are as guilty as any social institution in the promotion of an impoverished conception of freedom, what with their emphasis on the rights of the individual, to the near-exclusion of individual responsibilities. There are other interests besides client interests that matter *to society*, if not to the parties directly involved in a lawsuit. There is the notion of the common good, the public weal, though that is not a subject usually stressed in constitutional law classes.

Unfortunately, most law students would be hard pressed to articulate what constitutes a compelling government interest, so atomistic is their vision of society. Yet without an appreciation for the social and cultural bases of freedom, it is not clear how any lawyer can adequately address contemporary moral issues. Law schools would be doing a public service if curricular changes were made to mainstream the concept of the public good into constitutional law classes. Real reform means more than addressing societal interests, it means demanding that law students leave school with the same respect for the public weal that they now show for the rights of the individual.

The entire concept of no-fault legislation needs reexamining. Whether we would be better off without any no-fault legislation is uncertain, but what does seem certain is that justifications for such laws should be made on other than purely expedient grounds. Attention needs to be given in symposia, conferences, bar committees, law schools, and legislatures to the legitimate social and cultural side effects of promoting laws that exculpate wrongdoers. It is the moral fallout from no-fault legislation that needs due consideration; the lessons that the law teaches individuals regarding their responsibilities is one of the most important, and least understood, facets of a free society.

No reform of the legal system will have much effect unless the courts play a leading role. Rights mania could not have succeeded without the goodwill of the courts. Judges, as much as anyone, need to understand that there is such a thing as having too many rights, for when individuals are laden with rights they cannot help but lose interest in responsibilities. This does not mean that where fundamental human rights are at stake the courts should refrain from exercising their duly constituted powers. What it does mean is that judges should not be too quick to assume the mantle of arbiter to everyday disputes. More important, the courts should resist the temptation to *find* new constitutional rights. If new rights are deserving, then it is up to the people's representatives to proclaim them, and not unelected judges.

The idea that there can be such a thing as too many rights does not set well with many persons, especially those committed to the new-freedom agenda. Here is the problem: even in a nation that accepts the concept of natural law, it remains a function of the state to distribute rights, and when the distribution is carried out indiscriminately, without reference to social role and status, the prospects for ordered liberty are necessarily impaled. Society does not consist of beings functioning as atoms, but as men, women, or children complete with identifiable characteristics, situated within a social structure, embedded in a community, and partaking (for the most part) of the cultural expectations that accompany their role and status; even deviants owe their status to the normative order.

The point is that the law needs to be sensitive to existing social relationships and not to proceed willy-nilly to distribute rights. Laws that are made in a vacuum, without due consideration for social reality, cannot avoid upending authority, for authority is always built on inequality and the equal distribution of rights nullifies authority. Justice may demand that some forms of traditional authority be upended (for example, laws governing the sexes) and in these cases there is no problem. The problem to be avoided is the unintentional undercutting of legitimate authority (for example, laws governing the rights of students or prisoners), situations that arise more out of neglect or ignorance than design.

It is equally important that judges do not proceed without an appreciation for the role that tradition, custom, and social convention play in the ordering of society. Again, if ordered liberty is to be more than just a slogan, it needs to be operationalized, and that means that at the very least judges need to factor in what the social effects of negating tradition might be when considering challenges to it. It is no victory to freedom to be beset with deracinated individuals, all fully liberated from the customs of their past and shorn of any cultural imprint. If individual rights do not liberate, they are no friend of freedom.

Another problem that is often overlooked by those who want unlimited individual rights is that state power often grows enormously as a result of rights distribution, diminishing considerably the power of social institutions.

When the courts tell a Catholic university that it must give full recognition to homosexuals, in defiance of church teachings, they arrogate to government the kinds of powers that should give every student of freedom pause. A government that is powerful enough to police the mores of social institutions to that extent is powerful enough to trample on more substantive freedoms. That the trampling is done in the name of individual rights only makes the threat all the more awesome. Tocqueville had a term for this phenomenon: *democratic despotism.*

Any genuine reform must involve the family. Though there are only a limited number of things that public policy can do to meliorate family problems, there are many things that can be done to prevent further deterioration. To begin with, public policymakers need to know what constitutes strong families. It is regrettable that our interest in addressing social problems typically focuses on why some social institutions fail, instead of asking why others succeed. More specifically, it is regrettable that we do not study why some families succeed, despite being burdened, as many are, by lack of education and income, or by pervasive patterns of discrimination. Asian Americans are a case in point.

The work of Nicholas Stinnett and his Family Strengths Research Project provides evidence as to the nature of strong families. Stinnett's organization defined strong families as intact families with a high degree of marital happiness, parent-child satisfactions, and mutual response to one another's needs. After conducting a nationwide survey of such families, six qualities were consistently in evidence: (a) appreciation, (b) time spent together, (c) commitment, (d) good communication, (e) a constructive approach to crisis, and (f) very religious.

Perhaps the most striking aspect of Stinnett's research is the extent to which all the qualities that make for strong families are predicated on a "we-orientation." The first quality, appreciation, was said to be important because of the value that family members place on "building each other up psychologically." Feeling good about oneself, the findings indicated, was positively related to how much appreciation was expressed.

Spending time together is usually associated with a "we-orientation"; those who please themselves *through* their family clearly find the time to do things together. Similarly, a high degree of commitment assumes a willingness to give of oneself, being prepared to make sacrifices on behalf of one's spouse. A natural corollary to these features is the ability to establish good communication patterns, a trait that demands a "we-centered" relationship. Families that are able to deal effectively with crisis, and those that are quite religious in their orientation (two not unrelated properties), also exhibit a "we-ness" indicative of strong family bonds. It is significant that *all* strong families reported being very religious, citing prayer, regular church attendance, and participation in other religious activities as central to their support systems.[9]

There are two aspects of Stinnett's research that are worth noting. The first is the extent to which strong families embody characteristics that are directly contrary to the values made explicit in the culture of the new freedom; the "me-orientation" of the new freedom makes arduous the development of "we-centered" families. If we tried to nurture a culture more inimical to the establishment and maturation of strong families, it would be difficult to do so.

The second key aspect of Stinnett's work is its implicit support for the nuclear family. Where else but in the nuclear family are the six qualities that make for success likely to surface? They are not likely to do so in one-parent families, though that doesn't mean there aren't many strong one-parent families. It means that one-parent families are structurally handicapped in providing the requisites of strong family bonds. It is no reflection on women that the best one-parent family cannot match the resources, psychological as well as financial, that the best two-parent family can provide. If anything, it is a reflection of the multiple demands that children make on parents, and the taxing conditions that one-parenting necessarily entails.

This is the feature that public policymakers need to keep in mind: anything that makes it more difficult for the nuclear family to thrive—above all its competitors—is not in the best interests of society. Indeed, responsible public policy calls for jealously safeguarding the status of the nuclear family in an appropriately elevated fashion. That is why it would be a mistake for other cities to follow the lead of San Francisco and bestow legal recognition on so-called alternative life-styles.

The social meaning of strong families is that they grant a nexus for personal well-being, and thus facilitate social well-being. Since the advent of the new freedom, there have been many signs that personal well-being has suffered as strong families have declined. Adolescents, in particular, have fared poorly, as measured by almost any index. Since 1960 there has been a decisive decrease in academic achievement and a startling increase in juvenile delinquency, alcohol and drug abuse, illegitimacy, venereal disease, suicide, homicide, and accidental death. Moreover, it was reported in the late 1980s that adolescents were the only group in society in which mortality has risen since 1960. Fully 75 percent of all adolescent deaths are caused by accidents, homicide, and suicide, reflecting the degree to which adolescent risk taking has grown.

Sociologists Peter Uhlenberg and David Eggebeen studied adolescent well-being for the period 1960 to 1980, and after reviewing the standard explanations—not enough money spent on social programs, counseling, education, job training, and the like—they concluded: "We suggest that it is an erosion of the bond between parent and child—one characterized by parental commitment and willingness to sacrifice self-interest—that is a significant cause of the declining well-being of adolescents after 1960.''[10] Notice that the values mentioned by Uhlenberg and Eggebeen as being central to personal well-being are among the same ones mentioned by Stinnett as constitutive of strong families. And it is just those values, commitment and sacrifice in particular, that the new freedom paints as antagonistic to human liberty.

If it is the bond between parent and child that spells the difference between a socially healthy and unhealthy condition, it stands to reason that nuclear families have a decided advantage over one-parent families in passing this test. They do, but as everyone knows, there are many nuclear families where both parents have been delinquent in their obligations. Yet to say that many fathers and mothers have failed in their duties as parents is considered controversial in many quarters. Uhlenberg and Eggebeen correctly state that many will disagree with their conclusion that parents share much of the blame for adolescent problems because of ''its implication that individuals are in fact partially responsible for the deleterious changes of the past two decades.''[11]

It is not unexpected that in an age when irresponsible parents are all too common, there would be no shortage of social scientists prepared to exonerate their irresponsibility by blaming ''structural conditions'' for the problems that they have caused. The Carnegie Council on Children seems particularly given to exculpatory reports on the family. Kenneth Keniston and Richard deLone, for example, have independently written Carnegie studies on the family, and neither has seen fit to blame parents for contributing to family problems. Both prefer to blame social and economic conditions—anything but individuals— for the current state of affairs.[12]

Placing the blame on forces that lie outside the control of individuals has an appealing ring, especially in an age of declining individual responsibility, even if intellectually such notions cannot be supported. The commitment to equality is so intense among social scientists that research on the family is frequently skewed ideologically, with priority given to social equality, especially as it affects women and homosexuals, and to economic equality, especially as it affects the poor. Justice may demand more equality be rendered, but it is intellectually dishonest to force politics into scholarship and squeeze an activist agenda out of research undertakings. It is not likely that problems of the family will be overcome until and unless cultural expectations for parents change decisively, making outcasts out of the fathers and mothers who have shunned their responsibilities.

Is there anything specific that public policy can do to facilitate the growth of strong families? Yes, there are three things that would help: (1) make the family, and not individuals, the centerpiece of public policy programs; (2)

evaluate existing and proposed legislation with an eye toward its impact on the durability of the nuclear family; and (3) promote sexual restraint as the most effective and responsible conduct for adolescents and adults.

In their portrait of the sexes, Philip Blumstein and Pepper Schwartz opened their book with the remark, "The couple is a basic unit of society."[13] Of course, it is the family, and not the couple, which is *the* basic unit of society, but to acknowledge this truism would necessarily do violence to the predelictions of new-freedom celebrants, therefore the adoption of an appropriately atomistic lexicon.

More important, the language of the new freedom is demonstrative of a serious problem, namely, the readiness with which influential persons in our culture have come to treat deviations from the nuclear family as normatively acceptable social units. It is just this kind of thinking that allows legislators to consider cohabitation as the legal equal of marriage, or judges to dismiss the moral conduct of applicants for foster parenthood. Similarly, when government employees such as social workers give priority to the individual, and not to the family, certain behavioral consequences follow in train, and none of them are good.

Those inclined to adopt the relativism of the new freedom would do well to consider what has happened to Sweden, a nation where the primacy of the family has waned to an unprecedented extent. According to law professor Klaus Ziegert, one of the most salient changes in Swedish family law in the past fifty years has been the replacement of the stability of the family with the freedom of the individual as the prime focus of legal concerns.[14] The results are now in: the damage that has been done to the family, and most certainly to children, is enormous.

"Perhaps the most dramatic indicators of the condition of the family in Sweden today," writes Rutgers sociologist David Popenoe, "are the marriage rate, which is the lowest in the industrial world, and the nonmarital cohabitation rate and rate of family dissolution, both of which are probably the highest in the industrial world." The combined effect of high nonmarital dissolution and high divorce rates, says Popenoe, means that "it is reasonable to posit that Sweden has the highest rate of family breakup in the industrialized world."[15]

Popenoe maintains the net effect of these twin disasters is that Sweden now has "the lowest average household size and highest percentage of single-person households," making "contemporary Sweden a society in which people probably spend a historically unprecedented proportion of their daily, domestic lives living apart from the presence of others."[16] In this light, the high Swedish suicide rate, especially among those above the median age, becomes intelligible: the lack of social interaction leaves men and women without the necessary social supports that allow for psychological health.

So there is little reason that any nation should want to emulate Sweden; Japan, with its focus on the strong family bonds, would make more sense. But the pull of the new freedom, with its emphasis on unburdening the individual, leans heavily toward the Swedish model. The growing acceptability of cohabitation, along with a record high divorce rate, has meant that the average size of the more than ninety million households in the United States is at an all-time low, registering just over two and a half persons per household. The problem, as Rockford Institute family specialist Bryce Christensen argues, is that there is a host of negative physical and psychological side effects associated with single, widowed, and divorced life-styles, with much the same conditions found among one-parent families, for both adults and children.[17] The lesson for makers of public policy is to make sure that social programs promote family solidarity, discouraging wherever possible the growth of unattached individuals.

The second major objective of responsible public policy entails a review of existing and proposed legislation as it affects the nuclear family. Progress toward this end has already been made by Gary Bauer, President Reagan's chief domestic adviser and author of an executive order on the family. Under the executive order, all federal programs are to be evaluated as to how they impact on the family. What this means in practice is that agencies of the government must tailor new proposals to comply with a series of stipulations governing sound family policy. It is not a panacea, but it is a step in the right direction.

Child care legislation is one area that deserves to have the best interests of the nuclear family in mind. All too often such legislation is targeted at servicing special interest groups, bureaucrats, yuppie parents—anyone but the ostensible beneficiaries, namely, children. Even those who know better occasionally fall victim to crowd-pleasing gestures, as noted child psychologist Urie Bronfenbrenner has done. Bronfenbrenner admits on the one hand that every child "should spend a substantial amount of time with somebody who's crazy about him," and on the other hand counsels that this condition can be met by day care operatives.[18] Yet common sense informs that the kind of irrational involvement that Bronfenbrenner quite rightly recommends is not likely to occur in anything other than the traditional home-care setting.

A public policy that does not extol the virtues of the nuclear family is a delinquent one. All the talk about quality time is such a scam, presuming as it does that kids can calibrate their emotional needs to their mother's occupational clock. Yet the deceit continues, if only for political reasons. Child care legislation deserves to be carefully considered, deliberately avoiding any incentive for mothers to leave the home.

If mothers choose to work outside the home, they should not be penalized for doing so, but neither should they be invited to leave. It makes more sense to award generous child care credits than it does to create another bloated bureaucracy of administrators, none of whom can speak for the interests of parents. Fathers and mothers are the best judges of where their children should be cared for, and that is why programs that discourage such traditionally popular ways as home care, as well as provisions made by relatives, neighbors, and churches, should be rejected wholesale.[19]

It is one of the great anomalies of the day that despite heightened awareness of women's needs, there exist so many bad laws that work against women's interests, especially as they impact on mothers. What makes the situation so perverse is that those who assert that they represent women's interest are often responsible for promoting the very laws that mothers labor under. To be specific, divorce legislation and welfare programs have both emanated from circles usually held to be supportive of women's interests, yet both initiatives, as many now agree, have done as much to hurt women as any measure currently on the books. No-fault divorce legislation is to white middle-class women what welfare is to lower-class black women: in both instances, men get off scot-free, leaving women financially burdened and saddled with twice the level of parental responsibilities.

No-fault divorce legislation should be repealed. The fundamental problem with such legislation is that it treats adults as though they were socially naked individuals, instead of status-bearing men and women, many of whom are fathers and mothers. A law that blindly treats people that way creates immeasurable havoc, for it levels the distinctions that society has constituted. If men, for whatever reason, earn on the average more than women, then the law should be cognizant of such distinctions and not feign ignorance by treating men and women as if they were a tabula rasa.

Welfare reform should have one overriding goal: making able-bodied adults self-sufficient. That means empowering the poor with purchasing power, providing direct cash grants instead of in-kind services (excepting, perhaps, health care). It also means making low-interest loans available for tenant ownership, a policy that makes infinitely more sense than spending the same amount of money on staffing a welfare bureaucracy. Once welfare recipients are treated as adults—as men and women with adult responsibilities—and once they are required to budget their money the way everyone else does, the kind of discipline that such efforts exact will become manifest in other demonstrations of self-responsibility. And under no circumstances should fathers be allowed to escape their financial obligations; fathers who balk on child support should be sent to prison.

The third recommendation, that public policy should promote sexual restraint, is itself a reflection of the problem. It should be self-evident that sexual restraint is a defining characteristic of morally responsible individuals, and that responsible government programs would naturally incline toward such a stance, but given the wave of the new freedom, it actually has to be said in the way of advice. Be that as it may, the undisputable progeny of the sexual revolution are herpes, AIDS, and unwanted teenage pregnancies, making axiomatic to anyone with common sense that promiscuity is a moral outrage and social liability. Therefore, any government agency, institution, or program that does not affirmatively support sexual restraint is directly contributing to the problem.

When people like Admiral James Watkins, President Reagan's AIDS Commission chief, can issue a report on the deadly disease by saying, "I want to keep morals out of this,"[20] it is positive proof that government is actively contributing to the problem. Is it too much to ask that restraint be counseled? Is it so culturally unacceptable to say that behaviorally based diseases require behavioral changes before progress can be made? Is it Neanderthal to say that being promiscuous with sex and drugs destroys lives? If so, then there is little that science can do to stop the suffering. We should have learned by now that amorality in theory inexorably becomes immorality in practice.

Strong families need strong schools as a support, and vice versa. Probably no reform effort in the schools is more overdue than the reformation of the student as person. There are already a number of impressive proposals at work reforming teachers and curricula; reforming students should be the next step. To begin with, the present emphasis on students' rights should be replaced with a newly recharged emphasis on responsibilities. Any school that does not teach students that responsibilities are tied to rights is doing a disservice to young people, inviting them to think that rights carry no burdens. Early on children should be taught that the inalienable right that Americans enjoy to life, liberty, and the pursuit of happiness does not include the right to be irresponsible.

In terms of school policy, a dress code should be adopted, both for teachers and students, making clear what constitutes acceptable attire. The social message that a dress code sends is crucial to setting a tone of seriousness in the classroom, a quality that certainly needs upgrading. In addition, more autonomy needs to be granted to principals and administrators so that they may set their own disciplinary procedures, consistent with local concerns. Reinstating the tried-and-true measure of *in loco parentis* is a must, leaving to school officials the right to assume the authority of parents.

Moral education should once again be the focal point of education, and that means that no student should graduate who does not fully comprehend what constitutes morally responsible behavior, as defined by traditional community and religious standards. The virtue of restraint should be taught whenever possible, making sure that students understand why the absence of restraint is socially debilitating. In particular, sex education classes need to counsel restraint, emphasizing the real-life negative consequences that await those who abandon it. In this regard, no effort should be undertaken to reduce a healthy dose of guilt and shame, for when guilt and shame are weak, so too are the psychological deterrents to irresponsible behavior. That is why school-based clinics are a mistake: they lower the threshold of constraint by extending legitimacy to illegitimate conduct.

Bringing competition to the schools is important, but voucher programs and tuition tax credits, though worthy, will not in the end resolve the crisis in education. The public schools have always been, and will continue to be, the heart and soul of American education. That is why magnet-school programs and the like should be extended: most parents are still committed to the public schools; they simply want better ones.

A genuinely responsible vision of freedom does not regard religion as being the enemy of liberty, but that is the way we've defined freedom over the past few decades. The schools, for instance, have been so intimidated by the threat of lawsuits that many have literally prohibited any mention of religion on school grounds. So we now have the specter of students like Angela Kaye Guidry, a straight-A student at Sam Houston High School in Moss Bluff, Louisiana, being banned from giving a valedictory address because her speech included a quotation from Jesus.[21] Had she decided to quote Larry Flynt, editor of *Hustler*, that would no doubt have been acceptable.

The root cause of the present confusion over the public role of religion in American society is not so much a twisted interpretation of the establishment clause of the First Amendment as evidence of a profound ignorance of the relationship between religion and freedom. Organizations like the ACLU are hostile to public expressions of religion because they think that religion and freedom are polar opposites. That is why they meticulously examine every recess of society for any trace of religion, hoping to purge religious influence from public life. The distorted and historically inaccurate interpretation of the establishment clause that civil libertarians offer is symptomatic of their underlying belief that religion and freedom don't mix.

Reform efforts in this area should concentrate on a nationwide discussion of the relationship between religion and freedom. More efforts like the Williamsburg Charter are needed. The charter, a two-year labor of Christians, Jews, and secularists, was officially signed on June 25, 1988, in due recognition of the First Amendment principles on religion originally propounded by the Commonwealth of Virginia upon ratification of the U.S. Constitution. The charter, which forms the cornerstone of the Williamsburg Foundation, holds that "if religious liberty is neglected, all civil liberties will suffer." It notes "the striking absence today of any national consensus about religious liberty as a positive good," and presses for "a shared understanding of the relationship between the Constitution and the society it is to serve."[22]

Law school students are especially in need of greater appreciation of the moral bases of liberty. A concept of law that fails to emphasize the bond between religious precepts and the moral underpinnings of a free society is negligent and positively destructive of liberty in the long run. Law students need to be reminded of the primacy of the religious clause of the First Amendment, that is, they need to understand that religious freedom is the first freedom.

What constitutes freedom of religion also needs to be addressed. One major mistake that has been made in recent decades has been the tendency to think of freedom of religion in purely individualistic terms. Mention freedom of religion to most people and they think in terms of worship in a church or synagogue, rarely mentioning the institutional component of religious expression. An analogy with other aspects of culture will help.

Anthropologists have long known that religion is the most defining element of any culture, traditional or modern though the society may be. Along with religion stand art and music as features of cultural expression. Now consider this: What would be the likely public reaction to a proposal that would ban all public expressions of art and music, leaving protected by law only their private manifestations? Wouldn't most people be likely to see such a proposal as smacking of censorship?

Or try this: Would it sound credible if someone were to say that he has nothing against art or music, it's just that he thinks that if one wants to avail himself of either, he should do so in the privacy of his own home, or in a museum or concert hall, but not in a park where others might be exposed? No, we would say that such an attitude is hostile to art and music, for to deny them public expression is to squeeze the life out of them, gutting whatever contribution to culture they might have. But isn't this exactly what we are doing to religion right now? In this vein, the cause of freedom would be greatly enhanced if the dialogue that the Williamsburg Charter Foundation has begun were to continue, involving every segment of society.

Stronger families, more morally responsible schools, and a renewed respect for the public role of religion will do much to advance community and civility, but they need to be buttressed by a criminal justice system that makes accountability a priority once again. A good place to begin is with young people.

Crime prevention is a must, especially given the growing evidence that future adult offenders can be identified with increasing accuracy at younger ages. It makes little sense to lock these kids up, or even to "send them away," when the reality is that most will return to society as more polished deviants than ever before. It would make more sense to enlist these adolescents in a program of national service, paying them a livable wage, and removing them from the community that nourished their delinquency in the first place. For those who continue to act in a disorderly way, there is always the prospect of hard labor or imprisonment, a tactic long used by the armed forces to foster social control.

It would be an expensive project, but given the prospective cost to society that these youngsters pose, it wouldn't be prohibitively expensive. More important, it might work. If selling drugs is no longer an option, and a guaranteed job is, chances are progress could be made. The alternative of business as usual is almost too horrendous to contemplate, given the out-of-control situation that exists in many neighborhoods. Something must be done to rescue young men who are failing in society. Young men who fail become fathers who fail, inspiring families to fail.

One of the most irresponsible ideas to have surfaced in the past few years is the call to legalize drugs. Drugs destroy individuals and often wreck entire communities. A society prepared legally to sanction self-abuse yields whatever moral ground it previously had in counseling restraint. Drug addicts are a drain on society because they can neither work nor participate in the affairs of community. There is a limit, however, to what the law can do to control drug abuse. Support needs to be forthcoming from employers, including the commissioners of major league sports. For example, if professional athletes were summarily dismissed from the game after one bout with drugs, a message of seriousness would take hold, providing a deterrent that is badly needed.

The police deserve to be accorded more authority in apprehending criminals. If they were given more discretion to stop and frisk, to question suspects, and the like, crime control would be improved. Officers who abuse their powers should be punished severely, but it makes no sense to presume that the police are any more irresponsible than judges or reporters or any other segment of society that is given wide latitude in decision making. American crime control tactics should be brought into line with the standards used in other modern, democratic societies. Supreme Court decisions affecting the rights of the accused, such as pertaining to reading the accused his rights and the exclusionary rule, need to be pared back (as they have been), doing away with the most egregious loopholes while maintaining reasonable protections against police misconduct.

Prisoners' rights need more than paring back, they need to be substantially eliminated. Nowhere is there greater need to end the discussion of prisoners' rights than among those confined to maximum security prisons. The whole approach of granting rights to prisoners (above the most elemental level) has been a mistake, encouraging as it has a disrespect for the authority of prison guards and anger at prison officials for withholding whatever rights the convicted are still denied. Long-term sentences for repeat offenders are the only measure that will work, because the fact remains that age, more than any other factor, is the number-one deterrent to crime. Recidivists should be released only when they are too old to be much of a nuisance to society.

In the end, however, the crime problem must be solved by institutions other than the criminal justice system. Michael Novak put his finger on the problem by arguing that *"criminal behavior follows from a defect of virtue. Persistent criminal behavior follows from serious flaws in character. The criminal is a malformed or ill-developed human person."* When Novak says that "virtue and character have fallen into public neglect," due to a cultural ethos that has shifted "from one of self-control to one of impulse-release," he is describing the damage done by the new freedom. His prescription is the only one that will really work: *"A cultural ethos inculcating in every citizen the need for the acquisition of virtue, the imperatives of self-control and self-mastery, and the moral obligation to assume responsibility for the painstaking shaping of one's own character, will significantly decrease the frequency of criminal acts."*[23]

The unprecedented degree of psychological and social disorders that American society is plagued with will not go away until we redefine what freedom means. The makers of public policy and the courts can make a difference, but the reason they continue to make so little progress is that the new freedom remains the defining mark of our culture. If we come to a more realistic appreciation of what freedom means, and adopt a cultural definition that does not trash community and civility in practice, then many existing problems will become manageable as normalcy rebounds.

The present embrace of the doctrine of moral neutrality must cease. To establish a more viable sense of community, there needs to be a renewed consensus on what constitutes right and wrong behavior, and that means that defined standards of moral conduct must be upheld. The doctrine of moral neutrality has blunted our capacity for moral outrage, thereby allowing palpably outrageous behavior to go unchecked. Redrawing the parameters of acceptable behavior in a manner that accommodates a reasonably broad area of individual expression is one of the most pressing tasks that we face.

It was well understood by the ancients, as well as the founding fathers, that freedom was not possible without the successful acquisition of good character and virtue in the citizenry.[24] Nothing has changed in more than two thousand years to alter that belief. Lincoln knew that self-control was the bedrock of a free society, for without it the good society would prove unattainable. Yet we have brazenly acted as though these words of wisdom are no longer applicable, so thoroughly modern and enlightened have we become. The price we pay for this arrogance is all around us.

In 1978 Aleksandr Solzhenitsyn stunned the audience at Harvard's commencement exercises when he condemned in no uncertain terms the reckless quality of freedom that the West, and America in particular, had developed. To be sure, Solzhenitsyn was not talking about human rights abuses that American or European governments had created; having spent years in the Soviet gulag, Solzhenitsyn knew firsthand where human rights abuses flourished. His complaint was directed at the abuse of freedom that emanated from a culturally delinquent interpretation of liberty. It was the legalistic nature of our freedoms that bothered him most. "The defense of individual rights has reached such extremes," he said, "as to make society as a whole defenseless against certain individuals. It is time, in the West, to uphold not so much human rights as human obligations."[25]

"Liberty," as Edmund Burke once wrote, "must be limited in order to be possessed."[26] That may be a paradox but it is paradox born of experience; it is also an idea that is freighted with exciting possibilities. The most creative ages in history, as Robert Nisbet has noted, have been times when men and women have been able to escape the grip of tightly woven social strictures *without* dissevering themselves from society altogether. The nihilism in culture that the new freedom has spawned since the 1960s is testimony to what happens when limits are rejected. By accepting some limits, we liberate our resources and participate in the meaning of freedom. That is one of the most unlearned lessons of our time.

What it comes down to is that we have been living a lie. We have been acting as though we can have maximum freedom for the individual and a sense of community and civility in society as well. We have come to believe that psychological and social disorders can be mitigated without making personal sacrifices. We have convinced ourselves that the only alternative to the new freedom is moral despotism. But it is fatuous to pretend that we are stuck with only two choices; in between the two extremes is a great big middle area, and it is in this gray area that ordered liberty has been and can be found. We need not shove the pendulum between individual liberty and social well-being full force—a gentle push will do just fine.

Notes

1. Meg Greenfield, "Why Nothing Is 'Wrong' Anymore," *Newsweek*, July 28, 1986, p. 72.
2. Roger Rosenblatt, "The Freedom of the Damned," *Time*, October 6, 1986, p. 98.
3. "The Culture of Apathy," *New Republic*, February 8, 1988, p. 7.
4. John Patrick Diggins, *The Lost Soul of American Politics* (New York: Basic Books, 1984), p. 343.
5. Robert Bellah et al., *Habits of the Heart* (Berkeley: University of California Press, 1985), pp. 270, 287.
6. Ibid., p. 83.
7. Harry Jaffa, *American Conservatism and the American Founding* (Durham, N.C.: Carolina Academic Press, 1984), p. 34.
8. Quoted by Walter Goodman, "Dr. Kenneth B. Clark: Bewilderment Replaces 'Wishful Thinking' on Race," *New York Times*, December 27, 1984, p. A14.
9. Nicholas Stinnett, "Strong Families," in James M. Henslin, ed., *Marriage and Family in a Changing Society* (New York: Free Press, 1985), pp. 304–14.

10. Peter Uhlenberg and David Eggebeen, "The Declining Well-Being of American Adolescents," *Public Interest* (Winter 1986): 38.

11. Ibid.

12. See Kenneth Keniston and the Carnegie Council on Children, *All Our Children: The American Family under Pressure* (New York: Harcourt Brace and Jovanovich, 1977); Richard deLone, *Small Futures: Children, Inequality and the Liberal Reform* (New York: Harcourt Brace and Jovanovich, 1979).

13. Philip Blumstein and Pepper Schwartz, *American Couples* (New York: Morrow, 1983), p. 11.

14. Klaus A. Ziegert, "Children's Rights and the Supportive Function of Law: The Case of Sweden," *Journal of Comparative Family Studies* (Summer 1987): 169–70.

15. David Popenoe, "Beyond the Nuclear Family: A Statistical Portrait of the Changing Family in Sweden," *Journal of Marriage and the Family* (February 1987): 174, 178.

16. Ibid., p. 179.

17. Bryce J. Christensen, "The Costly Retreat from Marriage," *Public Interest* (Spring 1988): 59–66.

18. Urie Bronfenbrenner made his remarks to interviewer Susan Byrne in "Nobody Home: The Erosion of the American Family," *Psychology Today* (May 1977): 43.

19. Three of the most sensible articles on this subject appeared in the pages of the *Wall Street Journal*: Douglas J. Besharov, "The ABCs of Child-Care Politics," March 9, 1988, p. 26; Allan Carlson, "How Uncle Sam Got in the Family's Way," April 20, 1988, p. 22; Lawrence B. Lindsey, "Better Child Care, Cheaper," July 5, 1988, p. 20. See also Robert Rector, "The American Family and Day-Care," *Heritage Foundation Issue Bulletin*, April 5, 1988.

20. Quoted by Sally Squires, "Setting the Course on AIDS," *Washington Post* (Health Section), June 7, 1988, p. 14.

21. See Nat Hentoff, "The Censored Valedictorian," *Washington Post*, July 2, 1988, p. A23.

22. See Williamsburg Charter Foundation news release, "Williamsburg Charter Seeks Civil Debate on Religion in National Public Life," June 16, 1988.

23. Michael Novak, "Crime and Character," *This World* (Spring/Summer 1986): 26–54. The quotations appear on pp. 29, 53, 40, respectively.

24. The idea that the founding fathers did not take seriously the need for certain moral requisites in a free society has been effectively refuted by Thomas G. West. See his "Conservatives, Liberals, and the Founding: The Meaning of the Debate over Natural Rights," *The Heritage Lectures*, #184. West delivered his address at the Heritage Foundation on October 4, 1988, and has been widely disseminating his view.

25. Aleksandr Solzhenitsyn, "A World Split Apart," *East and West* (New York: Harper and Row, 1980), p. 49.

26. Edmund Burke, in Ross J. S. Hoffman and Paul Levack, eds., *Burke's Politics* (New York: Knopf, 1967), p. 109.

Index